HELLO! USA

Everyday Living for International Residents and Visitors

3rd Edition

by Judy Priven
© Hello! America, Inc. 2005

Hello! USA

for International Residents and Visitors

by Judy Priven

Published by:
Hello! America, Inc.
7962 Old Georgetown Rd. #B
Bethesda, MD 20814-2475
Phone: 240-497-1088
Fax: 301-215-4171
e-mail: judy@hello-america.com or helloameri@aol.com
www.hellousa.com

Library of Congress Cataloging-in-Publication Data
Priven, Judy.
   Hello! USA : everyday living for international
residents and visitors / by Judy Priven. -- 2nd ed.
   p. cm.
Includes bibliographical references and index.
   LCCN 2005920168
   ISBN 0-9635633-8-6

   1. Visitors, Foreign--United States--Life skills
guides. 2. United States--Guidebooks.   I. Title.

E158.P75 2002   973.931
                       QBI02-200090

Please note: Brand name products mentioned in this publication are proprietary property of the applicable firm, subject to trademark protection, and registered with government offices. The mention of a brand name product or service does not constitute an endorsement from the publisher.

While the publisher has made every reasonable attempt to obtain accurate information and verify same, occasional errors are inevitable due to the magnitude of the data base. All prices and costs are estimates and are subject to change. Should you discover any error, please write the publisher so that corrections may be entered in future editions.

ISBN 0-9635633-8-6

Hello! USA: Everyday Living for International Residents and Visitors, 3rd Edition

Acknowledgments

Author: Judy Priven
Writer/Researcher: Kate Goggin
Editors: Cheryl Anson, Alysa M. Dortort, Cecelia Williams
Artwork and cover design: Alma Lopez
Page design and desktop publishing: Sarah Withers, Lew Priven
Marketing: Alysa M. Dortort

About the Author

Judy Priven is the President and Founder of Hello! America, Inc., which publishes information for individuals and families relocating internationally. Her first publication, *Hello! Washington*, on which *Hello! USA* is based, won two awards from the National Directory Publishers Association—first prize for best page layout and honorable mention for best product.

As a certified language-arts specialist, Judy is the author of several adult-literacy books published by Simon and Schuster. She has also designed and provided content for nationally-distributed software on a variety of educational topics—including test-taking preparation, reading comprehension and American history.

In addition to publishing and writing, Priven has given seminars throughout the Washington Metropolitan Area—for example, at several major colleges and universities, the U.S. State Department, several embassies and private businesses.

Hello! America Publications

StaySafe!! for International Travelers and Residents. For Americans traveling and relocating outside the U.S. Topics include avoiding unsafe situations, even in high-risk countries, and teaching children about safety. (16 pages)

Choosing Elementary and Secondary Schools, 20 Plus One Questions Parents need to Ask. What to do—and not do—when moving to a new location, either inside or outside the U.S. (32 pages)

Jobs and Careers for International Spouses. How to get a job or find a satisfying alternative while you are away. For American spouses living outside the U.S. (16 pages)

Pets on the Move, a guide to moving your pet...here and abroad. Practical advice about transporting your pet safely and helping it adjust to its new home. (8 pages)

How to Use __Hello!™ USA__

Chapters

Chapter openers: maps, pictures of everyday objects & forms, sample conversations.

Chapter text: American customs and ways of doing things.

References:
> sample Banking/Money Matters: Look in the "Banking overview" section of the "Money Matters" chapter for more information.

1,2,3... step-by-step directions:
> (what you should do first, second...and last)

"Words to Know": American words used in everyday life.

 documents or papers you need

 time to start

 warning
(what *not* to do; what to watch out for)

 cost

 answers to questions you might ask

Table of Contents

Introduction: Our Country: Its States & Cities

The U. S.

maps: U.S. regions and states with state abbreviations and author's favorites
• *cities and climates* • distances

Coming & Going

1. Before You Come

chart: what to bring
  • *what to find out* • *what to bring* • *what to leave at home*
  • *international movers*

2. Just Arrived

illustrations: dollars & cents
charts: tipping • *tips on tipping* • *quick information*
  • *at the airport* • *where to stay* • *arrival checklist*
  • *translation services*

3. Getting Connected

illustration: using the telephone
  • *dialing a phone number* • *the operator* • *pre-paid calling cards*
  • *renting a cellular (cell) phone* • *accessing the Internet*
  • *telephone directories*

4. Your Legal Status

illustration: sample Social Security card • *sample VISA*
chart: types of non-immigrant visas
  • *overview* • *immigrant visas* • *non-immigrant visas* • *getting a visa*
  • *social security* • *how to avoid common problems* • *changes and extensions*
  • *choosing legal assistance*

When You Get Here

Settling In

 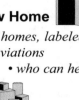

__Our Country__
Its States & Cities

Northeast

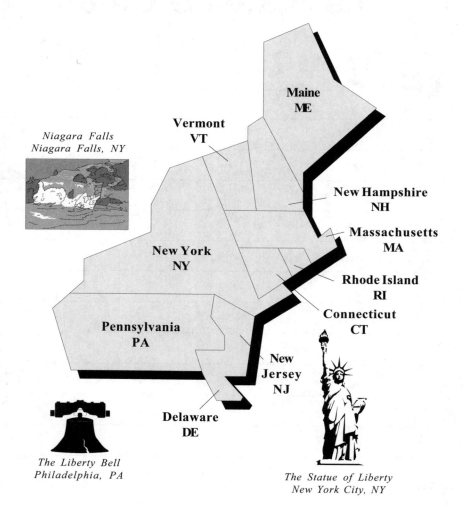

Niagara Falls
Niagara Falls, NY

Vermont
VT

Maine
ME

New Hampshire
NH

Massachusetts
MA

New York
NY

Rhode Island
RI

Connecticut
CT

Pennsylvania
PA

New
Jersey
NJ

Delaware
DE

The Liberty Bell
Philadelphia, PA

The Statue of Liberty
New York City, NY

Author's Favorites

Foods I love

 *Maine lobster.* Served boiled, broiled, steamed, or stuffed. Found all along the New England coast.

New England clam chowder. Thick and creamy soup. Different from Manhattan clam chowder, which has a tomato base.

Good times I've had

 *Buggy-riding through Pennsylvania Dutch country. Lancaster, PA. A trip into a different world, with Amish farmhouses and country roads. *Also take a guided tour through an Amish farm.*

"Dressing up" to see an opera at the elegant Metropolitan Opera House, Lincoln Center. New York City, NY.

Driving through the tree-lined streets in the fall. Anywhere in the Northeast. The leaves are bright gold and red.

Looking at photographs of people arriving in New York City. Statue of Liberty, New York City, NY. Learn about some of the history of the statue and of the newcomers who came to our country.

Riding into the Falls. Niagara Falls, NY. You feel the spray as the boat goes right up to the Falls.

Strolling through Harvard Yard and other college campuses. Boston, MA. Also, strolling down the Freedom Trail, a 2½-mile walk through American Revolution sites.

Whitewater rafting. New England Outdoor Center. Kennebec River, ME. A thrilling ride on fast-moving river waters. You can also hike, canoe, and cross-country ski at the Outdoor Center.

*Especially for children

South

The White House

Our Nation's Capital
Washington, DC

The Kentucky Derby
Lexington, KY

West Virginia
WV

Maryland
MD

North
Carolina
NC

Virginia
VA

Kentucky
KY

Tennessee
TN

Oklahoma
OK

Arkansas
AR

Georgia
GA

South
Carolina
SC

Texas
TX

Louisiana
LA

Alabama
AL

Mississippi
MS

Florida
FL

The Kennedy Space Center
near Orlando, FL

Author's Favorites

Foods I love

Crabs, boiled and spiced. Served in the shell, which you break open with a hammer. Maryland crabs are best. Also, soft-shell crabs in season, when the crab has shed its hard shell but has not yet grown a new one.

Southern fried chicken. Chicken dipped in a thick batter and deep-fried. Most popular all through the Southeast.

 Texas beef. Any way you like it—steaks, hamburgers, or pot roast. BBQ (barbecued) ribs are my favorite—grilled outdoors with a spicy tomato sauce.

Good times I've had

Climbing into the Apollo 11 space module. National Air & Space Museum, Washington DC. Also, the other nine Smithsonian museums and galleries, the White House and the Capitol—all free.

*Listening to Rock and Roll. Graceland, Memphis, TN. The estate of Elvis Presley, the famous rock and roll singer.

Nightclubbing. The French Quarter, New Orleans, LA. A historic area with jazz clubs, Creole restaurants, art galleries. The first Creoles were French settlers.

 *Riding down the Texas Cyclone. Astroworld and Waterworld, Houston, TX. A huge amusement park, with about 100 rides. Don't go on the Cyclone unless you like to be scared! Also, you can take a tram ride through NASA's Johnson Space Center.

*Shaking hands with Donald Duck and other Disney characters. Disney World, Orlando, FL

*Sipping free samples of Coca-Cola. The World of Coca-Cola, Atlanta, GA. A 3-story museum about the history of this famous drink.

Teeing off. The Pinehurst Resort, Pinehurst Village, NC. One of the top-rated golf courses in the country.

*Watching the racing horses. Kentucky Horse Park, Lexington, KY. Home of the famous Kentucky Derby. Horse shows, horse farm tours, and films on past races.

*Especially for children

Midwest

*Mount Rushmore
near Rapid City, SD*

*The Mackinac Bridge
Mackinaw City, MI*

*The Gateway Arch
St. Louis, MO*

Author's Favorites

Foods I Love

Macaroni & cheese. Best when baked with extra-sharp cheddar cheese from Wisconsin.

 Corn on the cob. Wrapped in tin foil and baked over the grille at a barbecue. Served with salt and butter over the corn; you pick up the cob with your hands and bite off the corn. The states of Illinois, Indiana, Iowa, and Ohio are known as "The Cornbelt."

Cherry pie. More than four million cherry trees grow around Lake Michigan. People from the Midwest also put cherries in soups, jams, and meat sauces.

Good times I've had

*Bicycling along the water. Mackinac Island, Mackinaw City, MI. Views of the bridge and ships. Also, horse-drawn tours to historic sites from the American Revolution and the War of 1812.

*Dancing the "frug." The Henry Ford Museum & Greenfield Village, Dearborn, MI. Exhibit of popular music from the '60s–'70s. Walk through the real rooms of famous Americans—such as Henry Ford and Abraham Lincoln. Also, an exhibit of antique cars such as the "Model T" Ford.

 Looking at Seurat's "Sunday Afternoon on the Island of La Grande Jatte." The Art Institute of Chicago, Chicago, IL. Western Art collection, exhibits of home decorations, and a re-creation of an old Stock Exchange Trading Room. Also in Chicago—Second City, one of the best comedy clubs in the U.S.

Photographing the busts of the presidents with the lights at night. Mt. Rushmore National Memorial, Keystone, SD. The busts of Presidents Washington, Jefferson, Lincoln, and Roosevelt (Theodore) carved in a granite cliff.

*Shopping. Mall of America, Bloomington, MN. The largest indoor mall in the world, with more than 400 stores and an amusement park.

*Especially for children

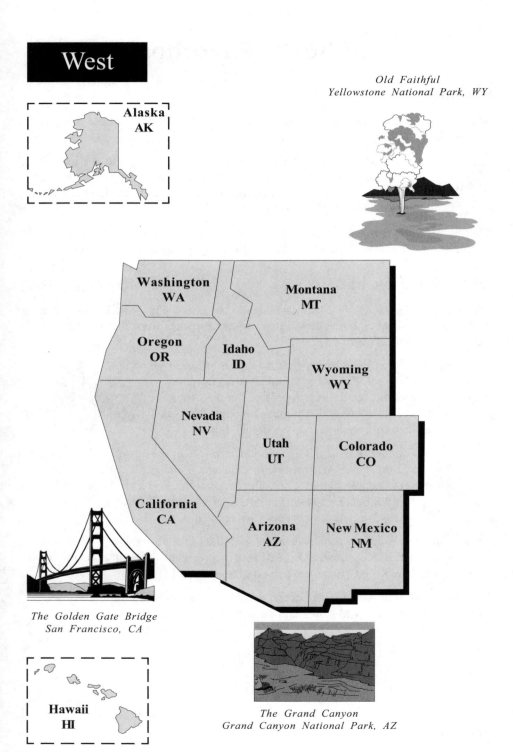

West

Alaska
AK

Old Faithful
Yellowstone National Park, WY

Washington
WA

Montana
MT

Oregon
OR

Idaho
ID

Wyoming
WY

Nevada
NV

Utah
UT

Colorado
CO

California
CA

Arizona
AZ

New Mexico
NM

The Golden Gate Bridge
San Francisco, CA

Hawaii
HI

The Grand Canyon
Grand Canyon National Park, AZ

Author's Favorites

Foods I love

Chili. Beans, tomato, and spices—especially chili powder. A thick "soup" made either "con carne" with meat or vegetarian. Usually served with cheese on top.

Baked potatoes. Idaho baking potatoes are best.

 Salmon. A red or pink fish most easily caught in fresh water. Best when broiled or baked. Smoked salmon, or lox, is also popular, but very expensive. You can buy salmon fresh from the stalls at Pike Place Market in Seattle.

Good times I've had

Photographing moose and bear in Denali National Park, AK. Also, flying above the mountains (weather permitting), fishing, hiking, and camping.

*Riding a mule down the Grand Canyon in Grand Canyon National Park, AZ. ½-day, full-day, or 2-day trips. Short rides for children.

Shopping for Native American (Indian) art at the pueblos near Santa Fe, NM. Also, taking a tour of the pueblo to see how Native Americans live today.

Sipping champagne in a hot-air balloon in Napa, CA. A "fun" way to see the Wine Country just north of San Francisco.

Skiing, downhill. Vail, CO. Probably the highest-rated ski area in the country; the Vail resort alone has 4,014 acres of runs, a gondola, 24 lifts, and a 3,250-foot drop. Also, cross-country skiing, ice skating, snowmobiling nearby, with golf in the warmer months.

Watching the song-and-dance shows at the big hotels in Las Vegas, NV. Bally's or Caesar's Palace is best.

*Especially for children

Cities & Climates

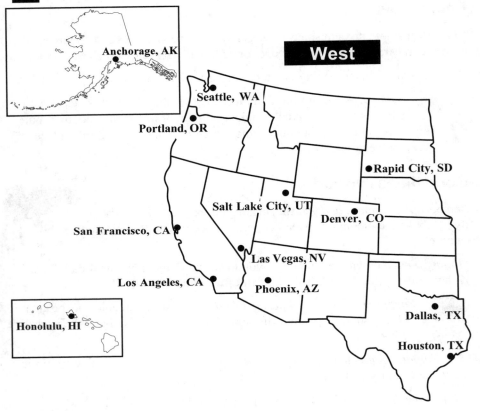

City	Average Temps		Sunny Days
	Lowest F° / C°	**Highest** F° / C°	**Average # per year**
Anchorage, AK	6 / -14	65 / 18	61
Dallas, TX	34 / 1	98 / 37	137
Denver, CO	16 / -9	88 / 31	115
Honolulu, HI	65 / 18	87 / 31	88
Houston, TX	41 / 5	94 / 34	95
Las Vegas, NV	33 / 1	104 / 40	211
Los Angeles, CA	48 / 9	84 / 29	186
Phoenix, AZ	39 / 4	105 / 41	212
Portland, OR	34 / 1	80 / 27	68
Rapid City, SD	9 / -13	87 / 31	111
Salt Lake City, UT	20 / -7	93 / 34	125
San Franciso, CA	44 / 7	69 / 21	167
Seattle, WA	34 / 1	75 / 24	57

Cities & Climates

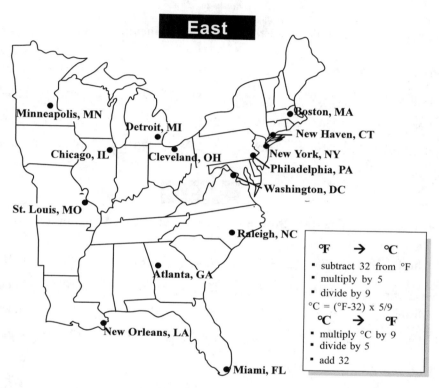

East

Minneapolis, MN
Detroit, MI
Boston, MA
New Haven, CT
Chicago, IL
Cleveland, OH
New York, NY
Philadelphia, PA
Washington, DC
St. Louis, MO
Raleigh, NC
Atlanta, GA
New Orleans, LA
Miami, FL

°F → °C
- subtract 32 from °F
- multiply by 5
- divide by 9
°C = (°F-32) x 5/9
°C → °F
- multiply °C by 9
- divide by 5
- add 32

City	Average Temps		Sunny Days
	Lowest F°/C°	Highest F°/C°	Average # per year
Atlanta, GA	33 / 1	89 / 32	110
Boston, MA	23 / -5	82 / 28	99
Chicago, IL	14 / -10	83 / 28	133
Cleveland, OH	19 / -7	82 / 28	70
Detroit, MI	16 / -9	83 / 28	77
Miami, FL	59 / 15	89 / 32	77
Minneapolis, MN	2 / -17	83 / 28	97
New Haven, CT	23 / -5	82 / 28	100
New Orleans, LA	43 / 6	91 / 33	103
New York, NY	26 / -3	85 / 29	107
Philadelphia, PA	24 / -4	86 / 30	93
Raleigh, NC	29 / -2	88 / 31	112
St. Louis, MO	20 / -7	90 / 32	103
Washington, DC	28 / -2	89 / 32	98

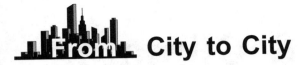 # From City to City

WEST

	Denver	Houston	Los Angeles	Phoenix	Seattle	
Dallas	799	242	1385	1015	2093	miles
Dallas	1286	389	2228	1634	3371	kilometers
Las Vegas	756	1484	265	292	1204	miles
Las Vegas	1216	2388	426	470	1938	kilometers

EAST

	Atlanta	Boston	New Orleans	St. Louis	Washington, DC	
Chicago	678	986	934	287	688	miles
Chicago	1091	1586	1503	462	1107	kilometers
Miami	665	1510	867	1222	1074	miles
Miami	1070	2430	1395	1966	1728	kilometers

From Coast to Coast

San Francisco → New York

2934 miles

4721 kilometers

1 mile = 1.6 kilometers
1 kilometer = .6 miles

Note: These are the distances for driving the fastest way from city to city.

Coming & Going

Before You Come

Money

Cash in U.S. dollars

Traveler's checks in U.S. dollars

Credit cards

Documents

Entry papers

Financial history/ bank routing information

Medical history/ medicine prescriptions

Birth and marriage certificates. Guardianship papers in cases of specific custody situations.

Driving history and auto information

Education records, diplomas, professional awards, publications you have authored

What to Find Out

Legal status

Your legal status determines:

- how long you can stay.
- who can come with you.
- how often you may travel outside the U.S.
- if your husband or wife will be able to work.

If possible, contact an immigration attorney before you leave (see "Choosing Legal Assistance/Your Legal Status"). Make sure you:

- have the type of visa that is best for you; your visa affects your legal and tax status.
- have all the documents you need and know how to fill them out (see section on "What to Bring" in this chapter).
- can get help if the regulations or your situation changes.

 Students should check with the foreign student advisor of the institution they will be attending–before they go to the consulate. Ask what papers you need to get your visa; the requirements vary.

Tax status

If you live or work here, you probably will pay U.S. taxes (see "Getting Help/ Paying Your Taxes"). You may be able to save time and money if you learn about U.S. tax rules *before* you leave. Ask an international tax professional what regulations you need to know before you leave.

Insurance

 Make sure you can get medical insurance *before* you come to the U.S. (see "Medical/Insurance You Need"). If you are coming here to study or work, ask your school or company for help. If you are coming on your own, call a few companies that offer insurance to internationals. Find out:

- how long you will wait for the insurance to be in effect. You need to get short-term insurance before your regular insurance begins.
- how much the insurance costs. Most employers and colleges pay for some of the insurance cost; you will pay the rest.
- how long the insurance lasts. Be sure you can get insurance for the whole time you are here.

 The insurance should cover any important condition you now have or may develop while you are here.

Cost of living

If you are coming here to study, you must sign a paper showing you have enough to live on (see "College Costs/ Colleges and Universities").

Homes and services

Every large city and county has an association of businesses, or Chamber of Commerce. If you know where you are relocating, the Chamber may help you find out about homes, schools, and services.

Banking information

Tip: You probably will need two banks: one in your home country and another in the U.S. (see "Choosing a Bank/Money Matters").

If possible, find banks that are compatible in the way they transfer and receive funds—either electronically, by fax, or by phone. Ask banks in both countries about:

- the time a transfer will take.
- an authorization signature. To avoid long delays, sign an authorization form for fax requests before you leave your home country.
- exchange rates.

To transfer money to the U.S., you need to know your home bank's:

- routing number.
- address.
- account number.

What to Bring

Money

Traveler's checks. Issued in U.S. dollars, these can be used as cash; if they are lost or stolen, you may get new ones.

Cash in U.S. dollars. Bring $500 U.S. dollars for things you will need right away—for example, taxis, tips, and food. If you arrive on a weekend, you may want to bring $200 more; most banks are closed. $100 of your U.S. cash should be in single dollar bills— $1, $5, or $10.

a credit or ATM card. Be sure you can use the ATM card in the U.S.

Tip: If the ATM card takes the money directly from your account, you may need to raise the withdrawal limit before you leave.

Tip: you may need a few dollars to get a luggage cart even before you exit the passport control area in the airport.

Charge or credit cards

Americans use credit cards to buy everyday items such as food, clothing, movie and theater tickets (see "Getting a Credit Card/Credit Cards and Loans"). If you will be here for more than six months, you may save money if you use an American credit card— rather than one from your home country.

⊗ Do not cancel your credit card at home right away. You may need to wait before you can get a credit card in the U.S. Also, if you know you will be returning home within a year, also keep your bank account and your credit card open in your home country. They will be handy when you return.

Your school, company, or organization may be able to get you a card right away. If not, ask an American Express® or similar office if you can get a card in your home country and convert it to a U.S. card after you arrive.

Documents

Entry papers. Have a certified translation of all legal papers—such as a birth certificate or a letter giving you permission to bring a child who is not your own into the country.

Tip: Make two copies of each person's visa and the passport page with his or her passport number and photo. These copies will be handy if your passport is lost, or if you just need the passport number.

Tell the truth whenever any immigration officer interviews you or you are filling out a government form. If you are having trouble entering the U.S., an attorney may be able to help you—as long as you have told the truth; if you have not told the truth, your problem may be more difficult to fix. You may even be deported, without the right to return (see "Overview/Your Legal Status").

You may not enter the U.S. as a married couple unless you are legally married in your own country, even if you have been living together for many years. Also, same-sex marriages are not recognized by the U.S. government.

A passport for each family member 21 years or older. Check the expiration date on your passport(s); if it expires less than 6 months from the time you plan to enter the U.S., ask for an extension. If the passport is less than one-year-old, bring both the old and the new passports.

Note: If your country does not give passports to young children, include your children in your own passport; you must accompany your children when they are traveling into or out of the U.S.

Bring:

- a birth certificate for each child.
- a notarized letter from the parent left at home if the children are traveling with only one parent or with another adult. The letter should give permission for the child to enter the U.S. with the accompanying parent or other adult.
- proof of guardianship if you are the legal guardian of any adopted children.

A visa for each family member 21 years or older. One family member has the visa status of "principal employee" or "principal student." Other family

Look up "Hello! America" (http://www.hellousa.com) for:

- books, information, and advice about U.S. cities and life.
- orientation services you can use before and after you arrive.
- information about choosing and applying to colleges.

One quick way to find out about your new neighborhood is to use the Chamber of Commerce Official Global Locator Internet site, where you may connect with real estate agents, apartment managers, relocation companies and other businesses in your new neighborhood.

members have "derivative status." The visa is attached to the inside of your passport at the U.S. Consulate; it tells

- the purpose of your visit.
- the expiration date, or last date, you may enter the U.S.
- how many times you may leave and enter.

The I–20 for students.

Note: All persons coming here as dependents who want to work in the U.S. must get a work visa independent of their spouse or parent. An immigration attorney may be able to help you.

Visitors from many countries may stay as long as 90 days—either for business or pleasure. Visitors may not earn money while in the U.S. See an attorney if you want to be paid for any work you are doing on your visit.

Most persons coming to the U.S. for more than 90 days need a visa.

 Your visa does not guarantee entry into the U.S. Once you have arrived, a U.S. immigration officer may ask you more questions—even if you have been interviewed at the U.S. embassy or consulate in your home country.

Apply for a visa as soon as possible; approval of your application may take a long time—especially if you are applying in June, July, or August.

Students will not receive a visa more than 90 days before the date on their I-20 form. To enter the U.S. more than 90 days ahead of time, apply for a visitor's

visa, as well as a student visa; be sure to let your student advisor know.

Financial information. To live and work in the U.S., you will need documents that show your income and assets outside the U.S., including:

- a copy of your latest tax returns.
- the deed for any property you own in your home country.

Financial history. To live and pay taxes in the U.S., you will need:

- a letter from your bank showing your financial history. Be sure the letter includes any loans you have had in the past. The letter may help you get a loan or credit card.
- bank statements and records of any other assets.
- credit or loan documents. Get a letter from anyone who has lent you money in the past.

Professional letter. If possible, get a letter from your employer on company stationery stating your name and the following:

- your professional title, or name of the position you will hold.
- the date you will begin your job.
- the approximate time you will stay in that position.
- your salary level.

Automobile information.

English-language international driver's license, in addition to the driver's license you are now using. The English-language international driver's license may be a useful identification card; it will also enable you to drive for a limited period of time before you get a local license (see

"Getting an ID/Driver's License/ Getting Around").

"No-claim letter" (in English) from your car insurance company, showing that you are a safe driver. This letter may reduce your car insurance payments in the U.S.

Car ownership records if you are bringing your car to the U.S., including your:

- bill of sale.
- international registration marker.
- car serial and motor numbers.
- insurance policy records.

Medical records.

- immunizations.
- medicines you take.
- illnesses you have had.
- reports, x-rays, or any other health information.

Birth certificates. Bring originals (preferably translated into English and notarized).

Education records, transcripts, diplomas, and test records (such as the TOEFL).

Job and professional records. These should include:

- reference letters (on company or university stationery).
- your résumé or curriculum vitae (CV).
- proof of your qualifications (see chapter on "Finding Work").

Copies of insurance policies.

Compare the cost of adding to the health insurance you now have versus buying insurance in the U.S. (see

section on "Insurance" in this chapter).

Inventory. List all items packed, shipped, or stored.

Communications equipment

If you plan to bring your own computer, you will need:

- a transformer, if your computer cannot operate with U.S. voltage.
- an electrical outlet adapter plug.
- a telephone adapter plug for accessing the Internet

Travel Discounts Passes. Some discount passes for travel inside the U.S. and other countries in North or South America are available only outside the U.S. For example, The USA Railpass is good for travel to and from most large cities in the U.S. Ask your travel agent or look online.

Useful items

Medical Needs.

Household medicine and antibiotics. Check with the U.S. embassy or consulate to see if you need a prescription for any medication you need— even if you do not need a prescription in your home country.

Eyeglasses. An extra pair of prescription eyeglasses.

A thermometer for measuring degrees Celsius.

Extra photographs (headshots). The photos should be passport size. You need these for the many forms you will complete.

Extra luggage keys.

What to Leave at Home

 Compare the cost of shipping or bringing an item versus buying it in the U.S. The best way to compare is through the Internet. For example, compare:

- large items—such as furniture. Furniture is usually cheaper in the U.S.—especially used furniture (see "Furniture/Moving In"). Also consider renting a furnished home.
- everyday items—such as medicines, shoes, or clothing.

Clothing.

- heavy indoor clothing. Almost all homes and buildings have air conditioning and central heating, so indoor temperatures are about the same throughout the year.
- extra children's clothing. Children who move to the U.S. often want what American children wear; since clothing in the U.S. is often cheap, you may want to buy it here.

Sheets. The bed sizes in the U.S. are different from those in most other countries. The following are the most popular sizes:

- king: 274x259 cm (108x102 in.).
- queen: 229x259 cm (90x102 in.).
- full: 206x244 cm (81x96 in.).
- twin: 168x244 cm (66x96 in.).

Electrical items. The electrical outlets and voltage here are different from those in most countries. The U.S. electricity standard is 110-120 volt, 60 cycles AC, so you will need adapters for all electrical equipment.

Before you come, be sure any electrical items you bring will work here. Go to a store that knows about international equipment. Check your:

- appliances. Most large appliances will not work in the U.S.
- TVs, video cassette players, and DVD players.

American equipment uses the NTSC system; most other countries use the PAL, SECAM, or MESELAM system. If your equipment has only one system, you may need to convert it.

Cars. Any car brought into the U.S. must meet U.S. highway safety standards and have a working catalytic converter. You will also need specific automobile documents. You may save time and money if you buy or lease a car in the U.S. (see chapter on "Buying or Leasing a Car").

If you want to ship your car overseas, find out:

- the regulations. For example, find out whether you:
  - may or may not import your car. Ask about fees.
  - will need to adjust your car so it meets U.S. standards.
- the way to get new parts, if you can get them.
- the type of gasoline it uses. You may import only cars that use unleaded gas.

Bringing items into the U.S.

 New U.S security regulations require detailed lists of all goods coming into the U.S.

Your mover should have forms for listing everything you pack. If your list is not detailed enough, the U.S. customs may delay or reject your shipment.

For more information on importing regulations, ask your mover or call the U.S. Consulate , or go to the U.S. Customs website.

Items from certain countries. You may not import some items from specific countries—for example, Cuba, Iran, Iraq, Libya, North Korea, Vietnam, or Sudan.

Items needing a special permit. Especially ask your mover about:

- firearms and ammunition.
- some drugs and medicines. Keep any medication in the box or bottle from the drugstore. If possible, the box or bottle should have
  - the name of the patient.
  - the name of the medicine.
  - the name, address, and telephone number of your doctor.
  - the name of the drugstore.
- plants and meat products such as fruits, vegetables, seeds, and un-tanned animal furs or skins.

Gold coins, jewelry, and medals. You may import only a limited amount.

Pets.

U.S. regulations. Contact the U.S. Department of Agriculture–Animal and Plants Health Inspection Service (USDA-APHIS) for regulations about bringing your pet into the country.

Ask a veterinarian to examine your pet. U.S. Customs will not admit a pet that may have certain diseases. If you have a dog or cat, bring a health certificate from the veterinarian. Have dogs three months or older vaccinated against rabies at least 30 days before arrival.

The trip. Call your airlines; check the hours of operation at your port of arrival to be sure that an officer will be available to inspect your pet.

Make plans for shipping your pet. Ask which pet carrier you need. Label all pet carriers with:

- your name and address.
- the name and address of the person who will be picking up your pet.
- a statement with the number of animals contained in each shipment.

Check to be sure your hotel or housing allows pets.

International Movers

Moving companies

Talk to a few companies about the issues below.

Compliance with the Customs-Trade Partnership Against Terrorism (C-TPAT). C-TPAT is a world-wide voluntary organization that sets standards for procedures such as hiring packers and keeping your goods secure while it is being transported. Movers participating may:

- reduce the number of times the U.S. Customs agents inspect your luggage. As a result, your goods move faster through immigration procedures, with less damage.
- keep your household goods safer.

Experience. Make sure the company has experience in moving from your home country to the U.S.

Reputation. Talk to at least three people who have used the company for U.S. moves.

Insurance. Be sure the mover is bonded (insured). Ask if the insurance covers all your belongings while they are on the ship and on the way to and from the ship.

Price. Get a written estimate from three or more companies. Find out what this price includes. For example, many larger companies help you:

- pack and unpack.
- get your appliances ready.
- tell you about the taxes and rules for bringing in certain items.
- prepare the shipping documents.
- arrange for customs procedures.
- give you booklets or videos about your new country.

Extra costs

Some costs that may not be in the estimate are:

- mattress bags and wardrobe boxes.
- extra pickups or deliveries.
- preparation of your electrical appliances.
- extra insurance for special items—such as antiques or jewelry.
- car shipment into the U.S. You may need to pay
  - taxes.
  - the cost of making your car meet government standards.

- fees and taxes for bringing some items into the U.S. Get a letter from an appraiser stating the value of any jewelry, furs, and antiques (items over 100 years old).
- storage of your goods—either in your home country or the U.S.
- tips. For example, a common tip is about $5-$10 a day for each worker.

Your records

Write down:

- the transit time (how long it will take).
- the itemized cost estimate, or an "order for service." If possible, get a "binding estimate" so the company cannot add extra costs.
- the amount of insurance. You can also buy separate insurance from an insurance company.
- an inventory of each item to be moved; it should list each item separately and describe any damage or marks already on the items before the move begins.

 Be sure you know about any special procedures, restrictions, or taxes for taking possessions (such as a car) back into your own country from the U.S.

If necessary, save receipts or proofs of purchase for items you bought here. These may include:

- cars.
- cameras.
- jewelry.

Words to Know

Antibiotic: a kind of medicine—for example, medicine for sore throats and other infections

Adopted (child): a child who is legally yours—but who was born to another parent

Appliances: electrical items such as refrigerators, toasters, and irons

Assets: your property and money

Bank statement: a paper showing the amount in your bank account

Bill of sale: a paper that shows what you bought and how much you paid

Binding estimate: the amount the service costs. The company cannot charge you more than this amount.

Birth certificate: an official document that shows when and where a person was born

Bonded: insured in case a worker steals or breaks something

Car serial number: the identification number of a car—often on the dashboard or under the hood

Central heating: a heating system that heats the whole house—not just one room

Certified translation: translation with a legal stamp showing that it is accurate

Chamber of Commerce: a group of businesses that can tell you about homes, schools, and businesses in a county or city. Almost every U.S. county or city has one.

Convert: change something (a video player or a machine). For example, you need to convert most foreign TVs so they will get American channels.

Correspondent (bank): having a special relationship with a bank from another country. Customers may get faster and better service from the bank in both countries.

Credit card: a plastic card used to buy things; you get the bill later

Curriculum vitae (CV): (see "Résumé")

Deported: forced to leave the U.S. and return to your home country

Derivative status: the legal status for families of the principal student or employee

Double size bed: a bed large enough for two people. It is smaller than a king or queen size bed.

Drugstore: a pharmacy; a place where you can buy medicine

Expiration date: the date your visa ends

Extension: getting permission to stay longer

Firearms: guns and other weapons

Full-size bed: see double size bed

Guardianship: having the legal responsibility to care for a child

Immunization: medicine or injection that keeps you from getting diseases

Inventory: a list of all items packed, shipped, or stored

King-size bed: an extra-large bed for two people. It is the largest size.

Mattress bag: a plastic bag to cover a mattress

Minor child: a child less than 18 years old.

"No-claim letter": a letter from your car insurance company that shows you are a safe driver

Pet carrier: a strong box that holds pets while traveling

Principal employee: the employee who holds the visa for himself or herself and for the family

Principal student: the student who holds the visa for himself or herself and for the family

Qualification: the ability to do a job

Queen-size bed: an extra-large bed. It is bigger than a double but smaller than a king-size.

Reference letter: a letter from a past employer that tells about your work

Résumé: a CV; a document that describes your education, employment history, and qualifications

Routing number: a bank's identification number for international wire transfers; a bank's electronic address

Standard calling card: a calling card that charges the cost of the call to your credit card or your phone bill

Tax return: a document you send to the government each year. It shows how much money you made and the taxes you paid.

Transcript: a person's official school record that shows the classes taken and the grades received

Twin bed: a bed for one person

United States Citizenship and Immigration Services (USCIS): a division of the Department of Homeland Security. The USCIS has responsibility for immigrant and non-immigrant visas, procedures for coming into the U.S., and working permits for international residents, financial benefits for immigrants.

Vaccinated: getting a shot or injection (see "Immunization")

Wardrobe box: a box movers use for clothes. The box lets you keep the clothes on hangers so they won't get wrinkled.

Will: an official document that shows who gets a person's money and property after he or she dies

____Just Arrived____

Dollars & Cents

With $1.00 you can:
• buy a cup of coffee

With $5.00 you can:
• rent two videos or DVDs for the night

With $10.00 you can:
• buy a tasty salad

With $20.00 you can:
• buy a fancy T-shirt

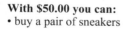

With $50.00 you can:
• buy a pair of sneakers

With $100.00 you can:
• see a popular musical

**A penny
= 1 cent
(1¢)**

**A nickel
= 5 cents
(5¢)**

**A dime
= 10 cents
(10¢)**

**A quarter
= 25 cents
(25¢)**

**A half dollar
= 50 cents
(50¢)**

**A dollar
= 100 cents
(100¢) or
$1.00**

Tipping

Occupation	Average Amount to Tip
Restaurants	
waiters/waitresses (except for employees at "fast-food" restaurants)	15% of food bill not including tax
coat checker	$1 per coat
valet parking	$2-$3

Note: You do not need to tip the maitre d' unless you ask for special services in advance—for example, reserving a group of tables for a meeting.

Airports, Trains, or Bus terminals	
baggage handlers–porters who carry your luggage (including curbside check-in)	$2.00 for the first bag and $1.00 for each additional bag

Barber shops/Beauty salons	
hairdressers and barbers	15%
shampooers	$1-$2

Note: You do not need to tip hairdressers or barbers who own the shop.

Taxis and Limos	
drivers	10%–15% of fare
person who gets you a cab (at the hotel or airport)	50¢ and $1-$2 for putting your luggage in the car

Hotels	
room service (delivering food or laundry)	$1.00 – $2.00

Do not tip:

- **officials** such as police officers or government employees.
- **service employees** such as bus drivers, theater ushers, museum guides, sales people, gas station attendants, elevator operators, receptionists.

Tips on Tipping

In general...

Are tipping customs the same all over the country? No. Leave a larger tip (about 20%) in major cities such as New York and Los Angeles. You may leave about 15% in smaller cities or in the country—but not less than 15%.

Why should I tip? Most waiters and other service people are paid less because they get tips. If you do not tip, you are cheating them out of money they earned.

Should I ever tip the employee of a store where I am shopping? In general, no. For example, do not tip a salesperson—even if that person spent a lot of time helping you. Many salespeople get a commission—that is, a percentage of the price you pay.

Note: In some food stores, shoppers give 25¢–50¢ to a bagger who carries groceries to the car. Other grocery stores do not allow tips. Watch what other shoppers do.

What are the customs for tipping at holiday time? (see "Cards and Gifts/ Meeting Americans").

Restaurants and Hotels

Should I tip the maitre d'? Usually, no. Tip only if you receive extra attention—for example, if the maitre d' helped with a large party or special group.

Should I ever leave more than 15% of the bill? Yes. The staff of a five-star hotel or restaurant usually expects about 20%–25%. Also, large groups (six or more) usually leave 18%–20%. Check to be sure the tip is not already on the bill.

May I leave a smaller tip if the service was not good? Yes, but only if the service was unusually bad. Many Americans leave a little less than 15% and complain to the manager. If you leave a smaller tip, be sure that the problem was the fault of the service person—not the kitchen.

Should I ever leave no tip at all? Do not leave a tip in cafeterias or informal restaurants—such as McDonald's.

Taxi and Delivery Services

Should I tip the person who delivers pizza or other restaurant food to my home? Yes, about 15%.

Should I tip the drivers for mail services, department stores, or flower shops? No.

Should I tip the messenger who delivers a special letter or package? No.

Quick Information

Arrival assistance

The information booth at the airport tells how to find out about transportation, hotels, and money.

Visitors' Information Centers help you get hotel reservations or general information about the city. Find the telephone number in the Yellow Pages directory under "Tourist."

Telephone

Finding the number. You may:

- press 411 or 1-411 from any phone for a local U.S. number; you may pay a small fee for this service. For numbers in other cities, press 1+the area code+555-1212. If you do not know the area code press "0".
- use the telephone directories for the telephone numbers of local residents, businesses, and government offices.

Note: The front pages of the telephone directories have useful general information and maps of the metropolitan area.

Read the chapter on "Getting Connected" for more information about telephone and Internet connections.

Airport bookstore

All major airports have bookstores with books, magazines, and newspapers for the city. If you are staying more than a few weeks, ask for a book that tells about *living* in the city (see "Publications/News, Sports, & Entertainment").

At the Airport

Entering the U.S.

Documents. When you enter the U.S., you will need to show the immigration officer your:

- visa, which is stamped inside your passport.
- I-94 card. The officer will attach this to your passport. The date on the I-94 card tells how long you are permitted to stay in the U.S.; you must apply for an extension if you want to stay longer than the date on the card. Do not remove the card after you leave the airport.
- U.S. Customs declaration card.
- entry papers—such as the IAP-66 form.

Transportation. Most large airports have transportation to the downtown area or the suburbs. You may take a:

- taxi. Tip the driver about 15% of the fare. In addition to the fare, the taxi may charge extra for

- tolls, or road fees.
- each extra passenger.
- luggage.
- shuttle service—either a van or a limousine. Shuttle services often cost less per person than taxis, but may take longer if the others in the limousine are going to different places. If two or more people are traveling together, the cost of a taxi may be the same or even cheaper.
- bus, subway, or train. Many airports have public transportation into the city.
- rental car (see "Renting a Car/ Traveling In & Out of the U.S.").

Where to Stay

Hotels

Most hotels have maid and laundry service, room service, and restaurants.

Some hotels also offer:

- suites with small kitchens.
- free parking.
- Internet/computer access.
- fitness centers and swimming pools.
- bilingual staff members.
- smoking and smoke-free rooms.

Motels

Motels are like hotels but usually cost less and have parking. Most motels are in the suburbs or near the road—rather than in the city center.

Guest houses

You may rent a room at a guest house or bed and breakfast (B&B) for a long or short term. With a few, you share a bathroom with other guests. Most offer breakfast; a few offer tea or cocktails in the afternoon.

Temporary homes

You may rent a temporary home for 1 week, 1 month, or more. Most temporary homes come with everything you need—such as furniture, linens (sheets and towels), bedding, dishes, kitchen utensils, and appliances (see "Renting/ Finding a New Home").

In general, furnished apartments cost about 50% more than unfurnished apartments. You pay a security deposit (about 1 month's rent) along with the first rent payment. The security deposit is for fixing any damage you cause to the home. Find out which fees and services are included in the rent.

Services. Some short-term apartments offer special services that may be included in the rental price. For example, you may get:

- 24-hour front desk service.
- maid service.
- newspaper delivery.
- transportation to airports.

American Youth Hostels. Travelers of all ages stay here. Usually, you share a bedroom and bathroom with other people. The cost is usually under $40 a night. You pay extra for sheets and blankets, towels, or meals. Members get discounts; the membership fee is about $25 a year.

Camping. The U.S. has many national and state parks where you can camp. Many camping grounds have cooking grills, toilets, and showers.

Some campsites are free; others charge a fee—usually under $30 a night. You often need reservations.

Arrival Checklist

- ☐ Find out what kind of help you can get from your employer or sponsor.
- ☐ Have all official documents translated into English.

    All translations should be notarized by a notary public or authenticated by your country's embassy. You will pay a small fee. You must show some form of identification—such as a driver's license or a passport. You can find a notary public at:

    - banks and law offices.
    - most real estate offices.
    - some translation companies.

- ☐ Open a bank account (see chapter on "Money Matters").

    You probably will need a checking account to rent a home. You may rent a safe-deposit box for all valuables.

- ☐ Find out about schools if you have children.

    The public school your child goes to depends on the area where you live (see chapter on "Your Older Child").

- ☐ Find a place to live.

    Pay the deposit with a check.

- ☐ Get a driver's license or identification (ID) card.

    If you drive, you need a local license within 30 days after you arrive. If you do not drive, get an ID card (see "Getting Around/ Getting a License).

- ☐ Apply for a Social Security card if you are eligible 3 weeks after you arrive.

    By that time, the U.S. Citizenship and Immigration Services (USCIS) will have your name in its database and will be able to process your application (see "Your Legal Status/Social Security").

Translation Services

Examples of official documents you may need translated are:

- school records.
- medical records.
- birth certificates.
- marriage certificates.
- a license to practice a certain profession.

The translation may take from one day to several weeks, depending on the language and the number of words. Most agencies offer a "rush" service, but prices are higher.

The price also depends on the:

- language used. The more common languages usually cost less.
- type of document. For example, a document with a technical language (such as medical or legal terms) will be more expensive.
- number of words. Usually there is a minimum cost for any document, regardless of its length.

What to look for

A general cost estimate. Most companies do not give estimates before they see the document.

Notarized documents. Some companies may notarize documents (put on a legal stamp), if necessary. Ask for someone who knows your language.

Client references or sample translations.

Other services

Translation companies sometimes offer other language services, such as:

- interpretation services at conferences, meetings, and seminars. You may also hire an interpreter to guide you around the area.
- audio tape transcriptions, which translate the contents of a foreign language tape into a written document.
- videotape dubbing for recording voices in any language over a film.
- language instruction.

Words to Know

Authenticate: to stamp a document. The stamp shows the document is true.

Bilingual: speaking two languages

Concierge: a person who works at the front desk of a hotel or apartment building

Customs inspection station: the place at the airport where officers look over your baggage

Customs declaration card: a card you get on the airplane. You write what you are bringing into the U.S.

Dependent: a person who gets a visa as a family member or employee (such as the driver of a diplomat)

Dubbing: recording voices in any language over a film or videotape

Extension: legal permission to stay in in the country longer

Guest house: a house where you can rent a room for a short or long time

I-94 card: a card that an immigration officer attaches to your passport

Interpreter: a person who repeats someone else's words in another language

Limousine: a large car, or "limo"

Motel: a kind of hotel. The rooms have outside doors and parking spaces.

Notarize: to make a document legal; to put an official stamp on a document

Notary public: a person who helps to make a document legal. A notary public signs that a signature is true.

Room service: food delivery to your room

Security deposit: the money you pay the owner of the house or apartment before you rent it

Social Security card: a U.S. government card that gives you permission to work legally in the U.S.

Suite: a group of rooms in a hotel

Temporary home: a house you can rent for a short or long time

Tip: extra money to a waiter or taxi driver. You are expected to give a tip even if the service was just OK.

Toll: fee for using the road

White Pages: the telephone book that lists people's names, addresses, and home numbers

Yellow Pages: the telephone book with business phone numbers and advertisements. You look up the name of a product or service to find out where to buy it.

Youth hostel: an inexpensive place to stay while you are on a trip. Usually, you share a bedroom and bathroom with others.

Getting Connected

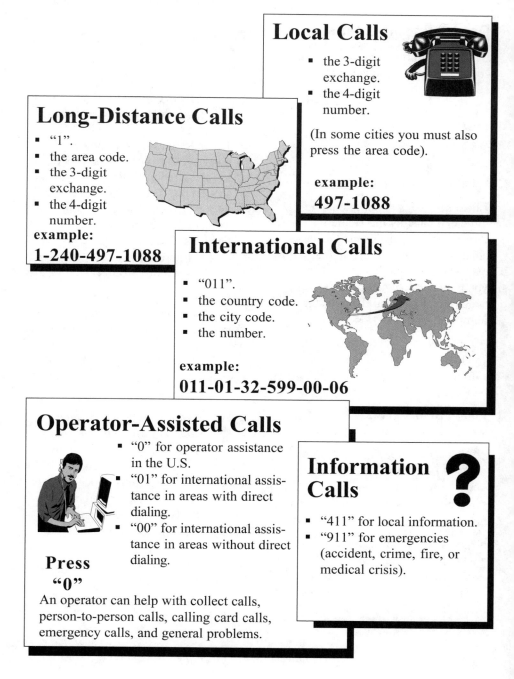

Local Calls

- the 3-digit exchange.
- the 4-digit number.

(In some cities you must also press the area code).

example:
497-1088

Long-Distance Calls

- "1".
- the area code.
- the 3-digit exchange.
- the 4-digit number.

example:
1-240-497-1088

International Calls

- "011".
- the country code.
- the city code.
- the number.

example:
011-01-32-599-00-06

Operator-Assisted Calls

- "0" for operator assistance in the U.S.
- "01" for international assistance in areas with direct dialing.
- "00" for international assistance in areas without direct dialing.

Press "0"

An operator can help with collect calls, person-to-person calls, calling card calls, emergency calls, and general problems.

Information Calls

- "411" for local information.
- "911" for emergencies (accident, crime, fire, or medical crisis).

Dialing a Phone Number

Domestic (U.S.) calls

Every U.S. number has a 3-digit area code, a 3-digit exchange, and a 4-digit number.

For example, in the number 240-497-1088:

- "240" is the area code.
- "497" is the exchange.
- "1088" is the number.

Local numbers. Your telephone directory (usually the White Pages directory) has a list of the local exchanges. In some cities, dial only the exchange and number. In other cities, you may need to dial the 3-digit area code before you dial the exchange and number.

Note: You may need to press "9" or "8" to get an "outside line" when calling from a hotel, campus, or office building.

Long-distance calls. Dial "1" + the area code + exchange + number.

 How can I tell if a number is long-distance? Most numbers are local if they are in the same city or town. To find out if a number is long-distance, you may:

- press "0" and ask the operator.
- dial the exchange and number. If you make the connection without pressing "1" the number is local; if it is long-distance, you will get a message.

Be aware of the differences in time when you are calling another part of the U.S. (see the map in the chapter on "Traveling In & Out of the U.S.")

What should I do if I don't know the number? You may:

- call "411" or "0" for any local or long-distance number. If you know the area code, you may also dial 1+ the area code +555+1212. Call 1+800+555+1212 to find out if a business has a toll free number.
- use the telephone directory (see the section on "Telephone Directories" in this chapter) for local numbers.
- look up the number of a resident or business in the "Yellow Pages" or on the Internet (www.switchboard.net).

In many cities, you can usually make three free "411" calls in one month. Then you will pay 75¢–$1.40 for all information calls—local or long-distance. You may need coins to pay this charge if you call "411" from a pay phone.

What if a recorded voice answers and tells me something I don't understand? Recorded messages are common in the U.S. The message tells which number to press; for example, if you call a theater, the message might say to "press '1' for more information on show times or '2' to order tickets." If you do not understand the recording, try one of the following:

- wait; do not press any buttons. Usually, someone will answer.
- press "0." Sometimes, you will get an operator.

- press the number when it asks if you want "to talk to a representative."

International Calls

To save money, dial direct; that is, do not use the operator. Dial "011" + the country code + the city code + the number; if the city code starts with "0," you usually do not dial the "0."

Special numbers

Phone numbers with letters. Some business numbers have letters instead of numbers. Press the letters on the phone buttons; for example, the number 800-WEATHER is the same as 800-932-8437.

"800" numbers. Numbers that have an area code starting with "8" are "800" numbers—for example, "800," "877," or "888." These are toll-free business numbers; that is, your call to them is free—even if the office is not in the local area. To call, dial "1" + the "800" area code + exchange + number.

"900" numbers. Numbers that have an area code starting with "9" are "900" numbers—for example, "915" or "976." The business will charge you for this call—sometimes, as much as $7 a minute or more. Check the cost before you call. To call, dial "1" + the "900" area code + exchange + number.

To find a telephone right away, you may:

- go to a pay phone on the street, near a gas station, a convenience store, or in a shopping mall. You will need coins or a calling card.
- go to a telephone center for international calls. These centers are usually in hotels or parts of the city with many foreigners. You may need to pay with cash.
- use the phone in your hotel. Local calls are usually less than a dollar. To make a long-distance or international call, use a calling card or other long-distance service.

⊗ Do not use the hotel telephone to make long-distance or international calls before you ask the price. For example, the fee for a call anywhere outside the U.S. may be $4 or more for a connection fee, plus $2.50–$5 a minute; if an operator dials for you, the fee will be even higher.

*To find a calling card right away…*Go to a gas station, convenience store, post office, supermarket, news store, hotel lobby, or printing shop. Check costs carefully, especially if you are using the card for international calls.

*To rent a cellular (cell) phone…*Ask at the car rental agency or call a phone-rental service (see section on "Renting a Cellular (Cell) Phone" in this chapter).

*If you will be here for 3 months or more…*sign up for phone service in your home and office as soon as you can (see chapter on "Communications at Home"). These services often have better rates with fewer surcharges.

The Operator

Help!

Tip: If you have trouble making any call, press "0" for the operator. After the operator explains what to do, hang up and dial yourself. If the operator makes the call for you, the cost will be $2–$7 more.

Call the operator if you:

- dial the wrong number on a long-distance call. With most services, the operator will not charge you for the call.
- are getting a noisy or weak phone connection. The operator will re-dial the number at no charge.
- lose money in a pay phone. Dial "0" for operator. For example, say, "I put two quarters in the phone machine. I dialed the number, but the line was busy. When I hung up, I didn't get my money back." The operator will re-dial at no charge.
- need to contact someone in an emergency and the line is busy. The operator may interrupt the call for you if it is a life-threatening emergency situation.

Special services

For the following calls, dial "0" + area code + exchange + number.

Collect calls. The person you are calling pays for the call. An operator will make the connection for you and ask the person you are calling to accept the cost for the call.

Person-to-person calls. Tell the operator the name of the person you want to talk to. If the person is not there, the operator will not connect you and will not charge for the call.

Pre-paid Calling Cards

To use most cards, first enter "1," the "800" access number, and then your personal code (card number).

Keep your calling card and personal code separate. Your personal code identifies your account. You will pay for any calls charged to this account. If your calling card has a pin number on the back, be sure not to lose it; anyone who finds the card will be able to use it.

Costs for pre-paid cards vary. Some offer a set number of minutes of calling time, plus some free minutes. For example, a $39.99 card may show 200 PLUS 60 free minutes for local calls. Other cards use units to calculate the cost of the call. If you can't find the unit cost on the card, ask the store manager.

Read everything on the card carefully before you buy it—especially the surcharges (see "What to Look for").

What to Look for

In addition to the cost of the card, check the following:

Per-minute rate. Check the rates for the cities and areas you call most often. International rates vary by more than $3 or $4 a minute; find a store with a calling card specifically for the area you are calling—for example, Latin America, Africa, Europe, or Asia.

Surcharges. Cards with lower rates often have higher surcharges, or extra fees—for example:

- connection fees, which may cost as much as $2.50 for every call.
- pay-phone surcharge (about 20¢-40¢ a minute) for calling on a pay phone.

Time Limit. Most cards you get in stores have an expiration date; you may not use the card after that date—for example 30 days after you make the first call.

Dollar Limit. Cards you buy from a store, usually have a dollar limit. For example, you may not use the card after you have spent the $10 or $20 you paid for the card. A few cards let you add to this dollar amount on the card. Ask when you buy the card.

Tip: You may also buy a card from a telephone service with a credit card. These cards usually do not have a time limit. You may also add onto the dollar amount on the card by calling up and giving your credit card information.

For more information about these cards and other communications services, see the chapter on "Communications at Home."

Note: If cost is particularly important, check the billing increments (time periods used to calculate the cost of the call).

Renting a Cellular (Cell) Phone

You may find a cell phone to rent at:

- a car rental agency. Ask when you rent the car.
- a cell phone service. Look under "Cellular/Telephones & Supplies" in the Yellow Pages directory.

The cost is about $3-$6 a day, plus 5¢-25¢ a minute for each call to a U.S. telephone number. Generally, you also pay taxes and a surcharge (an extra fee)—for example, a utility fee of about 8.5% of the total cost. You will need a credit card.

Tip: If you will be staying two weeks or more, consider buying a cell phone (see "Cellular Phones/Communications at Home").

Accessing the Internet

Finding a computer

Look in:

- the airport.
- a hotel business center or your hotel room. Hotel business centers usually charge about $15 a day–even if you use the Internet connection for only an hour.
- printing and office-supply stores (such as Kinko's) and Internet cafés rent computers with Internet

access for an hourly fee—generally around $6-$10 an hour.

- a public library. Most local libraries have free computer terminals, many with high-speed Internet connections. A few libraries let only local residents use the computers, but many have no restrictions. Generally, you may use the computer for a limited amount of time—about 1 hour. Ask around for the nearest

---

Finding the Number...

The name of a person or family. Look in the "Residence" section of the White Pages.

The name of a business. Look in the "Business" section of the White Pages.

A list of services or stores. Look in the Yellow Pages. For example, to find a list of Indian restaurants, find the:

- general category "Restaurants."
- sub-category "Indian."

An "Action Index" (list of categories) is in the back of the book; the pages are usually orange.

A government office. Look in the Blue Pages government section (usually in the White Pages directory). Use the quick "Reference" section at the beginning of the Blue Pages to find the government you want—United States, state, county, or city. Then look for the appropriate department; if you don't know which department you want, call the general information number at the top of the list or find the complete list of departments in the following pages.

Examples:

To find out about:

Immigration regulations: Look under: "United States Government/Immigration & Naturalization Service."

Requirements for getting a driver's license in Maryland: Look under "Maryland State Government/Transportation/Motor Vehicle Administration."

A list of the public schools in Montgomery County: "County/Montgomery County Government/Schools/Public."

A list of libraries with Spanish books: "County/Montgomery County Government/Libraries/Branch Libraries and Cultural Services/Cultural Minorities Services: English-Spanish

---

public library or find it in the Blue Pages of the telephone directory.

Note: Internet cafés may be harder to find in the U.S. than you expect. One reason is that many Americans have computers at home.

Tip: If you are traveling on a highway between cities, try a truckstop. Look for signs on the road or for a gasoline station with many trucks around. Generally, truckstops provide services for truck drivers. Many rent computer terminals to all travelers with a credit card.

Using your own computer

You will need:

- a telephone adapter-plug and an electric outlet adapter.
- a transformer to convert to the U.S. voltage. Many computers already have a built-in converter.
- Internet Service Provider (ISP) with U.S. service. Some hotels and apartments provide lines or terminals with Internet service. To get an ISP on your own, find a start-up disk for AOL or another ISP in a business supply store. The disk is free and has directions for setting up the service. You will need a credit card to use the service itself.

Telephone Directories

You may find telephone directories in most hotel rooms and near many pay phones. Use:

- the Yellow Pages for the numbers of stores and services. This directory has
  - an alphabetical list of different kinds of services—such as "Airlines," "Computers," and "Schools."
  - advertisements.
  - discount coupons for some of the stores and services listed.
- the White Pages for the telephone numbers of homes and businesses.
- the Blue Pages for the telephone numbers of government offices.

Other telephone directory information. The front of the telephone directory has information such as:

- telephone rates and services.
- instructions on using the telephone.
- emergency numbers.
- U.S. maps with area codes.
- local maps of the subway and city streets.
- numbers you may call to get the time and the weather for any major U.S. city.
- sports and cultural events.

Words to Know

"800" numbers: Toll-free numbers, or numbers with an area code that begins with "8"—for example, "800," "877," and "888." These are toll-free numbers. You do not pay long-distance charges.

"900" numbers: Numbers with an area code that begins with "9"—for example, "900," "915," "976." The business you are calling will charge you for each minute of this call— sometimes as much as $7 a minute.

Access number or code: a telephone number or code you dial to use a long distance or Internet service. You will pay for any calls made with this code; put the code and the number to call in separate places so no one can use the card without your permission. Usually, the number is toll-free.

Adapter plug (electric): a plug that allows the electrical connector on your equipment to fit the U.S. electrical outlet

Adapter plug (telephone): a plug that allows the telephone connector on your equipment to fit the U.S. telephone outlet.

Answering machine: a machine that takes phone messages

Area code: a 3-digit code for the region where you live—for example, "202" for Washington, DC.

Billing increments: the unit of time used to calculate the cost of a call. Usually, these units are either three minutes, one minute, 30 seconds, or 6 seconds. For example, if the billing unit is three minutes, you will pay for all three minutes—even if you talk for less time. The smaller the unit, the less you pay for each call.

Collect: a long-distance call that "reverses the charges." The person you are calling pays for the call.

Calling card: a card that allows access for making local, long-distance, or international calls.

Cancellation fee: (see "Termination fee")

Carrier: (see "Provider")

Connection fee: a fee you pay for starting, or connecting to, the service.

Convenience store: a small store that sells newspapers, groceries, and some medicine. Many are open 24 hours a day.

Country code: a number you dial to call a country. Each country has its own code.

Dial: press the numbers (or letters) on the phone to make the call

Dial tone: the humming sound you hear when you pick up the receiver

Domestic: inside the U.S.

Exchange: the first three digits in a telephone number—after the area code. For example, in the number "240-497-1088," the digits "497" are the exchange.

Expiration date: the last date when you may use a product or service.

Information: the number you dial to get someone's telephone number—usually "411"

Local: in the area where you do not pay extra for a call

Long-distance: not in the "free" area for your phone service. A long-distance number is outside your local calling area.

Outside line: line you use to reach a number outside a campus, office building, or hotel

Menu: a recorded message you get after you have dialed a number. The message lists the services or people you can access; you press a number for the service or person you want. If you cannot understand the message, just press "0" or wait for someone to come to the phone.

Personal code: the code, or group of numbers, that identifies your account. You will pay for any calls charged to this account.

Person-to-person: a kind of long-distance call. You tell the operator the name of the person you want to talk to. If the person is not there, the operator does not connect the call, and you are not charged a fee.

Phone card: (see "Calling card")

Pre-paid calling card: a calling card you buy with cash before you use it. Each card lets you spend a set amount of money on your calls.

Provider: company that sells you the service

Receiver: a part of the phone. You pick up the receiver and hold it in your hand; then you talk into the speaker at the end of the receiver.

Roaming charges: charges added to your phone bill when calling out long-distance on your cell phone

Standard calling card: a calling card that charges the cost of each call to your credit card or your phone bill. If you do not make any calls, you are not charged.

Station-to-station: a kind of long-distance call. You speak to anyone who answers.

Surcharge: any charge you pay in addition to the service unit (per-minute rate)

Termination fee: a fee you pay for canceling (stopping), a service before the time in the agreement

Toll-free numbers: calls for which you do not pay long-distance charges. For example, numbers with an "800" area code are toll-free.

Transformer: (see "Voltage converter")

Truckstop: a place where truck drivers can get gas, take showers, and sleep. Truckstop restaurants are popular with drivers of cars as well as truck drivers. Many truckstops have Internet terminals.

[Service] Unit: the amount used to calculate the cost of a call. The cost of each unit is usually on the card.

Voltage converter (transformer): a device for converting from U.S. voltage to the voltage needed by your equipment

White Pages: the telephone directory that lists people's names and home numbers

Yellow Pages: the telephone directory that has advertisements for products and services

Your Legal Status

Overview

There are two types of U.S. visas:

- immigrant, or permanent immigrant, visas for people who will be living and working in the U.S. permanently—rather than returning home.
- non-permanent, or non-immigrant, visas for foreign nationals who will be living and working for a specific period of time—and then returning to their home country.

All international newcomers need a visa to live in the U.S. Visitors from some countries may not need a visa to come here for business or pleasure; check with the U.S. Embassy in your home country.

What is a "green card" or a "pink card"? A "green card" shows that you have permanent immigrant status; that is, you may live and work here as long as you want (see section on "Immigrant Visas" in this chapter). Most newcomers with a green card may apply to become citizens after 3 or 5 years. The new cards from the INS are pink, rather than green. Carry a copy of this card all the time.

What is a "white card"? A "white card" shows that you have refugee status; that is, you left your country to escape persecution. You may live and work here as long as you want. You may also get immigrant status and apply to become a citizen.

The Federal Information Center has books and pamphlets on applying for jobs in the federal government, federal income taxes, immigration services, Social Security benefits, and other federal agencies, programs, and services.

Tell the truth whenever any immigration officer interviews you or you are filling out a government form. If you are having any immigration problems, an attorney may be able to help you—as long as you have told the truth; if you have not told the truth, your problem may be more difficult to solve. You may even be deported, without the right to return.

Both permanent and non-permanent immigrants must be sure not to break any U.S. law—for example, by shoplifting or driving while intoxicated. If you commit any crime at all, you may be required to leave the U.S.—with no permission to return. Both children and adults must know and obey the law.

Immigrant Visas

With an immigrant visa you may:

- travel anywhere in the U.S.
- leave the U.S. and return again as many times as you want.
- live here as long as you want.
- get a job here.
- apply to bring certain members of your "immediate family" into the country—for example, a spouse or a child.
- apply to be a citizen after you have lived here for 5 years (3 years if you came here as the husband or wife of a U.S. citizen).

Non-immigrant Visas

If you have a visa to live and work here, you may apply for a visa for others in your immediate family—that is, for a spouse or a child.

Your visa tells:

- how many times you may leave the U.S. and come back again. Some people may travel in and out of the U.S. as many times as they want. Others may not leave at all. If you have questions about traveling outside the U.S., call the U.S. Embassy or Consulate in your home country.
- whether you may work; often, the principal may work but the family member may not. For example, persons with an H1 or H2 visa can work, but their spouse, with an H4 visa, cannot. However, the spouse of a person with an L-1 visa may get authorization to work.

⊗ Do not confuse the date on your visa with the date on your I-94 or I-94W card. You must leave the U.S. by the date on the card or apply for an extension.

If you stay longer, you will be "Out of Status" and may be required to leave. You may not receive permission to re-enter the U.S. for a year or more.

Getting a Visa

U.S. Embassy or Consulate. Call the U.S. Embassy or Consulate in your home country or review its Website on the Internet. If you are applying for an immigrant visa, you may be able to apply for a Social Security Number (SSN) at the same time. Applicants for a non-immigrant visa must wait until they arrive in the U.S. to apply for an SSN.

⊗ Even if you and your partner have lived together for many years, you may not enter the U.S. as a married couple unless you are legally married in your home country. Also, the United States Citizenship and Immigration Services (USCIS) does not recognize same-sex marriages.

Do not try to avoid these immigration rules by coming in on a tourist visa and staying beyond the expiration date. Ask an immigration attorney to advise you.

Social Security

How to apply

The Social Security Card, with a Social Security Number (SSN) is like a national ID card. If you have come to the U.S. to work, apply for an SSN in person at a Social Security office about 3 weeks after you arrive. All supporting documents must be originals—not copies.

 You will need:

- a valid passport. The passport must be at least one year old. If not, bring both your current and your out-of-date passport.

Types of Non-Immigrant Visas

A visa: foreign government officials and employees such as ambassadors, public ministers, or career diplomatic or consular officers

B visa: people coming for a short while—usually less than 1 year

B-1: people coming here to do business. Find out from an attorney or from the U.S. Embassy or Consulate what kinds of business you can and cannot do.
B-2: tourists

E visa: treaty-traders and treaty-investors who want to trade with the U.S.

F visa: students in U.S. colleges, universities, seminaries (religious schools), language programs

G visa: representatives of international governmental organizations—such as the World Bank or the United Nations

H visa: people who will be here a certain amount of time—usually from 3–6 years. Most have a Bachelor's degree from a university.

- H-1: experts in business, science, or the arts—such as engineers, architects, teachers, or lawyers
- H-2: people who have temporary jobs in specific fields
- H-3: people in training programs

J visa: students, researchers, professors, and teachers—such as scientists for the National Institutes of Health. Usually, they are part of a U.S. Government exchange program.

K visa: men or women engaged to marry U.S. citizens (and their children)

L visa: employees who are transferred to the U.S. Usually, they:

- are executives, managers, or technical specialists.
- are employees of large companies with offices in other countries.
- have worked for the company at least 1 year.

M visa: students at a vocational school to prepare for a job. The school cannot be a language school, a college, or a university.

O, P, and Q visas: persons involved in cultural programs; people with exceptional ability in science, business, the arts, education, athletics, or the film industry

Tip: For a complete list, look in www.USImmigration.com

- a visa and I-94 form and visa application papers. The visa must be at least one year old; if not, bring both your current and out-of-date visas.
- a letter from your employer stating your position, salary, and the expected length of time you will stay.

Go to the Social Security website for more details, a list of Social Security offices, and an application form.

⊗ If you leave the country before you get your Social Security card, you will need to wait another 3 weeks after you return.

? How can I open a bank account while I am waiting for an SSN? Bring your passport, a mailing address, and $100 for your first deposit; you may use cash, a credit card, or a check from a U.S. bank.

Who may apply

If your visa allows you to work, you are eligible for a Social Security Card. For example, holders of E-1 or E-2, H-1 or 2, L-1 or L-2 visas are eligible. Other rules for spouses, students, and diplomatic families vary (see "Making It Legal/Finding Work").

To open a bank account, get a loan, or get a driver's license, students may need a letter from their foreign advisor stating their visa status. Diplomats and their families will need a letter from their employer stating their position, salary, and expected length of stay.

? *I cannot get a Social Security number. What should I do?*

If you cannot get a Social Security number, you will need other identification for business transactions or enrolling in a school. In some situations, you will need a copy of your passport and/or visa and proof of your street address—for example, a bill mailed to you in your new home.

If you cannot work, the best ID is a driver's license card issued by the Department of Motor Vehicles (DMV) in the U.S. state where you live. Even if you do not drive, you may still get an ID card from the DMV (see "Getting an ID/Driver's License/Getting Around").

Anyone who is not allowed to earn U.S. income must get an Individual Tax Identity Number (ITIN). Fill out and send an IRS W-7 form to apply (see "Paying Your Taxes/Documents you need"). The ITIN is useful only for paying taxes; you may not use it for any other purpose.

? *Should I carry my passport around?* No. Take it only when you need identification papers—for example, when you want to open up a bank account and do not have your SSN yet.

How to avoid common problems

1. Check your papers.

Be sure the officials have filled out your papers correctly (see "Documents/Before You Come"). If you find an error—for example, an incorrect date—you may want to see an attorney right away.

2. Keep a calendar of the important dates right after you arrive.

For example, write the dates when you:

- must leave or ask for an extension. That is the expiration date on your I-94.
- are leaving the country—whether or not you intend to return.
- need an extension.
- are changing your status (see "Changes and Extensions" in this chapter.

Also write the dates when you should see an immigration attorney or contact the USCIS.

⊗ Changing your visa may take up to a year; every case is different. To be safe, begin as soon as you know about a problem or a possible change.

3. See an attorney, your school advisor, or your company representative.

Go about 3 months after you arrive—even if you think you have no problems. For example, an attorney will talk about your future plans and look over your visa.

Changes and Extensions

Changes in status. Find out what to do if you are:

- changing jobs. Check with an attorney or other professional— even if you will be working for the same employer. For example, exchange visitors may need to fill out some forms to change from research to clinical work.
- changing schools. Go to the school's international office or the person in charge of the I-20 process at your new school.
- finishing school and going to work. Check with an attorney to make sure you are authorized to work before you begin.
- moving your home.
- getting married or divorced.

Note: Students generally may stay as long as the expected time of their study in school or college. Check with your foreign student advisor.

Extensions. To get an extension, you will need:

- an application to "Extend Time of Temporary Stay" from the USCIS.

- copies of the original I-94 forms for you, your spouse, and your children.
- other documents. The documents you need vary. Many times, you need a letter from your employer.
- the application fee.

File, or send, the application before, *not after*, the expiration date on your I-94 card. If you are sending the application yourself, start at least 3 months ahead of time. Your approval usually takes about 30–45 days, but special problems may cause delays. If you are still waiting, you may stay as long as 240 days after you file. To prevent unnecessary problems, ask an immigration attorney to file for you.

Choosing Legal Assistance

Attorneys. To find an attorney:

- ask your embassy for recommendations.
- call the American Immigration Lawyers Association.

Tip: Talk to an immigration attorney before you hire him or her. Be sure the attorney is experienced and specially trained in immigration laws.

Visa or "notario" services. Before you choose a visa service, ask:

- how much the service charges.
- what the service will do.
- how long the service has been in business.

Also ask for the names of references you can call. Be sure to get a signed, written contract.

Some visa services charge a lot of money for doing some things you can do on your own. Others have been charged with fraud or illegal practices. Be careful when choosing a service!

Words to Know

American Immigration Lawyers Association: a group that represents lawyers who practice immigration law

Attorney: a person who represents you in business and law

Dependent: a person who enters the U.S. as part of the family or household (servant or chauffer) of the main visa holder

Exchange visitor program: a program in which two people from different countries trade jobs

Extension: a written agreement that allows you more time to be in the country after a visa runs out

Fraud: a dishonest act, usually in business or law

"Green card" or "pink card": a paper, or document, that shows that you have an immigrant status; that is, you can live and work here as long as you want

"Immediate family": a father or mother, unmarried son or daughter under the age of 21, or husband or wife. Members of a U.S. citizen's immediate family are the most likely to get immigrant visas.

Immigrant visa: a visa that lets you live and work here as long as you want. You get an immigrant visa if you do not plan to live in your home country again.

Immigration and Naturalization Service (INS): the U.S. Government agency responsible for monitoring who comes into the country and how long they can stay

Individual Tax Identification Number (ITIN): a nine-digit number that the IRS uses instead of a Social Security Number (SSN). Only persons who cannot get an SSN may apply for this identification number. You may use the ITIN only for taxes; you may not use it for any other type of identification. It is not a permit to work in the U.S.

Mulitple entry visa: a visa that lets you leave and return to the U.S.

Non-immigrant visa: a visa that lets you live here for awhile—usually six months to five years. Non-immigrant visas are for people who will live in their home country again.

Non-permanent visa: visa for foreign nationals who will be returning to their home country after a specific period of time (see "non-immigrant visa").

Out-of-status person: a person who stays in the U.S. without applying for an extension or enters the U.S. illegally. Out-of-status persons may be required to leave, without permission to return.

Permanent visa. A visa for immigrants who will be living in the U.S. permanently—probably for the rest of their lives (see "Immigrant visa").

Persecution: actions against you because of your race, political ideas, religion, or nationality. Refugees come to the U.S. because their governments have persecuted them.

"Pink card": see "Green card"

Point of entry: the airport, port, or border crossing where you enter the U.S.

Principal: the student or employee who gets the visa; family members are dependents.

Refugee: a person who has come to the U.S. to escape persecution

Social Security Number (SSN): the number on the Social Security card that gives you permission to work legally in the U.S.

United States Citizenship and Immigration Services (USCIS): a division of the Department of Homeland Security. The USCIS has responsibility for immigrant and non-immigrant visas, procedures for coming into the U.S., and working permits for international residents, financial benefits for immigrants.

"White card": a paper, or document, that shows that you have refugee status; that is, you left your country to escape persecution. You have the same rights as immigrants with a "green card" or "pink card."

Traveling In & Out of the U.S.

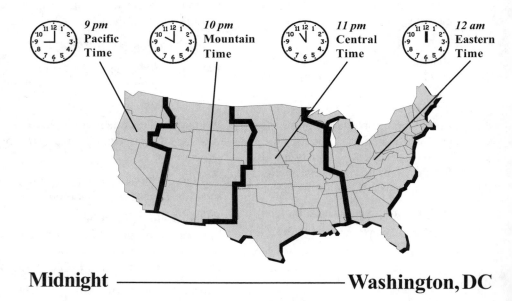

9 pm Pacific Time

10 pm Mountain Time

11 pm Central Time

12 am Eastern Time

Midnight ———————————————————— Washington, DC

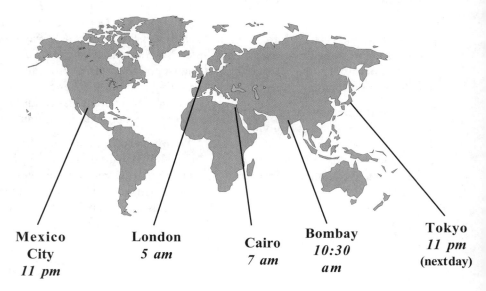

Mexico City *11 pm*

London *5 am*

Cairo *7 am*

Bombay *10:30 am*

Tokyo *11 pm* (nextday)

Renting a Car

When you plan your trip, try to stay away from big cities during the rush hours. If traffic is light, you can get from:

- New York City to Washington, DC—4½–5 hours.
- Atlanta to Miami—12 hours.
- Dallas to Houston—4 hours.

On some major highways, you will pay tolls; most are $2 each. For example, in the year 2004, tolls for driving from Washington, DC to New York City are about $20.

Tip: "On the Highway/Getting Around" has many tips on traveling from city to city. For example, on some roads, you may use a pass instead of cash. For example, the E-ZPass may save you hours on a trip from New York City to Washington (see "On the Highway/Getting Around").

You must be at least 25 years old to rent a car.

 You will need an international driver's license or a license from your home country.

 Prices vary according to the type of car, the rental company, and the city. Ask at the desk about discounts. The price per day will be less if you rent a car:

- for the whole week.
- on the weekend.

You may rent the following types of cars:

- economy, the least expensive.

- compact.
- mid-size.
- standard or full size.
- premium.
- luxury, the most expensive.
- specialty cars including convertibles, SUVs and pickups.

Gasoline. The car you get will have a full tank of gas. If you do not return it with a full tank, you pay for the gas you used. The price per gallon is often higher than the price at a gas station.

 You pay less if you pump the gas yourself (see "Service Stations/Getting Around").

Insurance. You may already have insurance with your auto policy. You may get more insurance coverage from the auto-rental company; often, this extra insurance is not necessary.

Tip: A few rental cars have an electronic Global Positioning System (GPS) that directs you to places in the area.

Riding Buses and Trains

Buses

Buses usually cost less but take longer than other ways of travel. Call and ask about express service.

 The year 2004 costs and times of some one-way trips are:

- $105 from Chicago to Houston—approximately 25 hours.
- $ 93.50 from Miami to Atlanta—approximately 17 hours.

- $ 44.00 from Los Angeles to San Francisco—approximately 8 hours.

 To get the lowest fares for trips over 800 miles, reserve tickets as soon as you can.

Trains

Amtrak is the only train that goes to most major sections of the U.S., but most routes are not direct. Call or check the schedule on the Internet. All AMTRAK trains have a café or dining car; some have sleeping cars.

 You can buy tickets at the station, by phone, or on-line with a credit card.

To buy tickets in advance, call any Amtrak station or use the Amtrak Website. If you want to tour the country by train, find out about Amtrak's discount passes.

Flying

Buying the tickets

Saving money. For domestic flights, start with the Internet. Start with "economy" airlines such as Southwest or JetBlue; register on their site, so you will get notice of discounts. Even major airlines often have cheaper prices on the Internet. When talking to the travel agent or the airline on the phone, have the Internet page handy so you can suggest different times; travel and airline agents do not always have complete information.

Shuttles. Some cities have shuttles between popular routes, for example, between:

- New York City and Boston.
- Los Angeles and San Francisco.

These shuttles fly every hour; you do not need to reserve your flight in advance.

 When buying tickets on the Internet, be sure to enter the correct information. For example, one common error is to mix up "am" or morning flights with "pm" or afternoon and nighttime flights.

When traveling on a holiday, get the tickets as soon as you can. Good tickets often sell out months in advance.

Frequent fliers. All airlines give frequent-flier miles or other awards for passengers who fly with them. Register as a frequent flier the first time you use any airline and make sure your frequent flier number is registered each time you fly. Some credit-card companies and hotels also award frequent-flier miles.

Tip: Often, your frequent-flier miles are valid with more than one airline; check if you want to use them for a particular flight.

Ask about discounts for all travel—especially if you are a full-time student or a senior citizen (usually a person over 60); the age for a senior-citizen discount varies. Discounts also may be available if you are a member of the American Automobile Association (AAA).

Refundable tickets. With a refundable ticket, you can get your money back if you cancel or change your flight. With a non-refundable ticket, you will not get your money back, but you may be able to apply the cost of the ticket to the price of another flight. Policies vary; ask your airline when buying the ticket.

Paper vs. electronic tickets. An electronic ticket (e-ticket) is just as valid as a paper ticket. With a paper ticket, the airline mails the tickets to you—unless you buy the ticket at the airport or other airline office. The cost for mailing the tickets is usually about $10.

With an electronic ticket, you get a one-page fax or email message with your name and flight information. One advantage of the e-ticket is that you may be able to check in electronically (see "Electronic check-in" below). The main disadvantage is that you will have more trouble changing your ticket if your flight is cancelled and you want to use another airline.

The airport

You will need:

- a photo ID for each passenger. If you do not have a photo ID, you will not be able to fly.
- a paper ticket or printed passenger receipt that shows you bought the ticket. If you have an e-ticket, your receipt is the information sheet with your flight schedule. Check with the airline for this and other security regulations.

Arrive early—usually 1–1½ hours ahead of time for a domestic flight and 2–3 hours early for an international flight. If you are driving, leave time for taking the shuttle from the parking (or car rental) lot to the airport terminal. Check with the airport or your travel agent.

Arrive even earlier if you are traveling around the time of a major holiday—especially Thanksgiving, Christmas, and New Year's Day.

You may not have any weapons or sharp instruments—such as guns, knives, scissors, or other cutting tools—in your carry-on bags.

Electronic check-in. With electronic tickets, you may be able to check in electronically; that is, you can print out a boarding pass, with a seat assignment. With some airlines, you may be able to check in, at home, one or two days before the flight. Many airlines have electronic check-in machines at the airport, close to the check-in counter. Use the machine if you have only "carry-on" bags and luggage.

Curbside check-in, or outside check-in, for domestic flights may be available at your airport. Often, the line for checking your luggage is much shorter.

Baggage. If you have a lot of luggage, call the airline ahead of time and ask:

- the weight, size, and number of bags per person.
- the weight, size, and number of "carry-on" bags per person.

53

Parking. Most airports have parking in:

- short-term lots. These may cost $5 an hour or more.
- long-term lots. These may be far away from the terminal; a shuttle bus will take you from the parking lot to the terminal for free.

Tip: Record the location of your car. If you cannot find your car when you return, ask the driver of a shuttle bus to call for someone who can drive you around.

Tip: Carry a cell phone with you. If your flight is delayed or cancelled, call the airline to make other arrangements. Often, calling on the phone is faster than waiting in line.

Getting Ready

Money

Travelers checks. Get them from your bank, an American Express office, or a foreign exchange office.

A major credit card. Write down the number of your credit card in case it is lost or stolen. Carry it separately from your credit cards.

Automatic teller machine bank card (ATM). You may use an ATM in most areas of the U.S.

Communications

The chapters on "Getting Connected" and "Communications at Home" have more information about cellular (cell) phone services, calling cards, and Internet access.

Cellular (Cell) phones. Most cellular (cell) phones will work in all major U.S. cities—but not in other countries. To rent an international phone with the same telephone number you already have, find a phone and service provider before you leave the country.

Calling cards. Look for a card with good rates to and from the cities and countries you are visiting.

Internet access. In many airports, you can access the Internet either with or without a laptop. Ask at the Information desk. When traveling internationally, bring telephone and electric outlet adapters, and a voltage transformer if necessary. See "Accessing the Internet/Getting Connected" for Internet options around town.

Tip: At some airports, you may rent a DVD player and DVD for the flight. This service is handy when traveling with children.

Travel insurance

You may buy travel insurance from:

- travel agents.
- health or travel insurance companies.

Trip cancellation or interruption insurance. If you need to cancel your trip because of an emergency, such as the illness or death of a family member, cancellation/interruption insurance will return any fees you have already paid for the trip.

Medical assistance insurance is for accidents or illnesses that happen on the trip. Check with your insurance company to see if you are already insured while traveling; ask what to do if you need to see a doctor in another area of the U.S. or in another country.

 When you arrive, put any valuables—such as jewelry, camera equipment, airplane tickets, and extra money—in a hotel safe-deposit box. Never leave your camera or any other costly item in the room.

Leaving the country

Your passport. Make a photocopy of your passport. Carry it separately in case the passport is lost or stolen.

Before you leave:

- Check your visa status; make sure you can return to the U.S. again.
- Find out if you need new entry papers.
- Inform the international students' office if you are a student.

How to leave your home

1. Arrange for someone to take care of your home.

Have a friend or neighbor watch your house or apartment while you are away.

Keep lights on at all times or use a timer that turns the lights on or off. Close all curtains and blinds.

2. Ask your newspaper carriers and post office to hold deliveries while you are away.

For short trips, ask a neighbor to pick up your newspaper and mail every day.

3. Get a pet-sitter or take your pets to a kennel.

A pet-sitter comes to your home and takes care of your pets while you are away.

4. Get your home ready.

Unplug all heating appliances and electronic equipment if you will be away for a long time. Do not unplug your refrigerator or freezer.

If the temperature may go below freezing while you are gone, "winterize" your home. For example, you may need to protect the pipes from freezing. Ask your neighbors or the home owner what to do.

5. Tell the neighbors you will be away.

Ask them to call the police or fire department if an emergency arises or if they see a stranger near your house. Leave a phone number where they can reach you.

Words to Know

Advance purchase: buying tickets in advance, or ahead of time

Airline: a company that owns and flies airplanes, such as British Airways

Automated teller machine (ATM): a machine for transactions such as depositing and withdrawing money

"Carry-on": bags you carry with you onto the plane

Compact (car): a small car—usually for 3–5 people

Curbside check-in: an airline stand where you check in your luggage for domestic flights. Often, the lines are shorter.

Electronic ticket (e-ticket): a type of travel ticket. With an e-ticket, you have an information sheet instead of a paper ticket. The "ticket" is on the airline database.

Economy (car): the least expensive type of rental car

Electronic check-in: a way to get your boarding pass and seat number ahead of time—either on a computer at home or on a machine at the airport. You may not check in electronically with a paper ticket or for an international flight.

Full size (car): see standard car

Frequent-flier program: A program that lets you earn free flights.

GPS: a system in your car that gives you directions as you drive. You give it the address, and then the system displays a map and a voice tells you how to get there.

Long-term parking lot: a place near the airport where you can park your car for more than one day

Luxury (car): the largest rental car. It can fit 5-6 people

Medical assistance insurance: insurance that pays for your medical care during a trip

Mid-size (car): a type of rental car

Non-refundable tickets: not able to be returned for money. You may be able to apply the cost to the purchase of a new ticket with the same airline.

Paper tickets: tickets for flying to and from your destination. The tickets are usually stapled together.

Premium (car): an expensive, large rental car

Refundable: able to be returned. You can get your money back if you cancel or change a refundable ticket.

Rush hour: the time of day when most people are driving to or coming home from work

Safe-deposit box: a safe for keeping valuables and important papers

Short-term parking lot: an airport lot. Short-term parking is more expensive than long-term.

Shuttle: a flight that goes every hour. You do not have to reserve a seat. You may pay on the plane.

Shuttle bus: a bus that goes back and forth from the parking lot to the main part of the airport

Standard (car): a good-size rental car

Toll: money paid for using some roads and bridges

Trip cancellation insurance: insurance that pays for your trip if you cannot go or have to come home early

"Winterize": get the house ready for winter

__Getting Around__

 Drive on the right. Pass on the left.

 Stop for a red light. In some cities, you may take a right turn at a red light if no one is coming; but first make sure there is not a "No Turn on Red" sign.

Stop for a flashing red light; look around and then go ahead slowly.

Go slowly for a yellow light.

 Stop for a stopped school bus with flashing lights. You must stop if you are:

- in back of the bus.
- facing the bus in the opposite lane.

Wait for the bus to turn off the flashing lights and start again. Then you may go.

 Go to the side of the road and stop if you see the flashing lights of, or hear a fire truck, ambulance, or police car.

In some states, the driver and any other person in the front seat must wear a seat belt—by law. The child safety seat law varies from state to state, but in general, children under 6 years of age or who weigh less then 40 pounds must sit in a child safety seat. Check with your local Division of Consumer Affairs of Police Department for the law in your state.

The police have the right to stop your car and test your breath for alcohol. If you have been drinking, you may:

- lose your license.
- pay a fine.
- go to jail.

 Carry your driver's license and car registration card whenever you are driving. Keep the car registration in your wallet—not in the car—in case your car is stolen.

Public Transportation

Railway systems

Subways. Many metropolitan areas have a rail system that runs through the city and nearby suburbs.

In most cities, you will not wait more than 15 minutes for a train.

Rail. You may also find commuter trains that connect "far-out" suburbs and smaller cities to the large metropolitan area.

Buses

Some cities and suburbs have buses that go through the city or connect with the rail system.

⊗ If you do not drive, find a place to live that is near public transportation. Make sure it runs at convenient times—including evenings and weekends.

Transfers

In most cities, you may get a transfer to go from a railway to a bus or from one bus to another bus. Most transfers are free; in a few cities you pay a small fee.

Discounts

Some people get discounts—for example:

- senior citizens (people over 65 years old).

- people who buy tickets for many trips at one time.

Taxis

If you are getting a taxi on the street, wave to a taxi with a roof light on. When the taxi stops next to you, look quickly inside, near the front window; you should be able to see a license with a photo identification (ID).

All cities have taxis that will pick you up at your door—even if you are in the suburbs. In most suburbs, you do not pay extra for this pick-up.

Usually, the taxi comes in about 15–20 minutes; ask how long you will wait, especially if the weather is bad. If possible, call 1–2 days before you go. Confirm on the day of the pick-up.

$ Ask for a "ball-park price" ahead of time—either on the street, before you get in, or on the phone. A "ball-park price" may not be exact, but should be within a dollar or two.

The cost depends on:

- the city. The taxis in each city charge different prices.
- the distance.
- the number of people in the taxi.
- the amount of luggage you have. Usually, taxis charge extra for each suitcase.
- the time of day; rush hour is most expensive.

In most cities, the taxis have meters. Other cities have taxi zones; the cost of the trip increases with each additional zone. Ask to see a map with the zones on it.

On the Highway

What to take

Bring:

- travelers checks or a credit card. Do not take more cash than you need; most places accept credit cards.
- a cellular phone (cell phone). You may need it to call for directions, reservations, or road service for your car.

Note: See "Accessing the Internet/ Getting Connected" for information about Internet access on the highway.

Internet Directions

Many Internet sites give routes for traveling inside and between cities. These routes may be helpful; if possible, check to be sure they are accurate and up-to-date.

Passes

Find out about "passes" for local or long-distance trips in the area where you are living or traveling. If you live in the Northeast—in Boston, New York, or Washington DC, an EZPass may save you hours of waiting at the toll booths on major routes.

Food

Most major highways have restaurants along the way. The restaurants usually serve cheap, fast food — for example, hamburgers, hot dogs, pizza, sandwiches, ice cream, and snacks.

Restrooms

All restaurants and gas stations have restrooms. Often you may use the restroom even if you do not buy anything.

Motels

If your trip will take more than one day, you may stay at a motel. Signs for motels are posted near most exits.

If you plan to stop late at night, make reservations ahead of time. AAA has free travel guides for members (see below).

Find out about joining auto clubs such as the American Automobile Association (AAA). With the AAA, you get services such as:

- free maps and advice on highway routes in the U.S.
- towing. If your car gets stuck, AAA will come and tow it for you.

In some states, you may find the AAA under the name of the state—such as the California State Automobile Association (CSAA).

Tip: You may also make reservations while traveling. If you see several motels with the same name, stop at one to reserve a room further down the road.

Safety

Speed. In general, do not go faster than 5 miles above the speed limit; otherwise, you may get a ticket.

Turning around. Keep moving if you miss your exit. Get off at the next exit. If the exit has an A and a B turn, get off at the B turn, and find the highway entrance that will take you back.

Hitchhikers. Do not pick up anyone standing on the side of the road. Hitchhiking is not safe; it is also against the law in most states.

Car trouble. If you see a car stuck on the side of the road, go to the nearest emergency phone on the side of the road and call for help.

If you must stop, park on the right-hand side of the road and turn on the emergency flashing lights. Lock your doors and close your windows.

Use your cell phone to call:

- AAA if you are a member.
- the official telephone number on a sign at the side of the road.
- the number of the rental company if you are renting a car.
- the local police or gas station. Call information—"411" or "0."

Note: If you cannot get anyone else and you are on a lonely road, call "911."

⊗ Do not get out of the car — even if you have no cell phone. Wait for help to come. Most likely, a police car will come in 10–15 minutes.

If someone comes up to your window to help, open the window about an inch — no more — from the top. Tell the person to get help from the nearest gas station or to use an emergency phone on the side of the road.

Parking

⊗ Look out for "No Parking" signs when you park on the street. If you park in a "no-parking" zone, your car may be towed, or taken off the streets.

Places to park

Garages. Garage parking in the city costs about $7–$12 an hour, or $20–$25 a day. Parking may be cheaper on Saturdays and Sundays or at night.

Meters. Usually, a meter takes quarters; some also take dimes and nickels. Check the number of hours you may park. If you stay too long, you may get a ticket and pay a fine—sometimes more than $100.

In most places, you may park for free:

- after 6:30 p.m.
- on Sundays.
- on holidays.

Parking validation. At some restaurants, stores, or movie theaters, you may park for free. Take your ticket with you and ask someone in the shop to validate ("stamp") your parking ticket. Give the ticket to the parking attendant when you leave.

Valet parking. On very busy streets, restaurants and stores often hire someone to park your car. Usually, you can see the sign and the price in front of the restaurant, on the sidewalk. Drive up and look for a parker at the door; if no one is there, just wait at the side of the road and blow the car horn.

 Valet parking usually costs about $5; tip about a dollar. If the service is free, tip about $2.

Service Stations

 The price of gas often varies; two stations right next to each other may have different prices. If you are using self-service, you may need to pay for the gas before you pump it.

Some stations give discounts for paying with:

- cash.
- the station's credit card.

Full service. The attendant pumps the gas, wipes the windshield, and checks the oil, if necessary.

Self-service. You pump the gas yourself. The self-service price is less than the full service. In most stations, you may use a machine to pay with

your credit card or debit card, so you may get gas any time—day or night.

The directions for using "self-service" are on the pump screen, but they are often difficult to follow. Ask an attendant to help you.

Getting an ID/ Driver's License

The driver's license is a useful ID in many situations—for example, for cashing a check, renting a video, or getting on an airplane. If you do not drive, you may get a non-driver's ID card at the state's Motor Vehicle Administration (MVA) or Department of Motor Vehicles (DMV). Bring the documents listed in this section for getting a license.

If you will be living in the U.S. more than 30 days, you must get a local driver's license in order to drive. You must be 18–21 years old or older; every state has different laws.

The best time to go to the MVA or DMV is in the morning or in the middle of the week.

If possible, do not go on:

- Mondays and Fridays.
- the first and last few days of a month.
- the day after a holiday.

Call and ask what you need to bring. Look under "Motor Vehicle Administration" or "Motor Vehicles-Department of" in the state government section of your phone book. Remember: All documents must be in English or translated and notarized.

You probably will need:

- an international driver's license or a translated driver's license from your home country. If you have one, you may not need to take the road test.
- proof of residence—for example, an electricity or telephone bill with your name and address on it. The address must be where you are living permanently—rather than the name of a hotel.
- proof of your name and age. Bring an original birth certificate (translated) or other official document—such as your employment authorization card.
- your passport, with your visa and I-94 card.
- your Social Security card. If you are not eligible for a Social Security card, request a letter of exemption from the Social Security office. Diplomats and their families should call their embassy or consulate.

Words to Know

American Automobile Association (AAA): a club for car drivers. It provides services—such as emergency repairs, maps, and tips on driving safely. The emergency repair service is especially useful; no matter where you are in the U.S., a AAA repair car can come and help if you are stuck.

Child safety seat: a car seat for a small child

Department of Motor Vehicles (DMV): (see "Motor Vehicle Administration" below)

Divided highway: a highway with grass, land, or a wall in the middle

Driver education: classes for people who want to learn how to drive and get a license

Driver's manual: a book that tells about driving and parking laws and gives sample driving test questions

E-ZPass: a pass that saves time on the highways. This pass is for driving in the Northeast, but most regions of the country have passes like it. You pay for the pass with a credit card, then put the pass on your windshield; the machine at the tollgate automatically charges the toll to your account. The lines for cars with the pass are much shorter.

Full service: complete gas station service

Gallon: 3.8 liters

Glove compartment: a small storage space in the dashboard of a car

Hazards: flashers; emergency lights on the side and back of a car

Letter of exemption: a letter from the Social Security office stating that you are not eligible for a Social Security number. You may need this letter in order to get a driver's license.

Licensed (taxi): allowed by the city or county government to drive a taxi

Meter: a machine in a taxi that tells the cost of the ride; also, a machine on the side of a road. You must put money in the meter to park your car there.

Motel: a hotel for people traveling by car

Motor Vehicle Administration (MVA): the state agency in charge of all traffic and auto regulations

Non-driver identification card: an identification card given by the MVA or DMV to people who do not drive

Notarize: to make a document legal; to put an official stamp on a document

Parking meter: see "Meter"

Peak hours: (see "Rush hour" below)

Public transportation: trains, buses, and subways

Registration card: a card that proves your car is registered by the MVA or DMV

Road test: part of the test you take to get a driver's license. When you take the road test, you drive the car with someone from the MVA sitting beside you.

Rush hour: the time of day when most people are driving to or coming home from work

Seat belts: safety belts attached to the car seats. You must wear seat belts in some states.

Self-service: to pump your own gas

Senior citizen: a person over 65 years old

Transfer: a piece of paper that lets you go from bus to bus or from the subway to the bus

Validation: a stamp on your parking ticket that gives you free or discount parking

Valet parking: With valet parking, a restaurant or business hires someone to park your car. The cost is usually $5; you may tip a dollar or two. If the parking is free, tip about $2.

Hello! America Publication List

¡Hola Estados Unidos! (Hello! USA in Spanish)

Check our website or call to receive notification of availability.

Availability date: December, 2002.

StaySafe!!

A 16-page booklet for American residents traveling or relocating outside the U.S. Practical tips on protecting yourself, your family, and your possessions in a variety of situations. Appropriate for both relatively safe and high-risk countries. The special section on "Teaching Your Children about Safety" explains how to instill good safety practices to children of any age, without increasing their anxiety. (available in packets of 10)

Choosing Elementary and Secondary Schools

A 32-page booklet for any parent relocating anywhere in the world. This comprehensive booklet contains 20 *Plus One* questions parents need to ask about all educational programs. Advice about what to do and what *not to do* from educators, parents, and students. Additional sections on special education, private day schools, and programs for families moving internationally (available in packets of 10).

Jobs and Careers for International Spouses

For American spouses moving internationally. Provides valuable information on getting a job or finding a satisfying alternative while you are away. The section on cultural differences in the job-search process is a must for anyone planning to look for a job in another country (available in packets of 10).

Pets on the Move

An 8-page booklet for individuals and families relocating with pets—including dogs, cats, birds, and horses. Comprehensive and practical information about transporting your pet safely and helping it adjust to its new home. A special section on international relocation explains rules and regulations you need to know ahead of time (available in packets of 25).

American Customs

A free newsletter about American culture and language

Holidays

Major sports events

Festivals and celebrations around the U.S.

Common idioms and expressions

Tips on everyday living

Visit our web site at: www.hellousa.com

Hello! America, Inc. 7962 Old Georgetown Road, #B; Bethesda, MD 20814-2475
Tel: 240/497-1088   Fax: 301/215-4171   E-mail: judy@hello-america.com

__Fun & Friends__

American Holidays

New Year's Day* (January 1): New Year's Eve (December 31). Many Americans have parties on New Year's Eve. They drink a toast to the new year at midnight. Local restaurants and clubs often have special dinner parties. On television, you can see a huge ball drop from a tall building in New York City at exactly 12 am.

Chinese New Year: Many cities—such as San Francisco—have parades with marching bands, dragon dancers, and clowns. Chinese restaurants often have special meals.

Martin Luther King, Jr. Day* (3rd Monday): Honors the civil rights leader. You can attend ceremonies in all major cities—for example at the Lincoln Memorial in Washington, DC, where Dr. King made his famous "I Have a Dream" speech.

Valentine's Day (February 14): Honors the people we love. Children often give cards to family members, teachers, and friends. Often, husbands and wives and lovers give each other gifts—such as candies, cookies, and red roses.

President's Day* (3rd Monday): Honors the birthdays of President Lincoln and President Washington.

Eid al-Adha (February): Commemorates the sacrifice by the prophet Abraham of his son Ishmael. Muslims celebrate this solemn day with prayer.

Black History Month: Special programs in museums and schools celebrate African-American history and culture.

St. Patrick's Day (March 17): Honors an Irish saint. On this day, people of Irish heritage wear green. Cities like New York and Boston have big parades.

Holi, or Festival of Color (March): Hindus celebrate the coming of spring by dancing, having fun with paints, and telling folk stories.

Easter (Sunday in March or April): A Christian springtime holiday. Most stores are closed.

Mother's Day (2nd Sunday): Honors mothers. Children and husbands give cards and gifts to the mothers in the family. Many restaurants have special meals for mothers.

Memorial Day* (last Monday): Honors soldiers killed in war. Many Americans visit soldiers' graves.

Father's Day (3rd Sunday): Honors fathers. Children give cards and gifts to their father.

 Independence Day* (July 4): Celebrates U.S. independence from England. Cities and towns have parades during the day and fireworks at night. Many Americans have outdoor picnics or barbecues.

 Labor Day* (1st Monday): Honors workers. A weekend of rest when many families go to the beach or the mountains. Outdoor picnics or barbecues are popular.

Rosh Hashanah and Yom Kippur (September/October): Jewish New Year. Schools and businesses may be closed in cities where many Jews live.

 Columbus Day* (2nd Monday): Celebrates the discovery of America.

Halloween (October 31): "Fun" evening for children. Children wear costumes and go "trick-or-treating"—that is, they visit neighbors' homes and ask for a "treat."

 Veterans' Day* (November 11): Honors U.S. soldiers and the end of World War I. Most big cities have ceremonies; the President often speaks at Arlington National Cemetery in Washington, DC.

Thanksgiving Day* (4th Thursday): Day for giving thanks for all we have. Families eat a big dinner; popular foods are turkey and pumpkin pie.

Diwali, or the Festival of Truth and Light (October/November): Hindus celebrate this New Year holiday with candle-lighting and fireworks.

Ramadan: The Eid al-Fitr festival ends the Ramadan (Muslim month of fasting) with food and celebrations in mosques and Islamic centers all over the country.

 Hanukkah (end of December): Jewish holiday that lasts eight days. Many stores, homes, and public places have a menorah (candlestick with eight branches).

Christmas* (December 25): Christian holiday. During the holiday season (Thanksgiving to New Year), many Americans give gifts and cards (see chapter on "Meeting Americans").

---

* National holiday. Banks and post offices are closed.

Note: Although Christianity is the most common religion in the U.S., many American citizens and residents practice other religions—such as Hinduism, Judaism, and Islam. Each religion uses a different calendar to set dates for their holidays. These dates change from year to year according to the "American" calendar.

__Dining In & Out__

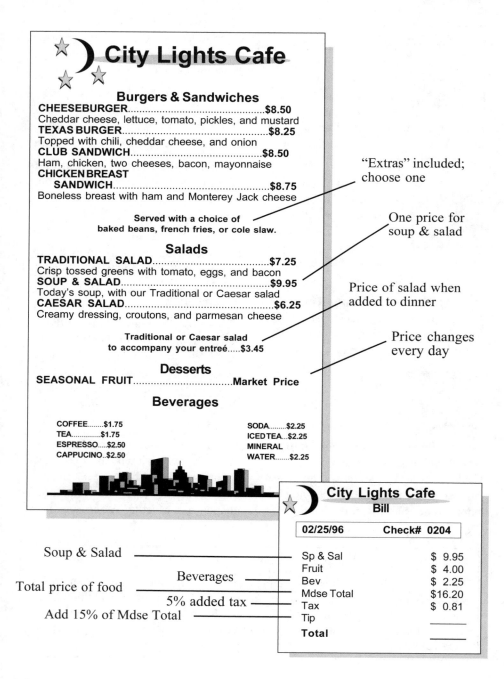

City Lights Cafe

Burgers & Sandwiches
CHEESEBURGER...$8.50
Cheddar cheese, lettuce, tomato, pickles, and mustard
TEXAS BURGER...$8.25
Topped with chili, cheddar cheese, and onion
CLUB SANDWICH...$8.50
Ham, chicken, two cheeses, bacon, mayonnaise
CHICKEN BREAST
  SANDWICH...$8.75
Boneless breast with ham and Monterey Jack cheese

**Served with a choice of
baked beans, french fries, or cole slaw.**

Salads
TRADITIONAL SALAD.......................................$7.25
Crisp tossed greens with tomato, eggs, and bacon
SOUP & SALAD...$9.95
Today's soup, with our Traditional or Caesar salad
CAESAR SALAD...$6.25
Creamy dressing, croutons, and parmesan cheese

**Traditional or Caesar salad
to accompany your entreé.....$3.45**

Desserts
SEASONAL FRUIT................................Market Price

Beverages
COFFEE.......$1.75
TEA.............$1.75
ESPRESSO.....$2.50
CAPPUCINO..$2.50

SODA.........$2.25
ICED TEA...$2.25
MINERAL
WATER.......$2.25

"Extras" included;
choose one

One price for
soup & salad

Price of salad when
added to dinner

Price changes
every day

City Lights Cafe
Bill

02/25/96	Check# 0204
Sp & Sal	$ 9.95
Fruit	$ 4.00
Bev	$ 2.25
Mdse Total	$16.20
Tax	$ 0.81
Tip	
Total	

Soup & Salad

Beverages

Total price of food

5% added tax

Add 15% of Mdse Total

American Foods

Meals

Breakfast. Common breakfast foods are: cereal; toast, bagel, or muffins; eggs; bacon or breakfast sausage; waffles or pancakes; fruit juice; coffee or tea.

Lunch. The most popular time for lunch is 12 noon or 1 pm. Restaurants serve lunch from 11 am–3 pm. Most Americans eat a light and fast lunch, since lunch breaks last only one hour or less. Common lunch foods are sandwiches, salad, and soup. Lunch menus at restaurants are usually less expensive than dinner menus; but the amount of food you get is less, too.

Dinner. This is the largest meal of the day. In the U.S., people often eat dinner earlier than most Europeans and South Americans—about 6–7 pm. Most restaurants serve dinner from 5–10 pm; restaurants in the suburbs and rural areas may close earlier.

Most dinners include a green salad before the main part of the meal; meat, chicken, or fish; cooked vegetables; and bread.

Some restaurants have "early-bird" specials—usually served around 6–7 pm. The "early-bird" specials are cheaper than the later meals. Usually you pay one price for a complete dinner.

Brunch. A brunch is one large meal for both breakfast and lunch—most popular on Sundays and holidays, from 11 am–3 pm. Many brunches are buffets; you go up to the food tables and fill your plate as many times as you want.

Restaurants

Many restaurants have menus in the window; you can check the prices and the type of food before you walk in. If a restaurant does not have a menu in the window, go in and ask to see one. It is not impolite to leave after you see the menu.

The prices on the menu do not include tip or tax. Tip waiters about 15%–20% of the bill—before tax. If you did not get good service, you may leave a little less than 15%; but make sure the problem was the *waiter*—and not the kitchen.

To find out about restaurants with foods from your home country, look up "Restaurants" in the Yellow Pages directory; you may find a list by type of food—for example, French, Chinese, Italian, or Japanese. If you do not eat meat or fish, you can also find "vegetarian" restaurants in this list. To find the names of restaurants with "take-out" or "carryout" menus, look under "Food."

Most bookstores have good restaurant guides—with the names of restaurants, their prices, and menus. Restaurant reviews are especially common in your local newspaper—particularly on Fridays and Sundays; many of these reviews are on-line under the name of the newspaper.

When you pay, first make sure the tip is not on the bill already; then leave the tip on the table or add it to your bill.

The tax will be added to the bill. In most cities, restaurant taxes are 5%–10%.

Types of restaurants

Tip: Some restaurants use symbols beside items on the menu to help you choose what to eat. For example, a heart usually means that the item is low-fat. Other symbols point out vegetarian or spicy items.

Tip: Some restaurants have a buffet. With a buffet, different dishes are on a long table; you take all you want. You pay one price—whether you eat a lot or a little.

Restaurants (full-service) may be informal or formal (tie and jacket).

Cafés, coffee shops, and diners serve coffee and pastries, in addition to typical meals. The costs and types of food vary.

Cafeterias are self-service restaurants. You take a tray and move through a line, choosing the food you want. Pay at the cash register before you eat. Cafeterias are informal.

Delicatessens (delis) serve sandwiches, salads, and soups. Some have no tables or chairs—you must take the food with you. Delis are informal.

Snack bars have snacks—such as potato chips, pretzels, and cookies—as well as fast-foods and some sandwiches. Usually there are no chairs—

just counters where you can stand while eating. Snack bars are informal.

Fast-food restaurants serve food that is prepared quickly or made ahead of time—such as hamburgers and french fries. You order "for here" to eat at the restaurant; to take the food somewhere else, order "takeout" or "to go."

Diners also serve food quickly. You can sit at the counter near the kitchen or in a booth. Many diners are open all day and all night. Usually you pay at the cash register when you leave.

Bar restaurants have a bar near the door and tables on the other side of the room; often you may watch a sports game or see a music video on TV. Many fine restaurants also have an open bar space for drinking with fine dining in another section.

Young people go to bar restaurants alone or with a friend; you must be 21 years or older to buy a drink. Bars often have "Happy Hours"—for example, 5–7 pm. on Friday nights; you can buy drinks at a low price or get hors d'oeuvres for free. Dress is often business casual or casual (see "Dressing 'Right'/Meeting Americans").

Note: You must be 21 years old to drink in many places. Bring an ID with a photo on it.

Dinner theaters have food and entertainment—including comedy, musicals, and mysteries. Tickets include entertainment and food. Drinks, taxes, and tip are extra.

Dinner cruises have full-service meals on boats that cruise along a river or harbor. Dinner cruises are popular for sight-seeing; some dinner cruises have dancing and live music. Tickets include food. Drinks, taxes, and tip are extra.

"Star" restaurants and cafés. Young people all over the world have heard of the "Hard Rock Café." The music is loud and the meals simple—usually pizza, hot dogs, and hamburgers. You may buy T-shirts and other souvenirs of famous movie or music stars. Dress is casual.

How to dine

1. Call ahead of time.

Make a reservation if the restaurant is very popular—especially on a Friday or Saturday night. Many restaurants do not take reservations.

Ask about the parking. Is it self- or valet parking? The cost for valet parking is usually $2–$5. If this service is free, tip the attendant $1–$2.

2. Arrive no later than 10 minutes after your reserved time.

Give your name when you arrive.

3. Ask for the smoking or non-smoking section.

By law, most restaurants must have a non-smoking area. A few restaurants do not allow smoking at all.

Note: It is not impolite to ask for a different table if your table is too noisy or crowded.

4. Order.

Usually, the waiter or waitress will take your drink order first. A glass of water is free; but you may have to ask. Most restaurants offer courses à la carte—you can order the courses separately if you do not want a full-course dinner. Salad is usually offered as a first course.

Tip: Ask the price for the "specials" that are not on the menu. They are often much higher than the menu items.

5. Pay the check (bill).

In some American restaurants, the waiter or waitress gives you the check before you ask for it—sometimes even before you finish eating; you may stay as long as you want, unless there is a long line waiting for a table.

Many Americans share the cost of a meal when they are with friends—that is, they "split the bill," or divide it evenly. At most restaurants, each person in the group may give a credit card; the waiter puts the same amount on each person's bill. If each person wants to pay separately, tell the waiter ahead of time.

6. Ask for a "doggie bag" if you have food left over.

Many restaurants serve lots of food. If you want to take some of the food home, ask for a "doggie bag." The waiter will put the food in a bag or plastic box.

Entertaining At Home

Kinds of parties

Common kinds of parties are:

- **open house.** A few hours when people can come and go as they like. You can serve just drinks and hors d'oeuvres, just dessert, or a buffet meal.
- **dinner party.** Serve buffet or "sit-down."
- **cocktail hour.** A few hours when people come and go as they like. Serve drinks and hors d'oeuvres.
- **barbecue.** An outdoor dinner party. Grill the food. Popular foods are hot dogs and hamburgers, chicken, and ribs.
- **"game" party.** A party when people come to watch sports on TV. Serve snacks or a light dinner. Popular foods are pizza, hot dogs, hamburgers, and beer.
- **social get-together**. An evening for conversation, usually starting around 8 pm on a weekend night. Serve hors d'oeuvres, then dessert and coffee or tea.

Invitations

You may:

- phone your guests if you are having just a few people. Tell your guests:
  - the time to come.
  - the kind of food you are serving. Guests will want to know if you are serving dinner; ask if they cannot eat any foods.
  - the type of clothing to wear.
  - directions to your home.
- mail an invitation. You may include a map with the directions to your house. You can ask for an R.S.V.P. (reply to the invitation) from
  - everyone. Just write your telephone number next to the R.S.V.P. line.
  - only the people who are not coming. Write your telephone number and "R.S.V.P. regrets only."

Saying "thank you"

If you are invited to someone's home, you may want to bring a gift. Call or write to say "thank you" after the party is over.

Note: For more information about parties in the home, see chapter on "Meeting Americans."

Caterers

Ready-made. Many gourmet delis, restaurants, hotels, supermarkets, and catering services prepare food platters for parties. You may pick up the food or have it delivered. Buying prepared platters costs less than ordering a custom menu or hiring a full catering service. Prices depend on the type and quantity of food ordered.

Prepared in your home. You may hire a caterer to prepare and serve a custom-made menu in your home. Most caterers will also help you plan the menu. Some services provide their own dishes, serving pieces, table-cloths, napkins, and decorations.

Words to Know

À la carte: a menu with a separate price for each item

Bagel: a type of bread. It is round with a hole in the middle. You can get many kinds of bagels—for example, poppy seed, onion, garlic, or "plain."

Brunch: one large meal for breakfast and lunch together

Buffet: a meal where you serve yourself. You eat all you want for one price.

Cafeteria: a restaurant where you serve yourself and take your food to a table

Cater: to provide food for a party. Caterers cook or bake for you.

Continental breakfast: a breakfast with juice, coffee or tea, and rolls or muffins

Counter: a long table where you sit and eat your food

Course: one part of a meal—for example, the appetizer or dessert

Delicatessen (deli): a restaurant with sandwiches, salads, and soups

"Early-bird" special: a meal served early in the evening—at a lower price

Entrée: main course

Fast food: food made and served quickly—such as McDonald's hamburgers

"For here": food you eat in the restaurant

Gourmet: special food—usually tastier than ordinary food

Platter: a large plate with meats, cheeses, fruit, or desserts

Reservation: a time when a restaurant saves a table for you

R.S.V.P.: a reply to an invitation. This reply tells whether or not you are coming.

"Sit-down" meal: a meal where the guests sit at a table and the host or hostess serves.

"Take-out": food you get at the restaurant and then take home to eat

"To go": food you take out of the restaurant

Valet parking: personal parking. Someone takes your car when you arrive at the restaurant or party and gets it for you when you leave.

News, Sports, & Entertainment

American Football

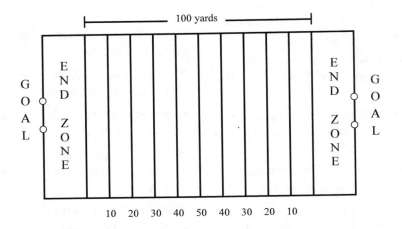

American Baseball

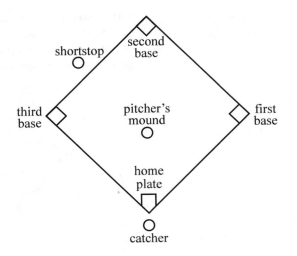

Publications

Your city paper

The city newspaper is the best place to get general information—for example:

- religious events—with lists of religious organizations (see "Where to Go/Making Friends").
- real estate—with articles and advertisements about new homes.
- business and employment sections—advertisements for jobs. This section is more likely to advertise higher-level jobs than the employment section.
- the "arts"—with interviews, reviews, and upcoming events.

Newspapers are cheaper if you subscribe (get home delivery); to call the newspaper; look in the Yellow Pages under "Newspapers" and call the number for "Home Delivery."

Most major newspapers also publish their news on the Internet.

Other popular dailies

Two daily newspapers read all over the country are:

- *The Wall Street Journal* (business).
- *USA Today* (a popular, easy-to-read newspaper).

Community and ethnic papers

Community newspapers give the news about a local area—for example:

- stores and sales.

- nearby movies.
- clubs and classes (see "Fun Classes and Clubs/Making Friends").
- jobs—especially jobs for the home, such as home repairs, babysitting, and tutoring.

Most community newspapers are published weekly; many are delivered to your home for free. You may also get them at the library or at small food stores in your area.

Out-of-town and international papers

Most big cities also have foreign language, out-of-town, and ethnic newspapers.

International newspapers cost 75¢–$3 a copy for the daily paper. You can get many of these newspapers on the day of publication, but others (especially international ones) may be 2–3 days late.

Check the Yellow Pages directory or the Internet.

Magazines

Most cities have magazines on special subjects such as the theater and the arts. You can also find national magazines on any hobby—for example, travel, autos, hiking, and photography.

Books

Many cities have guidebooks with information about schools, shopping, area businesses and jobs, and activities for children.

Radio & TV

Note: The number of advertisements may be surprising. Some programs have ads every 10 minutes or even more frequently.

Public television and radio

The money for public television and radio comes from the government, private businesses, and individuals. The programs on these stations have few advertisements.

AM/FM radio

Your radio has two settings:

- AM stations often have more
  - programs with many advertisements.
  - rock programs.
  - 24-hour news programs.
  - "talk shows" that let people call up, ask questions, and tell what they think.
- FM has the most classical music and public radio stations.

Cable television

This is a paid service that gives you:

- more stations or channels, including:
  - CNN.
  - public TV.
  - the Weather Channel.
  - special interests such as history or movies.
- better reception on all channels.

You can find out more about cable TV programs by looking at:

- a cable guide—a magazine with all the cable listings. It costs about $1 a month.
- the weekly TV guide in your newspaper or at your local supermarket.

Videos/DVDs

Renting

Video stores rent VCRs and DVD players, as well as videos and DVDs. Most stores have movies (including foreign films), documentary films, exercise programs, and concerts. Some video stores specialize in foreign films from all over the world or from one country.

 You may pay a membership fee in some smaller stores. If you don't return the videotape on time, you pay a "late fee." Most video stores have a "return box" if the store is closed.

Some public libraries will permit you to borrow videos either for free or for a smaller fee than a video store.

Buying

You may not be able to use the TV set, VCR, or DVD player from your home country (see "What to Leave at Home/Before You Come"). Find out what you need for any electronic equipment before you plug it in. Otherwise, you may damage your equipment.

A company that specializes in international electronics can help you choose the attachments or adapters you need. Look in the Yellow Pages directory under "Sound Systems," "Television," or "Video Recorders." If you need new equipment and plan to return home again, find out which equipment will work in your home country before you buy it.

Most foreign-recorded videotapes must be converted for American equipment.

To find a service that converts videos, look under "video production" in the Yellow Pages directory.

Movies

 Most movie theaters, or cinemas, show each film three or four times a day, especially on weekends. Many movie theaters have 6–8 theaters; you buy tickets for one movie and leave when the movie is over. Seats are unreserved.

Tip: If you want to see a popular movie on a weekend night, come early or the movie may be "sold out." You may want to buy the ticket in advance. Call the theater to find out if you may buy the tickets online or on the phone with your credit card. Often, you will pay $1 or more for each ticket you buy in advance.

Many movie houses have special "early-bird" prices (discounts for shows that start before 6 pm).

Watching Sports

Overview

Baseball, American football, basketball, and ice hockey are the most popular team sports. If you live in a city with a good baseball or football team, many Americans you meet—especially men—will want to talk about the "game." In some cities, football is so popular that you cannot get tickets for any of the home games. You may watch many professional and college games for these sports on TV.

You may save money by buying a group of tickets—for example, season or half-season tickets (tickets for all or half the home games). Tickets for college games are usually free for students. If you are not a student, call the college and ask for the "sports information center."

"Sports parties." Many fans watch sports such as football every week on TV—often with friends. Pizza and beer are popular at these get-togethers. If you are invited to a "sports party," dress casually—for example, wear jeans, a shirt and sweater, and sneakers.

Ask about discounts when you buy tickets for the movies, concerts or plays, or sports events if you are a:

- student. You must show your ID.
- senior citizen (person over 60–65; the required age varies).
- parent calling for your child. The age varies.

Baseball

Professional baseball starts in April and ends with the World Series in October. Each team belongs to the American League or the National League. During the World Series, the top teams from each league play each other. The team that wins four out of seven games wins the Series.

Football

Professional football has two conferences—the American Conference and the National Conference. The season starts in September and ends with the Superbowl on the last Sunday in January.

Almost all professional players played in college first. The best college teams are picked for different "bowls," such as the Cotton Bowl or Rose Bowl.

Sports Words

Amateur: a player who does not get money for playing a sport

Cheerleader: a woman or man who marches, dances, and leads songs to cheer on the team

Conference (football and hockey), division (basketball), or league (baseball and soccer): a group of teams. During the season, the teams play each other. At the end of the season, the best teams from each conference (division or league) play each other.

Defense: the team that does not have the ball or puck, or is not batting. It tries to keep the other team from scoring.

Division: (see "Conference")

Foul: an action that is not allowed and is usually penalized

Goal: place, or area, where hockey or soccer teams score

League: (see "Conference")

Offense: the team with the ball or puck, or that is batting

Pass: to throw or send the ball or puck to another player on the same team

Playoffs: games at the end of the season. The best teams play each other to determine the champion.

Professional: player who is paid a salary for being on a team

Referee or umpire: the person who decides if the players follow the rules

Season tickets: tickets for all the games played in the home city during the season—not including the playoffs

Basketball

The professional games begin in October. National Basketball Association (NBA) teams from the four divisions (groups) play a season that lasts until April. Playoffs then continue until the end of June.

The college season starts in November and ends with the National College Athletic Association (NCAA) tournament in March. In the tournament, 64 college teams play for 3 weeks to see which team will be the champion.

Ice Hockey

The National Hockey League (NHL) has two conferences—with 26 American and Canadian teams. Professional hockey begins in October and ends with the Stanley Cup in June.

Soccer

Soccer is becoming more popular—especially with young people. The term "soccer mom" is often used to describe a young suburban mother who drives her kids back and forth to soccer practice and other activities.

Since 1996, the U.S. has had a professional league with eight teams.

The Arts

 Most art galleries and some museums are closed on Mondays.

Galleries

Most galleries with art for sale are free. You may come in, look at the art, ask questions—and leave. To get notices of special events and shows in the mail, sign the guest book.

Museums

If you plan to visit a museum often, you may want to pay to become a member. Members enter for free, get information about the museum's activities ahead of time, and often go to special exhibits before the rest of the public.

Music and Theater

In some cities, you may get discounts or tickets for half-price on the day of the show. Call the theater and ask how to buy them. For example, in New York City, you may get half-price tickets for many shows at Times Square; but you may wait in line a long time.

Most counties and cities have sports teams for children of all ages. Usually, the fathers coach the teams (see "Fun Activities/Older Children").

Libraries

Public Libraries

 Public libraries are free.

What they have. In addition to books and magazines, libraries often have:

- music on records, audio cassettes, and compact discs.
- video cassettes and DVDs.
- newsletters about topics such as job openings and adult education.
- foreign language books, magazines, and newspapers. Ask which library in your county or city has the language you want.
- reference books—such as encyclopedias and travel guides—in the reference section.
- computers you may use for writing, editing, printing, or browsing on the Internet.
- activities—such as book discussions and children's storytelling (see "Family Activities/Your Young Child").

To borrow, or take out, books and videos, get a card at the information desk; you must show proof of residence—for example, a utility bill or copy of your lease. Each member of your family may get a separate card.

Rules: Find out:

- how many books, cassettes, or DVDs you may take out.
- how long you can keep borrowed items—usually 2–3 weeks for books and 1–7 days for a cassette or DVD.

Football Words

Interception: a play. A player on the offense passes the ball to a team member, but a player on the defense catches it instead.

Fumble: a play. A player for the offense drops the ball and any player on the field can pick it up.

Half-time: the time in between the first and second parts of the game. Usually, the cheerleaders and band from the home team entertain the audience.

Tackle: a play. A player on the defense forces a ball-carrying player on the offense to the ground.

Quarterback: a player on the offense who passes the ball. The quarterback is one of the most important players on the team.

Touchdown: a play that gets the ball to the goal line for six points. Usually, the offense runs with the ball or passes it to get a touchdown.

- how much you will pay if you do not return the borrowed items on time.
- what the hours are.

 Return the books and cassettes before or on the due date; if you are late, you will pay a fee. For example, the late fee for a videotape is $5 a day in some cities.

If the library is closed, look for a "Book Drop" slot on the outside wall. In some counties or cities, you may return your books to any library branch within the same county.

? *What if I want to keep an item past the due date?* You probably can renew it in the library, on the phone, or on the Internet; call and ask.

Baseball Words

Base: padded objects at three points in the diamond that runners touch as they try to score.

Batter: an offensive player at home plate who tries to hit the pitched ball with a bat

Bleachers: the cheapest seats—usually in the outfield. They do not have a cover or roof overhead.

Catcher: the defensive player who stands behind home plate and catches the ball the pitcher throws

Home plate: the place at the bottom of the diamond where the batter stands and where runners must reach to score

Home run (or homer): A hit (usually out of the ballpark). With a home run, the batter has the time to run all the bases and return to home plate. If any players are on base, they run to home plate too. The team gets one run for each player who gets to home plate.

Infielder: a player on the defensive team who stands near first, second, or third base. Shortstops stand between second and third base.

Inning: a segment of the game. Each game has nine innings. Both teams get a turn at bat during the inning.

Out: a play that prevents the batter from running around the bases. After three outs, the team gives up its chance to score runs and the other team tries to score.

Outfielder: a player who guards the field behind the bases

Pitcher: the player who throws the ball that the batter tries to hit

Run: a point. The team with the most runs after nine innings wins the game.

Umpire: person who decides if the player has followed the rules

Words to Know

AM radio: a kind of radio station. Most AM stations have rock music and talk shows.

Broadcasts: programs on the radio or TV

Cable television: a paid TV service. You get extra channels and better reception on your TV.

Conversion: changing something (a video cassette or a machine)

Dailies: newspapers published every day

Ethnic: belonging to a certain group of people in the U.S.—such as African-Americans, Asian-Americans, or Latin Americans.

FM radio: a type of radio station. The broadcast is clearer than most AM stations.

Home delivery: a service that brings the newspaper to your door

Home games: sports games played in the team's home city.

Public television or radio: a channel or station that gets money from the government, businesses, or individuals. They have fewer advertisements than other channels or stations.

Season tickets: tickets for every home game or performance for the season

Subscribe: to pay for a newspaper or magazine to be delivered regularly to you

Talk shows: a kind of radio or TV program. People call in and ask questions or tell what they think.

Video machine (VCR): a machine to watch videotapes or record TV shows

Meeting Americans

Saying Hello

Marcia: Hello! How are you?

Ahmed: OK. How are you?

Marcia: I met your friend last night… You know, the one who is a writer. I told him I know you…

Note: Marcia and Ahmed say "hello" with "How are you?" They do not tell each other how they are feeling.

Saying Good-bye

Marcia: Ahmed, I'm late for an appointment right now, but I'd like to get together. Can I call you back?

Ahmed: Sure. Call this evening. I'll be home.

Marcia: Thanks. Talk to you then.

Note: Marcia says "good-bye" with only a few words.

Tip: Americans often say they would like to "get together" but never call back. If you want to meet again, set a time.

Saying "Hello"

Names

First and last names. Most Americans use first, or non-family, names when they are meeting for the first time. They also use nicknames—such as Jim for James or Judy for Judith.

Middle names. Some women use their maiden (unmarried) name between their first and last names—such as Carol Smith Taylor.

Mr. and Ms. (pronounced "Miz") To be more formal, Americans use:

- Ms. for married and unmarried women—for example, Ms. Smith. Some women prefer Miss for unmarried women and Mrs. for married women.
- Mr. for married and unmarried men—for example, Mr. Harrison.

Use Mr. or Ms. if you are meeting:

- your boss for the first time.
- someone much older than you.

Sir, Miss, and Ma'am. Use these titles for people you don't know personally—such as a waiter or waitress, mail person, or clerk in a store.

"Ma'am" is especially popular in the southeastern part of the U.S.

Do not whistle or make loud noises to get someone's attention.

Titles of respect. Use a title of respect for a:

- college or university official: President Marcus, Professor Smith, or Dean Harrison.
- high government official: Senator Lombardi, Mayor Ferris, or Ambassador Evans. Use "Congressman" or "Congresswoman" for members of the U.S. House of Representatives.
- religious leader: Reverend Samuels, Father O'Connor, or Rabbi Cohen.
- medical doctor or dentist: Dr. Peters.
- person who has earned a doctoral degree: Dr. Halley.

Body language

Shaking hands and kissing. Shake hands when you are meeting a man or woman for the first time. Women often kiss on one cheek if they are friends—that is, they put their cheeks together and kiss in the air; they often hug each other at the same time. Male

---

Remember: You need not act "just like an American" if you do not want to. These chapters tell what Americans expect—*not what you must do.* In general, Americans do not mind if you dress differently or do not speak English perfectly. Other differences may cause problems. For example, Americans may notice—but never mention to you:

- being on time.
- personal hygiene.
- eye contact.
- personal space.

friends shake hands or pat each other on the back. Shake hands or kiss again when you say good-bye. A man and a woman may kiss on the cheek if they are friends.

Smiling and eye contact. Americans smile and look each other in the eye when they meet. Look at an American's eyes for just a few seconds when you meet. Look again once in a while you are talking; again, eye contact lasts just a few seconds. In the U.S., eye contact helps people trust each other.

Smiling is also important. Americans smile often—sometimes even at strangers. For example, a stranger may look at you and smile when you are walking on the street or riding the subway. The smile and eye contact are a way of saying "hello"; if you smile back, people may even say "hello" or "hi" as they pass. The smile and the "hi" do not mean the person wants to stop and talk.

Personal space. Americans expect you to stand about 2 feet (approximately ½ meter) away during the conversation. How can you tell if you are standing too close or too far? An American might keep stepping backward if you are standing too close, or forward if you are too far away.

Dressing "Right"

Overview

(See chapter on "Shops & Malls" for a chart of European and American sizes). American dress may vary with:

- the time of day. Get-togethers are often more formal in the evening than in the afternoon.
- people's age. Younger people are more casual than older people. For example, people in their 20s may wear jeans and T-shirts to most social get-togethers.
- the region. People may dress more casually in some regions or cities— for example, in areas near San Francisco and San José, CA.
- the season. For example, a restaurant may be more formal in the winter and casual in the summer— especially if it has outdoor tables.
- the business or corporation. In some offices, men wear a tie and jacket every day; women wear suits (jackets and skirts), pants suits (jackets and pants), or dresses. In other offices, men and women wear jeans and loose sweaters. In most cases, people who meet customers or clients usually dress more formally.

Most American buildings have the same temperature all year round—no matter what the weather. In the summer, wear a light jacket or long-sleeved shirt to a restaurant or theater; otherwise, the air conditioning may be too cold for you. In the winter, be ready to take off a heavy sweater; most places are well-heated.

Dressing "Right"

Casual or "sporty"	Shopping malls; sports games; barbecues and picnics; informal restaurants; everyday errands.	Jeans or shorts; T-shirt, long- or short-sleeved sports shirt; sweatshirt; sneakers.	Jeans or shorts; T-shirt, long- or short-sleeved sports shirt; sweatshirt; sneakers.
Business casual	Social get-togethers; most restaurants; many offices. Afternoon plays, ballets, and concerts; all performances for small theaters.	Skirt or long pants, sometimes with a jacket; blouse or sweater; low-heeled or flat shoes.	Long pants; short or long-sleeved shirt; jacket with no tie; shoes (rather than sneakers).
Everyday business	Most offices; dinner parties and dinner at fine restaurants; evening plays, ballets, and concerts.	Dress or suit; blouse or sweater; shoes with low or high heels.	Suit and tie; long-sleeved white or light-colored shirt; shoes.
Formal	Formal cocktail parties and special occasions, such as weddings. (Usually the invitation says "black tie" or "formal.") Operas at major opera houses, especially at night. (Opening night is usually fancy.)	Fancy dress or suit; low- or high-heeled shoes.	Tuxedo; white shirt and cummerbund; black tie; dress shoes.

Note: Adults and children change their clothes every day. Most have 5–6 outfits or more, so they don't wear the same clothes in 1 week.

 Women do not wear "topless" bathing suits on most public beaches or at pool parties.

Tip: Many offices have "casual Fridays," when employees dress more casually than on other days. For example, employees in some banks wear jeans and a shirt, with no tie, on Fridays.

Tip: If you do not know what to wear to a party, ask:

- your host or hostess when you are invited.
- a salesperson in the clothing store. For example, if you are invited to an evening wedding, ask the salesperson if the dress is "right" before you buy it.

National dress. In most major cities, Americans are used to clothing from other countries and will not stare. You may wear the dress or head covering from your homeland in most offices and at any social get-together—either casual or formal.

Personal Habits

Smoking. Smoking in public places is often illegal. If you do not see ashtrays around, ask if you can smoke. Usually, you may not smoke in the rest room.

Look for "smoking-designated areas" in public places such as:

- restaurants. The host or hostess will ask if you want "smoking" or "non-smoking" when you enter. Some restaurants are "smoke-free."

- shopping malls. Many shopping malls are "smoke-free"; look for the "no-smoking" sign at the door to the mall.
- airports. Sometimes the whole airport is "smoke-free." If you don't see any ashtrays, do not "light up."
- buses and trains. Look on the window of each car for the "smoking" and "non-smoking" signs.
- office buildings. Most offices are smoke-free; many smokers stand outside and smoke during their break.
- doctors' offices and hospitals. Most do not allow smoking at all.
- schools and universities. Most have strict rules about smoking.

Alcohol. Wine and beer are popular with dinner or at evening get-togethers.

You must be 21 or older to buy any alcoholic drink in a liquor store, supermarket, or bar or nightclub. If you are young, you may need to show an ID that shows your age.

All states have strict laws against driving after drinking alcohol. In many states, a policeman can stop you and test your breath; you will pay a fee or even lose your license if you drink and drive.

Private homes. Many Americans do not like smoking in their homes; ask. Guests often go outside to smoke; just say "Excuse me. I'm going outside for a cigarette."

Personal hygiene. You probably will notice that:

- most Americans bathe or shower every day; in general, they do not like body odor, strong perfumes, or strong after-shave lotions.
- American women usually shave their legs and underarms.

⊗ At a party or in the work place, you may meet others from your own country. Do not have a long conversation in your own language and ignore the others around you.

Being on Time

In general, Americans expect you to come at the exact time. If you:

- know you will be late, call ahead and tell the person you are meeting.
- are already late, say "I'm sorry" and explain why you were not on time.

Social get-togethers

Parties at home.

Do not come more than 5 minutes early for any party at a home; often, the host or hostess is still getting ready.

In general, if the invitation gives the starting and ending times, you do not need to be on time. For example, if the invitation is from 2–5 pm, you may come at 2:30 or even 2:45 pm; people often stay about 30 minutes after 5 pm—usually no later.

Dinner parties. Arrive no more than 15 minutes after the exact time; the hostess probably has a meal planned for a certain hour. Do not leave right after the meal is over; wait at least 30 minutes.

Cocktail parties. The invitation will tell you the party hours. You may come 30-45 minutes late if you like.

Informal get-togethers. Come no later than 20 minutes after the exact time.

Open house parties. Come any time during the hours on the invitation.

Restaurants. Come no more than 10 minutes early or 10 minutes late. At some restaurants, you will wait—even if you have reservations. Other restaurants will not save your table if you are more than 15 minutes late.

Appointments. Come at the exact time. Many Americans do not like to wait; in fact, if you are more than 20 minutes late, the person may not wait.

Surprise parties. If the invitation says that the party is a surprise, come 10-15 minutes early or right on time. If you must be late, ask the hostess when you should come.

After a party, call up or write a thank-you letter to the host. Your "thank-you" should be short. You may tell the host that the food was good or that the people were "interesting" or "fun to be with."

Business situations

Come at the exact time for all meetings—no more than 5 minutes early or 5 minutes late. Being on time is especially important for:

- lunchtime meetings or meals. Often the person has only an hour for lunch.
- job interviews. Be about 10 minutes early.

Cards & Gifts

The "holiday season"

The holiday season starts after Thanksgiving and lasts until New Year's Day (see chapter on "Holidays"). Many Americans send cards or gifts.

Cards. You may buy sets of cards at the store or order "personalized" cards from a stationery store. Cards to people who do not celebrate Christmas (for example, Jews and Muslims) should say "Happy Holiday"—rather than "Merry Christmas."

If the person is married, address the card to both the husband and wife—even if you do not know both of them. Mail cards to:

- co-workers you see every day; include secretaries (see "Business giving" in this section).
- friends who live out of the country. Americans often put a family photograph in the card.
- friends you see regularly.

Business giving. Each office has different customs. For example, managers may thank their secretaries by:

- giving them a gift.
- taking them out to lunch.
- sending flowers.

Some offices have rules against sending or giving any gifts. Ask.

Holiday tipping. Tip people who serve you regularly. Put the tip in a card; the amount depends on how much they have helped you. You may tip:

- people who deliver your newspaper or mail. Put a small tip ($5–$10) in the card. If you have more than one mail person, you do not need to tip.
- door people in your building. Put a tip in the card if the door person has helped you during the year; check with your neighbors to see how much to give. Tips are usually $15–$100.
- hairdressers. If you have a regular hairdresser, you may give a small tip (less than $15) or a small gift.

Gifts. Most gifts are small ($5–$10); many people bake cookies and wrap them with a bow. You may want to give to:

- your child's teacher. The gift is a "thank you"; the teacher will treat your child the same—whether or not you give a gift.
- good friends. Many Americans give a special gift to their two or three "best friends" or to people who have helped them out during the year.

Special occasions

Other holidays (see chapter on "Holidays").

Celebration parties. In general, bring a gift for all celebration parties. It is not impolite to ask what the person "would like"; call the person giving the party. Some types of parties are:

- wedding and bridal shower. Many couples make a list of the gifts they want; then they "register" the list at a store. Ask the couple if they are "registered." Then go to the store with the list and choose something to send (see "Special Services/ Shops & Malls").
- graduation, confirmation, bar or bat mitzvah. Popular gifts are books and gift certificates at book and record stores.
- baby shower, baptism, christening, or bris. Many couples "register" for baby showers.
- surprise birthday party. Bring a gift for the birthday person. If the invitation says not to bring a gift, come with a bottle of wine, candy, or flowers for the host or hostess.
- invitation to a new home. Bring a "house gift" when you are going to the new home of a friend—even if it is not for a party.

Home parties. Bring a gift for:

- dinner parties. Popular gifts are bottles of wine or sherry, candies, and flowers. When you are invited, ask: "What can I bring?" Sometimes, the dinner is "potluck"—that is, everyone brings a dish of food.

- cocktail parties. The most popular gift is a bottle of wine, sherry, or other type of liquor.

Words to Know

Baby shower: a party for a woman expecting a new baby, or for her husband

Baptism: a Christian religious ceremony mainly for babies. The ceremony is usually in a church, with a celebration afterward.

Bris: a Jewish celebration for a newborn boy. The boy is circumcised when he is eight days old. The bris usually takes place in the home.

Bar or bat mitzvah: a religious service and celebration for a Jewish boy or girl at age 13

Bridal shower: a party for a woman who is going to be married

Christening: a Christian religious ceremony that includes baptizing and naming a baby

Cocktail party: a party with appetizers and drinks. Usually, many guests are invited.

Dean: a person in charge of a group of students or study programs at a college or university

First name: the name parents give their children—such as Amy, Robert, Gloria, or Mark. Americans say this name first, then the last, or family, name.

"Housewarming" party: a party for someone who has just moved into a new home

Jeans: pants made of thick, blue cloth

Maiden name: a woman's family name. Most women use their husband's family name after they are married. A few women keep their maiden name.

Last name: the family name—such as Smith, Harrison, or Evans. Americans say this name last.

"Potluck" (meal): a get-together for dinner. Everyone brings a dish to share.

Open house: a kind of party. The host or hostess tells you the hours—such as 2–5 pm. You can come any time after 2 or before 5.

"Smoke-free" environment: a restaurant, shop, mall, or office where you cannot smoke

Sneakers: sports, tennis, or running shoes. The bottoms are rubber and the tops are cloth.

Sweatshirt: a loose, thick cotton shirt. The shirt is soft with a fluffy lining inside. You may wear a sweatshirt for jogging or other sports.

Making Friends

Jack: Greta, it's so good to see you! How are you?

Greta: Fine, thanks. I'm glad to see you, too.

Jack: I wanted you to meet some of my friends… Let me introduce you.

Note: Men and women shake hands. If they are good friends, they may kiss.

Jack: Greta, these are my neighbors, John and Barbara Weedon.

Greta: *(shaking hands)* Pleased to meet you.

Jack: And this is Carl Post. Carl used to live here, but he's moved away.

Greta: *(shaking hands)* Oh, where do you live now?

Jack: *(leaving)* Someone's at the door. Greta, I'll let you introduce yourself to the others…

Note: Jack expects Greta to introduce herself and start a conversation. Common questions for starting a conversation are: "Where do you live?" or "What do you do?" (that is, "What kind of work do you do?")

Overview

Many Americans move to a new city every few years. Each time they move, they make new friends. To some, a friend is a person you meet socially—even once in a while; for example, people who stop and chat at work may call each other friends.

Often, Americans may seem too busy to make new friends—especially in large cities. Some newcomers say that people smile, look friendly, and say, "Let's get together sometime"; then they walk away. If you want to meet friends, often *you* must be the one to start.

Where To Go

Getting information

Newspapers. In general, you may get the names and numbers of clubs, religious organizations, and classes from:

- the major newspaper in your city (see "Publications/News, Sports, & Entertainment").
- the local newspaper for your town or county. These newspapers usually have the names of community centers, clubs, and classes in your area.
- ethnic newspapers.

The Chamber of Commerce for your town or county. Find the name in the White Pages directory—for example, "Riverton Chamber of Commerce."

The library, restaurants, and stores. Look in the area near the entrance.

The Internet (see "Accessing the Internet/Getting Connected").

The White and Yellow Pages directories. Look in the front sections for the names of religious organizations and clubs.

Places to go

Your neighborhood. In some areas, your neighbors may come to say "hello" when you move in. Often, they bring cakes or cookies. In other neighborhoods, no one seems to notice you. They may not be unfriendly—just "busy." If you feel lonely, introduce yourself when you meet your neighbors on the street. Chat awhile; then ask the person to come and visit.

Religious organizations. Churches, synagogues, mosques, and all other religious organizations usually have:

- groups for singles or couples.
- Bible and history classes for adults and children.
- nursery schools and day care centers.

Look in the Yellow Pages under "Churches," "Synagogues," "Mosques," or under "Religious Organizations."

Ethnic organizations. Most large cities have ethnic groups—such as Korean-Americans, Chinese-Americans, Polish-Americans, or Hispanic-Americans. Sometimes the members have been born in the U.S., but their

"Fun" Classes and Clubs

4-year or 2-year colleges	Professional and "fun" classes such as music, art, history, cooking, and dancing. Classes about finding a job or the right career are also popular. Two-year colleges may cost less for county residents.	Find "Schools-Academic-Colleges & Universities" in the Yellow Pages.
Public schools	Professional and "fun" classes.	Find "Schools-Academic-Secondary & Elementary" in the Yellow Pages.
County and city recreation departments	Fun classes. aerobics, nutrition, and arts and crafts are popular. Many recreation departments have adult teams for sports such as softball, basketball, and soccer.	Find the number of the nearest recreation center in the city or county government section of your phone book under "Recreation."
Libraries	"Book discussion groups" that meet to talk about a different book each month. These may be free.	Find the number of the nearest library in the city or county government section of your phone book under "Libraries."
Community centers	Aerobics and other fun classes. Book discussion groups. Some communities have "welcome clubs" for newcomers; most clubs meet about once a month.	Call the Chamber of Commerce for the names of community centers in your city or county.

⊗ Check to see if you are a resident in your county. For example, in some counties you are a resident if you have paid county property taxes in the past year.

"Fun" Classes and Clubs (cont.)

Young Men's (or Women's) Christian Association (YMCA/ YWCA)	Water sports, basketball, aerobics, and fun classes. Men and women of all religions may join. Usually, you pay an initiation fee and monthly dues.	
Women's centers	Classes and discussions— particularly about choosing the right career, getting a job, and improving professional skills.	Call the Chamber of Commerce or look under "Women" and "Career" in the Yellow Pages.
Health clubs/ fitness centers	Aerobic classes, exercise programs and equipment, swimming. Usually, you pay an initiation fee and monthly dues.	Find "Health Clubs" in the Yellow Pages.
Outdoor clubs	Bird-watching, hiking, biking, or camping.	Ask at a good sporting goods store or find "Clubs" in the Yellow Pages.
Tennis clubs	Group tennis lessons, indoor and outdoor tennis courts for rent. Public courts cost less than private clubs.	Find "Tennis Courts-Public" and "Tennis Courts-Private" in the Yellow Pages.
Country and golf clubs	Social get-togethers, golf courses and lessons. Often, a member must invite you to join a private club; some clubs have a waiting list. The initiation fee may be thousands of dollars. Usually, you also pay annual dues. Public courses cost much less.	Find "Golf Courses-Public" and "Golf Courses-Private" in the Yellow Pages. *Note:* Some golf clubs let non-members play for a fee— usually only during the weekday when they are not so busy.

To join some health clubs, you must sign a contract. Read the contract carefully; have someone translate if you do not understand it. If you sign a 2-year contract, you will have to keep paying, even if you move out of the area. Most clubs will give you a 6-month contract if you ask.

With many health clubs, you may negotiate the price and terms of the contract.

parents or grandparents were immigrants. These organizations may have:

- social get-togethers—such as picnics and parties.
- business networking groups ("Looking for a Job/Finding Work").
- schools where children learn language and history on Saturdays or Sundays.
- nursery schools and day care.
- volunteer work to help the poor.

You may find ethnic organizations:

- from the Chamber of Commerce for your city (see "Moving In/ Chapter Information" in Appendix B).
- in the business section of the White Pages or Yellow Pages. Look for any organization starting with the name of your ethnic group.

Professional associations. All professions have an association. Many have local chapters; almost all have national and state meetings at least once a year. Look up the name and number under "Associations" in the Yellow Pages.

Volunteer work. Americans often volunteer, or work for free, in their extra time. Women who do not work often volunteer more than men; but many people with jobs volunteer in the evenings or on the weekends. Some volunteer work may help your career (see chapter on "Finding Work"); but volunteering is also a good way to meet others who have the same interests. Some suggestions are:

- the Parent-Teacher Association (PTA) or other parent organizations. If you have children in school, the PTA gives you the chance to meet other parents and find out more about your child's school. The general PTA meetings are large, and you may not meet anyone. Volunteer to help
  - raise money. For example, many schools have fairs to raise money for extra equipment or field trips.
  - teach or supervise the children in the classroom, computer lab, or library.
- churches and other religious organizations. You may teach a class, visit the sick, raise money, or deliver food to the poor.
- museums. For example, you may take classes and learn about art, then guide visitors through the museum. Many museums have research programs that use volunteers.
- libraries. For example, you may help put books away or read to children.
- hospitals, old-age homes, and child-development centers.

International student organizations (see "Colleges and Universities"/ "Chapter Information" in the Appendix).

Newspaper "dating" ads. Many newspapers have ads for singles who want to date; the people in the ads tell a little about themselves—their hobbies, age, and gender (male/female), religion, or race. Usually—but not always—the male pays for any food or entertainment; on a "Dutch Treat" date, each person pays his or her own bill.

Dating services. A dating service will match you up with someone for a fee. Be sure you know the cost of the service before you begin.

Bars and nightclubs. Many singles go to bars and nightclubs on Friday or Saturday nights. Usually, they go with a friend. Some restaurants have "happy hours" when you may buy drinks at a discount or get free hors d'oeuvres.

 When you meet someone at a bar or nightclub:

- Do not give your address or telephone number to any person you just met; get to know that person first.
- Do not go home with anyone alone. If you want to meet someone again, choose a public place with lots of people.

Words to Know

Aerobics: activities and exercises that take a lot of energy

Chamber of Commerce: an organization of businesses. Most counties, cities, and states have a Chamber of Commerce. The U.S. Chamber of Commerce is for the whole country.

Community center: a public club house for the town or village. Usually, you can take classes or join clubs there.

Country club: a club where members can get together socially. Most have a dining room and sports facilities— such as a golf course, swimming pool, and racquetball or tennis courts. Usually, you join for the year.

Ethnic group: group of Americans with families from a different country or area of the world—such as Korean-Americans, Chinese-Americans, Irish-Americans, or Hispanic-Americans

Fitness center: (see "Health club")

Health club: a place to go for exercise, swimming, and fitness classes

Initiation fee: a one-time payment to join a club

Mosque: a place where Muslims pray and celebrate their holidays

Parent-Teacher Association (PTA): an organization for the teachers and parents of children in a school

Recreation department: a program with sports, arts and crafts, music, and other classes. Usually, the county or city runs the program. Some programs are only for children; others are for adults and children.

Synagogue: a place where Jews pray and celebrate their holidays

Volunteer work: work you do for free to help a person or an organization. Volunteer work is a good way to help others, improve your job skills, or meet others.

Welcome club: a club for people who are new in the area. Most clubs meet once a month.

White Pages directory: the telephone book that lists people's names, addresses, and home numbers

Yellow Pages directory: the telephone book that has advertisements for products and services and the phone numbers of businesses. You look up the name of a product or service to find out where to buy it.

Young Men's (or Women's) Christian Association (YMCA or YWCA): an organization with sports, classes, and clubs. Men and women of all religions can join. YMCAs are often cheaper than other clubs.

When You Get Here

Food Shopping

Brand name

Average amount used at one time

1/2 less fat
1/3 fewer calories than similar product

Pepe's Spicy Tomato Soup

Lite

Ingredients:
Water, Diced Tomatoes, Onions, Peppers, Apple Cider Vinegar, Cilantro, Garlic, Herbs and Spices.

Serving size .... 1 Cup
Servings per jar 1

Nutrition Facts

Calories 210	Calories from Fat 15

% Daily Value*

Sodium 60 mg	
Total Fat 1.5g	**2%**
Saturated Fat 0g	**0%**
Cholesterol 0mg	**0%**
Total Carbohydrate 49g	**16%**
Dietary Fiber 8g	**32%**
Sugars 7g	
Protein 9g	

Net Wt. 15½ oz. (439 g.)

High levels may lead to heart disease.

*Daily values are based on a 2,000 calorie diet.

High levels may lead to heart disease.

Salt; higher levels may lead to high blood pressure.

Oven Temperatures

Heat	Fahrenheit	Centigrade	British
Very low	100-250°	40-120°	Regulo 1-5
Low	300°	150°	Regulo 6
Moderate	325-350°	165-180°	Regulo 6-7
Hot	400°	205°	Regulo 8
Very hot	450-500°	235-260°	Regulo 9-10

Note: Most recipes assume that the oven has been *preheated* to the indicated temperature *before* the food is placed in the oven.

Allow about 15 minutes for the oven to preheat before you put the food inside. If you like, you may buy an oven thermometer to be sure your temperature control is accurate.

You may also buy a *meat thermometer,* which shows the temperature inside the meat, so you can tell when it is ready.

Note: The climate and altitude may affect your cooking. For example, in Miami, the humidity makes baking bread or pie crust difficult. In Denver, the high altitude affects the temperature you need for cooking; in that city, you need to keep the oven about 25° hotter than it says in the recipe.

The Supermarket

 If you have the time, visit a few stores before you need to buy anything.

Most supermarkets are open 7 days a week. On Mondays through Saturdays, they are usually open 6 am–11 pm; on Sundays, they close in the early evening. Some supermarkets are open 24 hours every day. The hours should be posted on the door.

Most stores close early or all day on Thanksgiving, Christmas, New Year's Day, and other major holidays.

How to shop

1. Find what you need.

Use a cart or a small basket to carry your food. Above the aisles, or rows, are the names of the items in that aisle. Also, your shopping cart may have a small chart under the handle.

2. Get your check approved.

If you will be paying by check now or in the future, go to the manager's office. The manager will sign your check. Fill out an application for a courtesy card (see "Special Services" section in this chapter).

3. Go to the checkout counter.

If you are buying only a few items, look for the "express lane." With some express lanes, you must pay cash; with others, you may pay with a check or credit card. In most stores, you can find a lane with "No Candy" near the cash register; look for the sign overhead.

Tip: If you are in a hurry, look for a counter where you pack the groceries yourself. You must pay with a credit card.

4. The checkout worker scans each item.

You can see the price up on a screen above the cash register.

5. Give the checkout worker your discount coupons and bonus card (see "special services" in this chapter).

The checkout worker subtracts the value of the coupons from your total price.

6. Pay the cashier.

Most supermarkets accept cash, checks, debit cards, and credit cards. Most also have bank machines where you can use your Automated Teller Machine (ATM) card.

7. Take your cart to the car or leave it near the door.

In some areas, the bagger takes the cart to your car. In other areas, you may leave your bags in the cart and drive back to pick them up.

? *What if I don't have enough money at the register?* Most stores take a credit card. If you have a bank card, look for an ATM machine.

? *What if I want to return something the next day?* The large supermarkets let you return most items if they are spoiled or if you have changed your mind. Take the item and the sales slip to the manager. Do not return fresh items such as eggs or milk.

What you can find

Produce. Most fresh fruits and vegetables are sold by the pound. They may come packaged or loose. At the checkout counter, the worker weighs and prices the food.

Meat. The meat counter has fresh or frozen:

- beef.
- chicken and other poultry.

Meats are usually graded.

- Prime meat is the best quality and the most expensive. It has more fat and is more tender.
- Choice meat is the most common grade. It has less fat and is less tender.
- Select, or lean, meat is trimmed of fat. It can be tougher than other cuts, but most major supermarkets tenderize the meat.
- Ungraded meats can still be good, but they are usually cheaper and less tender.

To get help, ring the bell near the butcher's window. You may ask the butcher for a special cut of meat or for a package weighing the exact amount you want (see section on "Special Services" in this chapter).

Poultry. Chicken, Cornish hens, turkey, and other poultry are usually graded AA or A. The most expensive is AA. It has less fat and is the freshest and most tender.

Seafood. The seafood counter has fresh, frozen, and "previously frozen" seafood. Some common kinds of fish are grouper, salmon, swordfish, flounder, halibut, catfish, and tuna. Common kinds of shellfish are shrimp, clams, mussels, and oysters. In general, though, you will find fish from all over the world in most stores.

Dairy products. The dairy case has eggs, milk, cheese, yogurt, and fruit juices. You may also find pickles, sauces, dips, and fresh pasta.

Butter comes by the pound or the stick (¼ lb.). Eggs come in cartons of six

Keeping Food Fresh

Check the date on the package of fresh food. This shows the last day on which the product can be sold. Use the following guidelines for keeping food:

eggs	5 weeks
meat (unground)	2–3 days
meat (ground)	1–2 days
meats (unopened deli)	7 days
milk	7 days
seafood	1–2 days

Several Internet sites give advice on keeping foods fresh, with recommended times for storing canned and refrigerated items.

(½ dozen) or twelve (1 dozen); the price depends on the size.

Check the expiration date before you buy.

Delicatessen. The deli counter has fresh salads, hot barbecued chicken, appetizers, and other kinds of prepared or cooked foods. Order about ¼ pound (lb.) of meat or salad per person.

It is not impolite to ask the employee to show you food; you may ask him or her to "add a few slices" or "take away a few spoonfuls" or for "a taste," if you like.

Bakery. Baked goods are usually made every day. Sometimes you may buy "day-old" breads or pastries for half-price. If your area has a wet climate, be sure the bread is wrapped tightly so it stays fresh.

You may need to take a number at the bakery or delicatessen counter. The number shows when it is your turn to be waited on.

Frozen foods. These include frozen vegetables, juices, ice cream, meats, fish, breads, and desserts. Frozen prepared meals include lasagna, burritos, and TV dinners.

Special diet foods. By law, foods with labels such as "low-fat" or "low-sodium" must meet guidelines set by the federal government.

Food Labels

By law, the labels on food must mean what they say. For example:

Key Words	What they mean
Fat Free	Less than .5 gram of fat per serving
Low Fat	3 grams of fat (or less) per serving
Lean	Less than 10 grams of fat, 4 grams of saturated fat, and 95 milligrams of cholesterol
Light (Lite)	Less than 1/3 the calories; no more than ½ the fat of similar products; or no more than ½ the sodium of similar versions
Cholesterol Free	Less than 2 milligrams of cholesterol and 2 grams (or less) of saturated fat per serving
Organic	Natural foods, or foods that are free from processes such as genetic engineering or radiation and that have no man-made ingredients such as preservatives or pesticides.

To make health claims about...	The food must be...
Heart Disease	Low in fat, saturated fat, and cholesterol.
Blood Pressure	Low in sodium

Baby items. These include strained foods, baby cereal mixes, infant formulas, and even diapers.

Ethnic foods. You can find ethnic foods such as Oriental, Italian, Hispanic, and kosher canned goods.

Baking goods. These include ingredients for baking or cooking—such as sugar, flour, and spices. You can also find "mixes" for breads, cakes, cookies, and puddings.

Food bar. You choose hot and cold foods and pay by the pound. The prices are posted for such items as:

- the hot food bar, with cooked meats, chicken, pasta, soups, and chili.
- the cold salad bar, with mostly fresh vegetables and fruits; sometimes it has tuna or egg salad.
- the frozen yogurt machine; the yogurt often comes in two different flavors every day.

Take as much food as you want. The cashier at the counter weighs and prices the food.

Pharmacy. The pharmacy, or drugstore, has over-the-counter and prescription medicines (see "Medicine/ Medical Care"). You may also find products such as toothbrushes, sanitary napkins, sunglasses, combs and brushes, and shaving lotion.

Photo center. You may buy film or have color photos developed here.

Calculating the Price

Labels. Look for the store's own label. These products often cost less and may be just as good as the food with more famous labels.

Item price. The item price is the price of the package. If two boxes have the same amount of food, you can calculate quickly which brand is cheaper. If not, check the unit price.

Unit price. If two products are not the same size, the unit price helps you calculate which product is cheaper. For example, a unit price may show the price per ounce. You may use it to compare two cans of soup—one large and one small. Look for this price on the shelf edge just below the item.

Coupons. Cut these out of the "Food" section of the newspaper or out of magazines or advertisements that come in the mail. Coupons give you a discount on a specific item. Often, you cannot use the coupons:

- after the expiration date printed on the coupon.
- in every store. For example, they may be good only in the store where you found the coupon.

Sometimes a store has "double" and "triple" coupons (two or three times the value of the coupon). For example, if you have a coupon for 25¢ off Kleenex tissues and it is a double coupon, you will get a 50¢ discount.

Large supermarkets usually have public rest rooms. Ask an employee where they are.

Sales tax. Items that are taxed have a "T" after them on the sales slip. In general, basic foods such as meat, milk, bread, and produce are not taxed. Snack foods and some household items are taxed in some areas.

Special Services

Special orders. Most stores take advance orders for meat, fish, or pastries. For example, you can order a turkey or ham about a week before Thanksgiving or Christmas. If you are having guests, you may order special cuts of meat, deli platters, or desserts.

Repackaging. You may buy a smaller slice of watermelon or a smaller piece of fish than is on display; ask.

Coffee. Many grocery stores grind fresh coffee beans for you to take home. Some have coffee grinders next to the coffee beans so you can grind the coffee yourself.

Check cashing. The courtesy or check-cashing card lets you cash a check easily. The card is good at all stores with the same name. If you need money, some large supermarkets also let you write a check for $20–$50 more than the amount of the bill; you get the money back in cash.

To get a courtesy card, go to the manager's office and ask for an application. If you have a bank account in the area, you should get a card in the mail within a few weeks. Some stores give temporary cards.

Bonus cards. Many large grocery and drug stores use bonus cards that let you get a discount on some items. If

you shop often at one store, get a bonus card and give it to the clerk when you check out.

Specialty Stores

Natural Foods

Many supermarkets carry natural, or organic, foods—that is, foods with no chemicals. You can also find natural food stores in many communities.

Ethnic Grocers

Every large city has ethnic grocery stores where you can meet people from your home country and get the kinds of foods you like. You may find videotapes, audiotapes, books, and newspapers in your own language.

Look under "Grocers—Retail" in the Yellow Pages directory. Also look in the Business Section of the White Pages directory for business names that start with the name of your country.

Warehouses

The suburbs of most American cities have large warehouses that sell food and other items at a discount. With many, you must pay a small annual fee to shop there—usually $25–$50.

Each discount store is different. With some, you must bring your own bags to carry the groceries. With others, most of the items come in bulk; that is, you must buy large quantities.

In general, you may buy most of your food items in a warehouse; but you may need to shop somewhere else for a specific item. In addition to food, some warehouses sell items such as clothes, electronics, bicycles, and toys.

Gourmet Foods

Gourmet food stores usually have higher prices than other chain stores. Most offer a wider variety of:

- organic foods and drinks. Most carry both organic and "regular" items, so you have a choice. Many do not offer items with artificial ingredients such as sugar substitutes or preservatives.
- fresh fruits and vegetables. For example, you may find fine peaches in the wintertime or fresh figs and dates that are not offered in other stores.
- meats, fish, chicken, cheeses, coffees, and teas.
- pre-made items such as "store-made" pasta sauces, crab cakes, or soups.

Home Delivery

Home delivery. Some stores offer home delivery. You can give your order over the telephone and have the groceries delivered to your house on the same day. You may have to pay for this service.

On-line services. Many cities have one or more services with on-line ordering and home delivery. You may order groceries or even meals.

In general, the prices are about the same as those in grocery stores; but you may have more choices if you go into a grocery store.

Most on-line services have a minimum order—usually about $75. You pay on-line with a credit card; the services do not accept coupons.

Words to Know

Altitude: height, or number of feet, above sea level. If your area is high above sea level, you may need to change the way you cook.

Bonus card: a plastic card that lets you get discounts at grocery stores or pharmacies

Brand name: the name of a particular type of product. For example, kleenex is the brand name of a type of tissue.

Checkout counter: where you go to pay for items

"Choice": the most common grade of meat

Coupon: a piece of paper that gives a discount on the price of a specific item

Courtesy or check-cashing card: a card that lets you pay with a check

Dairy products: products made from milk—such as milk, cheese, or yogurt

Debit card: a bank card used to pay for something. The money is taken out of your account right away.

Drugstore: (see "Pharmacy")

Deli platter: a large plate with meats and cheeses, and sometimes salads

Expiration date: ending date. For example, you may not use a coupon after the expiration date. Do not buy foods after the expiration date.

Express lane: "fast lane"; lane for shoppers who have only a few items

Genetic Engineering: changing the genes of the plant or animal

Gourmet food store: a store with more kinds of fine and organic foods than other grocery stores

Graded: a way of telling how good a product is. For example, meat is graded "prime," "choice," or "lean."

Home delivery: a service that sends the groceries to your home

Humidity: wetness in the air. The humidity may affect the way you bake.

Item price: what one box or package costs

Lean: a type of meat with very little fat

Natural foods: foods grown or made without chemicals

Organic foods: natural foods—with no chemicals, such as sugar substitutes for adding flavor or preservatives for keeping foods fresh. Organic meat comes from animals that have eaten only naturally grown feed. Man-made processes, such as radiation, are forbidden for all organic foods.

Pesticides: chemicals added to plants to keep bugs from eating them

Pharmacy: a store (or section of the grocery store) where you can buy items such as medicine and vitamins.

Preservatives: chemicals added to keep food fresh

"Prime": the best and most expensive cut of meat

Produce: fresh fruit and vegetables

Radiation: using energy waves to keep food from spoiling

Repackaging: to pack again; putting less or more food in a package

Sales slip: a paper that lists what you bought and how much it costs

Sales tax: the value-added tax. Meat, milk, bread, and produce are not taxed. Snack foods, such as potato chips, are taxed.

Scan: to pass an item in front of a machine so that it can "read" the price

Select: a type of meat with very little fat; lean

Special order: an order for meat, fish, or pastry that the store will make at your request—for example, deli platters or fresh whole poultry

TV dinner: a frozen meal that comes in a tray, to be heated

Unit price: the price for each unit of measure—usually pounds or ounces

Ungraded: a cheaper and less tender type of meat

Warehouse: a large store that sells food and other items at a lower price

Shops & Malls

"Misses" Dresses, Coats and Skirts

American	3	5	7	9	11	12	13	14	15	16	18
European	36	38	38	40	40	42	42	44	44	46	48
British	8	10	11	12	13	14	15	16	17	18	20

Sweaters and Blouses

American	10	12	14	16	18	20
European	38	40	42	44	46	48
British	32	34	36	38	40	42

"Junior Miss" Dresses or Suits

American	3	5	7	9	11	13	15
European				34	36	38	40

Shoes

American	5	6	7	8	9	10
European	36	37	38	39	40	41
British	3½	4½	5½	6½	7½	8½

Men's clothing sizes

Suits, Overcoats and Sweaters

American	34	36	38	40	42	44	46	48
European	44	46	48	50	52	54	56	58
British	34	36	38	40	42	44	46	48

Shirts (Neck sizes. Sleeve sizes are 32–36)

American	14½	15	15½	16	16½	17	17½	18
European	37	38	39	41	42	43	44	45
British	14½	15	15½	16	16½	17	17½	18

Shoes

American	7	8	9	10	11	12	13
European	39½	41	42	43	44½	46	47
British	5½	6½	7½	8½	9½	10½	12½

____Measurements____

American & Metric Systems

	American	Metric
Length	1 inch (1")	2.54 centimeters
	1 foot (1')	0.305 meter
	1 yard	0.914 meter
	1 mile	1.609 kilometers
Area	1 square inch	6.452 sq. cm.
	1 square foot	929.030 sq. cm.
	1 square yard	0.836 sq. m.
	1 acre	4,047 sq. m.
Volume/Capacity		
	1 pint	0.473 liter
	1 quart	0.946 liter
	1 gallon	3.785 liters
Weight	1 ounce	28.350 grams
	1 pound	453.592 grams
	1 ton	0.907 metric ton

	Metric	American
Length	1 centimeter	0.394 inch
	1 decimeter	03.937 inches
	1 meter	39.37 inches
	1 kilometer	0.621 mile
Area	1 square cm.	0.155 sq. in.
	1 centare	10.764 sq. ft.
	1 hectare	2.477 acres
Volume/Capacity		
	1 deciliter	0.211 pint
	1 liter	1.057 quarts
	1 decaliter	2.642 gallons
Weight	1 decagram	0.353 ounce
	1 kilogram	2.205 pounds
	1 metric ton	1.102 tons

Overview

Comparing

Americans are used to "shopping around"; that is, they compare before they buy.

When you "shop around," it is not impolite to talk about the item with a sales clerk for a while and then say you want to think about it.

Paying

 Most stores expect you to pay with a check or credit card; if you pay with a check, you usually need two forms of identification (ID), for example:

- a photo ID—such as a driver's license or employee ID.
- a library card.

Adding up the cost. Often, the price you see on an item is not the price you pay. Most states and cities have a sales tax. This tax is like a VAT (value-added tax); but it is added to the price you see. The tax is a percentage of the price. For example, with a 6% sales tax, you will pay $10.60 for an item listed at $10.

Returning and exchanging

Sales slips. Always save sales slips (also called "receipts"). Most stores will return your money if you are unhappy with a product. Some require that you return it within a specific time period—for example, within 2 weeks.

Many small stores offer "store credit only" for returns—that is, you can get something else in the store for the same or greater price; but you will not get your money back.

Returning items. Go to the department where you bought the item. Ask to see a salesperson; if possible, have the product and the sales slip with you. Explain why you are unhappy with the product.

Tip: You do not need a "good" reason for returning most items. Just say you changed your mind.

? ***What if I buy a defective product and the sales clerk will not refund my money?***
Ask to see the manager and explain the problem. If you still cannot get your money back, ask to see that manager's boss. If you still are not satisfied, contact the Office of Consumer Affairs in the city or county where the purchase was made. The number is in the county or city government section of your telephone book under "Consumer Regulatory Affairs."

Shopping Malls

Mall hours are different in each region; but the hours usually are:

- during the week, 10 am–9:30 pm.
- Saturdays, 10 am–5 or 9 pm.
- Sundays, 12 pm–5 or 6 pm.

Around Christmas time, most malls are open from 9 am–10 pm every day.

Stores and services

Stores. Most malls have:

- specialty stores, or stores specializing in books, electronics, furs, shoes, gifts, clothing, toys, jewelry, sporting goods—and anything else you can name!
- department stores, or large stores with many kinds of items. You may buy linens, jewelry, shoes, pajamas, TVs, and stationery. Many department stores also have beauty salons and photography services.

Directories. Usually, you can find store directories, or maps of the mall, near the entrances. You may also ask at the information desk.

Rest rooms. Every mall has at least one public rest room on each floor, especially near the food court. Department stores also have rest rooms.

Restaurants. Most malls have food courts, or large areas with tables and many types of foods. The food is served "over-the-counter," or cafeteria style. You may also find more formal restaurants around the mall or in some department stores.

? *What if a salesperson comes to the door or calls me on the phone?* You will get many sales calls on the phone—especially around 7 or 8 pm. A few salespeople will come to your door in the middle of the day. *Remember:* it's your money! You do not have to buy anything. Just close the door or hang up the phone if you like.

Special Services

Alterations

Many stores do alterations (tailoring for clothes you buy there). The service is convenient; but the cost is usually higher than the cost of tailoring from a dry cleaning shop.

Personal shoppers

Some department stores have personal shoppers. This service is free for items bought in that store. Personal shoppers can help you:

- choose gifts.
- buy clothes.
- decide what to wear for different occasions.
- choose makeup and hair styling.

Some personal shoppers even bring items to your home; find out if they charge for the visit. If you find a personal shopper you like, you may call ahead of time and make an appointment.

Home decorators

Like personal shoppers, home decorators give personal attention. You may use department store decorators for free. Often, they come to your home and give advice on furniture, carpets, drapes, and wallpaper. Private decorators may charge by the hour or by the size of the job.

Special orders

? **What if a store does not have the item I need?** If the store sells the item but does not have it in stock, you may be able to order it. For example, if the store does not have the correct size for a shirt you want to buy:

- The clerk may be able to send out a special order for the item.
- The clerk may be able to have the item shipped from another store. Ask if you must buy the item after it arrives.
- You may be able to order the item on-line from the store's website. You probably will pay for shipping and handling.

Shipping

Many stores will ship an item anywhere in the U.S. for a small fee. This service is convenient for sending gifts out of town. If you like, someone may gift wrap the present for you; then you may attach a card and send it—all from the store where you bought it.

Gifts

Gift wrapping. Usually, the store will give you a free box if you ask. Many stores gift wrap for a small fee; some stores have cards to put inside the box.

Gift certificates. Gift certificates are common for graduations, birthdays, and Mother's or Father's Day. For example, a person who has a $50 gift certificate can spend $50 in that store. You may buy gift certificates at many kinds of stores—such as department stores, record stores, and small specialty shops.

Bridal registry. Brides often register at a store to help people choose gifts. The bride and groom make a list of the items they want and give the list to a store. Most stores have the lists on computers you can use. When you look up the name of the bride or groom, you will see a list of the items they want; the list also tells you which items other people have bought for them already. If you like, ask a salesperson to show you an item you want to buy; the store will also send out the item for you. Ask for a card to put inside.

If you have a credit card, you may buy and send the gift over the telephone. You may choose the gift, charge it, and have it mailed—without ever leaving your house!

Baby registry. The baby registry is like the bridal registry. Ask for the children's department.

Catalogs

Kinds of catalogs

Store catalogs have many more items than the store itself. For example, if a store does not have the size or color of an item you want, you may order it from the catalog. Many stores also mail out their catalogs to their customers.

Mail catalogs, like L.L. Bean® or Land's End®, do not have stores at all. If you get catalogs you don't want, call the company and ask to be "taken off the list."

For more about catalog and Internet shopping, see below.

How to order

You may order by mail, fax, telephone, or on-line. The catalog company will need the number and expiration date of your credit card.

 The delivery cost is usually a percentage of the cost of the item; add this to the price. You may or may not pay a sales tax—depending on the location of the store or catalog company.

E-commerce

You may buy almost anything on-line—including clothes, electronic equipment, books, and flowers.

Note: You always pay with a credit card. Generally, your credit card information is as safe as ordering on the telephone.

 Look on the left side of your screen for the "safe" symbol—a closed lock or key.

Advantages

Convenience. You may order from your home 7 days a week, night or day—to any place in the U.S. Many sites also mail outside of the U.S.

Add-on services. For example, many florists remind you of birthdays and other special occasions. Other sites keep you posted about new products.

Choice. The choices on the Internet are greater than anyone can imagine—and they are growing every day. The Internet is particularly convenient if you are looking for specialty items such as clothing with an unusual size, out-of-date music CDs—even especially tender steaks!

Disadvantages.

Shipping costs. Usually, you do not pay taxes. But you pay a shipping and handling charge—often 5–10% of your purchase. If you return the item, you pay the shipping cost to send it back.

Dissatisfaction with the item. For example, you may be unhappy because the color of the item is not what you expected or because the item does not fit. Check the return policy before you buy. Most large companies let you return easily.

Delivery delays. If the company does not have what you ordered "in stock," you may need to wait. Sometimes the delay is only a few days, but it may be a month or more. Most large companies call and ask if you want to wait for the order or cancel it.

On-line auction sites

A few sites auction off their items. In an auction, the seller posts an item and people "bid" for it, or tell how much they will pay. One popular auction site is eBay, where you may buy used baby clothes, theater tickets, rugs—even paintings. The rules for buying and selling are on the site.

Bargain Hunting

In general, do not bargain in stores—even when items are on sale. Often, you may bargain if you are buying from individual sellers.

Advertisements

Classifieds. The classified ads in the back of the newspaper are mostly from people who want to sell something secondhand (used).

Store ads. Stores often advertise sale items in newspapers. If you see an item that interests you, call the store to find out more about it. Make sure you know when the sale ends and if there are any restrictions (circumstances under which the sale price is not good).

Special sales

When you go to a store for a sale item, take the ad with you. If the store has no more of that item, a dealer will sometimes give you a "rain check"; that is, you may buy the item at the same sale price at a later time.

It is not impolite to ask the salesperson if an item will go on sale soon.

What if I have just paid full price for an item and then see it on sale? Show the salesperson the item and your receipt; you usually get the discount.

Discount shopping

There are discount stores for almost every kind of item. Pay special attention to the return policies; sometimes there are no refunds.

Warehouse clubs are huge stores that sell name-brand products at lower prices. The prices are cheaper—sometimes almost half those in the regular stores.

About 25% of the items in a warehouse club are food products that are frozen, canned, and boxed; some warehouse clubs do not have fresh food. Most clubs also have office supplies, small appliances, sporting equipment, household products, clothes, and many other kinds of products.

To shop in a warehouse club, you may need to pay an annual membership fee—around $35.

Discount stores are smaller than warehouse clubs; their prices may not be as low, but you do not have to buy in bulk or pay a membership fee. You can find discount stores for almost anything—including clothing, furniture, leather goods, shoes, and sporting equipment. Look at the ads in the newspaper to find the discount store you want.

Outlet malls get their products right from the factory and sell them for a lower price. Ask if the item is a "second," or slightly damaged; if it is, look closely to see what could be wrong. For example, look for stains, missing buttons, loose threads, and holes.

Garage/yard sales are usually in private homes. Most items for sale are used. You may find antiques, old books, furniture, clothes, or dishes. You cannot return what you buy, but you can bargain.

Consignment shops sell used items, such as clothing, home lamps, or books. You cannot return what you buy. Usually, you cannot bargain.

Flea markets are public markets with many kinds of items. Most flea markets are outdoors, but some larger ones are indoors.

Flea markets usually sell used items, such as furniture, clothes, jewelry, and antiques. As with yard sales, you cannot return items, but you can bargain.

Words to Know

Alteration: the changing of clothes so they fit you

Auction: In an auction, people bid each other for an item; that is, each person tells how much he or she is willing to pay; the highest bidder gets the item. On sites like eBay, sellers may start the bidding with a minimum price, or lowest price they will accept.Then they set a specific amount of time—for example, one week—for the bidding.

Baby registry: a list of gifts that parents want for their baby

Bridal registry: a list of gifts for the bride and groom

Bulk: (items) in large quantities. Usually, you get a discount for buying "in bulk."

Cafeteria: a restaurant where you serve yourself and bring the food to a table

Catalog: a book that shows pictures and tells about the items for sale. You can call or mail in your order.

Classified section: a section of the newspaper that lists items for sale

Consignment shop: a store that sells used items

Defective: having something wrong with it. For example, a defective computer may shut down frequently. A defective dress may shrink a lot with one washing.

Discount store: a store that sells items at lower prices

E-commerce: a way of buying and selling on the Internet

Flea market: an open area where people sell items on tables or in tents. Flea markets are good for items such as antiques, furniture, jewelry, audio and video cassettes, and clothing such as jackets and hats.

Food court: an area in a mall or shopping center with many types of fast-food restaurants

Garage/yard sale: sales in private homes. Usually items for sale are used.

Gift certificate: a kind of gift. To buy someone a gift certificate, go into the store and pay for the certificate at the cash register. When you give the certificate to your friend, he or she can use it to buy something at the store.

Gift wrap: to cover a package with pretty paper and a bow

"In stock": an item that is available. If a store has an item in stock, you can take it home with you.

Mail-order company: a company that sends you products in the mail. You order by calling or by sending a check.

Mall: a large shopping area with many kinds of stores under one roof

Name-brand product: a product made by a major company with a recognizable name

Outlet mall: a mall with stores owned by the manufacturer (maker of the product). Usually, the manufacturer is well-known for high-quality and expensive merchandise. Some outlet malls have 90 or more stores.

Personal shopper: a person who helps you choose gifts and buy clothes

Rain check: a paper that lets you buy an item for a lower price after the sale is over

Receipt: a paper you get from the store when you buy something which shows the items purchased and the amount paid; also called "sales slip"

Refund: to return money

Sales taxes: the taxes you pay when you buy something

Sales slip: (see "Receipt" above)

Second-hand: used

Specialty store: a store that sells only a few types of items—such as lamps, jewelry, or antiques

Store credit: credit you get for returning an item

Warehouse club: a big store that sells items at lower prices

Your Mail

International

Return address

Air Mail stamp

Tomiko Yamada
1716 Woodmont Ave.
Bethesda, MD 20814
U.S.A.

Air Mail

Miss Akiko Yamada
7-3-6 Kyodo, Setagaya-ku
Tokyo, Japan F156

City, Country

Domestic

Tomiko Yamada
1716 Woodmont Ave.
Bethesda, MD 20814

Mr. Thomas Barett
066 Berkeley Ave.
Albany, CA 94706

City, State (California), Zip Code

Getting to the Post Office

Location. Most post offices have a U.S. flag near them and the words "U.S. Post Office" on the building.

Services. At the post office you can:

- mail letters and packages.
- weigh a letter or package and find out the cost to send it.
- buy stamps and supplies—such as envelopes and boxes.
- buy money orders (see "International Transactions/Money Matters").
- rent a post office box.

How to pay. You can pay with:

- cash.
- a check. You will need an ID—such as a driver's license.
- a credit or debit card.

The post office is usually open Monday through Friday, 8 or 9 am–5 pm. Many post offices are also open on Saturday mornings until 12 noon or 1 pm.

Domestic Mail

Ways to send

First class. This is the most common way to send letters and postcards. Mail usually arrives in 2–3 days, depending on the distance.

Fourth class ("parcel post"). Regular mail service for packages that weigh 1 pound (lb.) or more. Packages may take up to 8 days to arrive.

Book rate. A lower rate for sending books, records, and magazines.

Express. Overnight mail. You get tracking; that is, you can find out where the package is if it is not delivered on time. You will also get delivery confirmation (the date and time it was delivered), plus the signature of the person receiving it.

Priority. First-class mail that weighs more than 13 ounces, with a 2–3 day delivery time. If you want tracking and delivery confirmation, ask to send it certified. To get the signature of the person receiving the mail, ask for a "return receipt."

Collect-On-Delivery (COD or CASH in some countries). You pay for an item when the letter carrier delivers it.

Do not mail cash; if the money gets lost, you will not be able to replace it. Use a check or money order.

Note: You may insure any package or get proof of delivery for a small fee. Ask the clerk at the post office.

To mail a letter or package in the U.S., you must include the zip code in the address. The zip code is a 5- or 9-digit number that indicates the U.S. postal area. To find the zip code for an address: Call or go to any post office or look it up on the post office's website.

How to mail a domestic letter

1. Write the addressee's name, street address, city, state, and zip code.

2. Write your own address in the upper left-hand corner of the envelope.

If you have the wrong mailing address, the letter carrier will return the letter to you.

3. Buy a stamp if you are sending the letter regular first class.

You can buy stamps at any post office or at some supermarkets. (For certified or registered letters, go to the post office.)

4. Put your letter in a *blue* mailbox.

You can find these boxes:

- on the street—especially near the post office.
- at airports.
- in shopping malls.

Note: Read the words on the box. Some mailboxes are only for express mail.

You may also leave your letter in the mailbox outside your door or the mail slot in the door of your house; the letter carrier will pick it up.

Mailing packages

Wrap the package. Mark the box in large letters on the front and back:

- "FRAGILE" for objects that could break.
- "DO NOT BEND" for photographs or documents.
- "DO NOT X-RAY" for computer disks and film.
- "PERISHABLE" for foods that might spoil.

Bring the package to the post office. A clerk will weigh the box and put on the postage.

If your package weighs 1 pound or more, take it to the post office. The postal service will not pick up these packages from a mailbox.

International Mail

Letters/packages

Airmail letters take about 4–7 days.

The U.S. Post Office delivers the mail to the country where it is going—not directly to the person who is receiving it. In countries with poor domestic postal services, the mail may not arrive until much later. For door-to-door delivery, use a private service such as United Parcel Service (UPS) or Federal Express.

Express

International express mail takes 2–3 days. If the package is lost, the postal service will be able to trace it—until it reaches the destination country; after that, the U.S. Postal Service is not responsible.

The number of delivery days is not guaranteed. For guaranteed, door-to-door, overnight delivery to another country, use a private service.

 Some countries limit package weight. Ask the postal clerk about the rules for a specific country.

Private Services

Mailing

Private services do some jobs that the post office does not. For example, some services such as Federal Express and UPS:

* pick up the mail at your door.
* mail overnight to countries outside the U.S.

 Be sure to use an address with the name of the street and the number of the house.

Services such as FedEx and UPS do not ship to addresses with a post office box (P.O. Box #) address.

$ You will pay a pick-up fee. Some services have letter-size mailing envelopes, but you must seal and label any boxes yourself, if you are mailing them from home.

How to pay. Most private services let you pay with a credit or debit card. If you have an account with the service, you may charge it on the phone.

Other services

Wrapping. Often, private services have more packaging and office supplies than the post office. Also, the clerk will do the wrapping for you.

Mailboxes. Some private services rent mailboxes by the month. When you travel, the service will forward your mail to the city where you are staying.

Telegrams ("Mailgrams"). You may use a telegram to send a message quickly here or abroad. Western Union, the only company that sends telegrams, has an "800" service number to take orders and answer questions (see "Chapter Information" in the Appendix).

Look up the U.S. Post Office's website at www.usps.com. For example, you may find:

* a list of U.S. zip codes.
* a complete list of mailing options—with easy-to-understand descriptions.
* customs regulations.
* instructions for sending money orders or bill payments.
* postal rates.

You may also order stamps, phonecards, and stationery on-line.

Faxing and copying. You may send faxes inside or outside the U.S. at most private mail centers. Copies may be made at printing offices, office supply stores, libraries, private mail services, and at a few post offices. The price ranges from 5¢–25¢ a page.

Words to Know

Book rate: a lower rate for sending books, records, and magazines

Certified mail: a type of first-class or priority mail. You get a mailing receipt. If you want proof of delivery, you need to request return receipt service.

Collect-on-delivery (COD): a type of shipping from a store or catalog company. You pay for the item when you get it.

Domestic: within the United States

Express mail: overnight mail

First-class mail: the most common way to send letters and postcards; for domestic mail only

Fragile: an item that can break easily

Money order: a special check you can buy at the post office or bank. You can send the check in the mail. A mail order is handy when you want to mail cash or when you need money right away. For example, newcomers may use money orders instead of checks for a rental deposit.

Parcel post: regular mail service for packages that weigh one pound or more

Post office box: a locked box in the post office where your mail is kept until you pick it up

Priority mail: first-class mail that weighs more than 13 ounces. The mail usually arrives in 2–3 days.

Registered mail: mail that is guaranteed special care and security

Return receipt: a card signed by the person who receives the mail, which is mailed back to the sender as evidence of delivery

Surface mail: mail sent by ground or boat (usually slower), in contrast to air

Tracking: a service that tracks your letter or package—that is, it finds out where your mail is. The U.S. Postal Service can track your mail if you send it certified or express. Private services such as Federal Express or UPS always are able to track the item.

Zip code: a 5-digit or 9-digit number that indicates the U.S. postal delivery area in the United States

__Money Matters__

Your Bank Check

Joe Sanchez
Marie Sanchez
701 Montgomery Place
Bethesda, MD 20814

0001

1/5 20 02

PAY TO THE
ORDER OF *International Center* $ **42.76**

Forty-two dollars and 76/100 DOLLARS

Washington Bank
1 Pleasant Street
Washington, D.C. 20005

FOR *tapes* *Joe Sanchez*

⑆012486⑆ ⑈067003442⑇

Your Check Register

Check No.	Date	Payee	Payment	Deposit	Balance
0001	1/5	Int'l Ctr	$42.76		$ 96.12
	1/6	Transfer		$200	$296.12
0002	1/6	Giant	$31.19		$264.93

International Transactions

International money wires

Tip: To send money quickly, use Western Union or another wiring service; with most wiring services, you must go in person to the wiring service's offices; the person receiving the money must also go to the office once the funds have arrived. Banks are often more convenient if you wire to and from the same accounts regularly—or if you want the money to go directly into someone's account.

 You may pay:

- a transaction fee—usually about $15–$75.
- a currency conversion fee. If you are converting from a foreign currency into U.S. dollars, this fee may be included in the exchange rate.

To shop around for the best price, call a few banks, private services, and currency exchanges; ask about pick-up and delivery when you call. Compare costs at the same time of day. You probably will get the best rates early in the morning, when European markets are open and trading.

International services.

Banks. Many banks will not wire your money if you do not have an account with them. The fee for transferring money outside the U.S. is usually about $20–$40; most banks will deposit money wired from another country for free if the money is going to one of their accounts.

Wiring money to and from the bank with your account is usually convenient. For example, you may be able to transfer money:

- at the bank.
- by fax; ask the bank ahead of time how to set up fax transfers.
- on-line.

Generally, wiring to and from banks in developed countries takes 3–4 days. The transaction may take much longer if you are wiring to or from an undeveloped country or a bank with little international experience.

When asking about the transaction time with any bank representative remember: Although banks may send out the money within 1 or 2 days, no bank can guarantee that the bank receiving the money will make the deposit right away. Be sure the sending bank can find out what has happened to the transfer if it takes too long.

If you need money right away for a down payment or large purchase, find an ATM with the same network you already have from your home bank or get a money order from the nearest post office; you may use your credit card to purchase the money order and use it instead of cash.

If you are using a bank, you will need:

- the names and addresses of the foreign bank and of the U.S. bank's main branch.
- the routing number, or electronic address, of each bank—if possible. You may also need the international routing number of the main bank; ask.
- the account number and account title or name for both banks. In most cases, people transferring funds must have an account and adequate funds in the bank from which they are wiring the money.

If you are not using a bank with your account, you will also need:

- identification—for example, a driver's license, passport, student card, or credit card. Ask ahead of time.
- a cashier's check, cash, or a credit card.

Private delivery services. For example, Western Union transfers money to and from Western Union locations in just a few minutes. The rates vary according to the amount of money being transferred and the country where it is going.

With Western Union, the person receiving the money must go to the office in order to pick up the money.

You may transfer the money:

- on-line with a credit card.
- by phone with a credit card. You may pay $10–$15 more—depending on the state you are sending from.
- in person, at a Western Union location. Payment is with cash only. You will need a picture ID, such as a driver's license.

Currency exchanges. For example, Travelex/Thomas Cook can wire money to major European banks in 48 hours; the fee is less than $50 for all transfers to all locations anywhere in the world. You can also transfer money in just a few minutes—at a higher cost.

Look on the Internet for more information about wiring inside and outside the U.S.

Money Orders. If you are sending money to a country with good mail service, you may also send a mail order. Bring cash to your nearest post office and buy one or more money orders; each money order has a limit of $70, but you may buy as many as you like. The U.S. mail can deliver the money orders to a foreign post office within 2–3 days, depending on the country. The additional delivery time depends on the country.

Americans generally pay for most services with credit cards and checks. Few banks automatically pay bills such as rent, electricity, or credit-card payments. You probably will need to pay these bills every month—either through on-line banking or with a check. If you are paying rent to a large management company, you may be able to arrange for the company to automatically withdraw the rent payment from your account.

Banking Overview

Why you need a bank account

If you are planning to stay for more than 1 or 2 months, you need a checking account. You may use your account to pay:

- monthly bills—for example, bills for the phone, gas and electricity, cable TV, and rent.
- grocery bills. Most supermarkets offer courtesy cards for cashing checks (see "The Supermarket/ Food Shopping").
- day-to-day expenses—such as dry-cleaning and home-cleaning services.

 Do not carry large amounts of cash (more than $100). Pay with traveler's checks, a bank check, or a credit card.

Kinds of institutions

The U.S. has three main kinds of banking institutions:

- banks.
- savings and loans (S&Ls).
- credit unions.

All three have the same basic services. Banks and S&Ls are private corporations, but credit unions are owned by the members themselves. Usually, you may get a loan or a credit card more easily from a credit union than from a bank.

You may join a credit union only if you are a part of a group that has one. Many large institutions have credit unions for their employees.

Choosing a Bank

International experience. For example, if you will be transferring money to your home country, make sure your branch can do international transfers conveniently.

Tip: A few banks have branches in foreign countries. If you have an account in both branches of the bank, you may be able to do the following more easily:

- transfer money.
- get a credit card, loan, or emergency funds.

Location. Usually, Americans choose a bank close to their home or office. You may be able to withdraw money from any U.S. branch—at no extra cost. But some banks accept deposits only at the branch with the account. Many charge for using the ATM of another bank.

ATM network. If you travel frequently to specific locations outside the U.S., be sure you can find a compatible ATM network easily.

Direct deposit: With direct deposit, your employer wires your salary into your account. You may have direct deposit with almost all U.S. banks and with many—but not all—employers. The advantage to direct deposit is speed; you can use the money right away.

Credit card and loans. Ask if you can get a credit card. Check the limit of charges you may have on your account at any one time; Americans use credit cards for so many transactions that insufficient credit may be inconvenient. Also ask about loans (see chapter on "Credit Cards and Loans").

Tip: If you cannot get a credit card, ask your employer to write a letter stating your salary and position. The letter is sometimes helpful.

On-line banking. Most banks offer on-line services such as balance updates, money transfers between accounts, and on-line bill paying.

Hours. Compare bank hours if you will need personal services such as wiring money internationally.

Federally insured (FDIC, FSLIC, or CUIC). Most banking institutions are federally insured. If the institution fails, the U.S. Government will give you up to $100,000 of your money back.

Interest rates. All banks pay interest for savings accounts. Most pay interest for personal checking accounts, too.

Overdraft protection. If you have overdraft protection, the bank will "honor," or pay for, a check when you overdraw your account. Without overdraft protection, your check will "bounce"; you will pay a fee—sometimes as high as $30.

Cost of services. Many banks charge for services such as cashing a check.

Minimum balance. The minimum balance is the amount of money you must keep in the account to avoid extra fees.

To open an account, you will need to deposit about $100 for each account. You may pay with cash, a credit card, or a check.

Call ahead to find out what documents you need, for example:

- proof of your name and address. Use
    – a letter or bill sent to your home or office address.
    – a work or student ID.
- a letter from your employer or university stating the length of time you will be here and your salary (if appropriate).
- your Social Security number. If you do not have one yet, the bank may accept your passport, but you may need to complete an Internal Revenue Service (IRS) W-8 form.
- your passport.
- your employer's name and address or your student ID.

Most banks are open from 9 am to 2–3 pm; in some areas, banks are also open at least one night a week or on Saturdays. To do everyday transactions, you may use the ATM or the drive-through window (see section on "The ATM" in this chapter). The best time to open an account is Monday through Thursday mornings. Plan to spend about 30–60 minutes.

How to open an account.

1. **Call the bank and ask what documents you need to bring.**

2. **At the bank, ask for the "new accounts" person.**

You will decide:

- which accounts to use. You will probably open both a savings and a checking account.
- whether each account will be single (for one person) or joint (for more than one person).

If you have more than $100,000, ask how all your money can be federally insured.

3. **Fill out a form for each account.**

4. **Make a deposit.**

5. **Choose your checks.**

Decide what will be printed on your checks (name, address, phone number). You will get temporary checks to use until the printed ones come in the mail (about 7–10 days).

6. **Get a Personal Identification Number (PIN).**

This is your code for using the ATM.

Your Checkbook

Check register. Record every deposit and withdrawal in the check register.

Bank statement. At the end of each month, you will get a statement listing:

- all your transactions.
- the interest earned.
- the service charges.
- beginning and ending balances.

Check this information against your register and make any corrections.

Check clearance. When you deposit a check, you may be able to use $100 of the money right away. The rest of the money has to "clear." By law, banks must give you access to:

- a local check for $5,000 or less in 2–3 business days.
- a local check for more than $5,000 in 6–7 business days.
- an out-of-state check for $5,000 or less in 4–5 business days.
- an out-of-state check for more than $5,000 in 8–10 business days.

Checks from other countries may take as long as 3 weeks to clear.

The ATM

The ATM is convenient because it lets you make transactions:

- 24 hours a day, 7 days a week.
- at another bank's machine within the same network.

To use an ATM, you will need a card and a PIN. You will choose your PIN when you open your account. The card comes in the mail about a week later.

 Your PIN is confidential. It is the number you need to make transactions using the ATM. Do not tell anyone this number. Do not write the number on the ATM card.

Be sure to take both your card and your receipt when you are finished. If you leave your card in an ATM, call the bank as soon as possible.

? *What if I lose my card?* Call the bank right away so that no one else can use it. You will get a new card.

? *What if I punch in the wrong PIN?* The ATM will ask you to try again, but if you punch the wrong number two or three times, the ATM may keep your card. Call the bank to get your card back.

Words to Know

Automated teller machine (ATM): a machine for transactions, such as depositing and withdrawing money from your bank account

Balance: the amount of money in the account

Bounced check: a check you cannot cash because there is not enough money in the account

Cashier's check: a check made out by the bank. The money is immediately withdrawn from your account.

Checking account: an account in which to keep money for writing checks

Credit card: a plastic card used to buy things; you get the bill later. This bill will include a "late charge" if you pay after the payment due date.

Credit union: a type of banking institution. You can join only if you are part of a certain group, such as employees of an organization.

Currency conversion fee: a fee, or cost, for changing currencies—for example, from English pounds to U.S. dollars

Deposit: to place money in an account; the money placed in an account

Federally insured: (deposits that are) guaranteed by the Federal Government

Interest: money the bank pays you for keeping money in its account(s); money you pay for borrowing or for having an unpaid balance on a credit card

Interest rate: a percentage paid to you by the bank for the use of money on deposit; a percentage charged for having an unpaid balance on a credit card

Money order: a document you buy from the U.S. Postal Service. You may send the document to someone in another country instead of cash.

Network ATM: a system of connected ATMs

On-line banking: making electronic transactions such as transferring money between accounts or paying bills on-line

Overdraft protection: a way of making sure all the checks you write are cashed—even when you don't have enough money in the account

Overdraw: to write checks for more money than is in the account

Personal identification number (PIN): your number, or code, for using the ATM

Savings account: an account in which to keep money you are saving

Savings and loan (S&L): a banking institution specializing in home mortgages

Service charge: money paid to a bank for a specific job, such as cashing a check

Transaction: an exchange of money; a deposit, withdrawal, or transfer

W-8 form: an Internal Revenue Service (IRS) form. You need this form in order to open a bank account if you do not have a Social Security card. This form says that you will not be able to use some of the funds in your account if you do not inform the bank of your Social Security number before a specific date.

Paying
___ Your Taxes ___

Income Tax
- U.S.
- most states and Washington, DC
- some counties and cities

Social Security (FICA) Tax
- U.S.

Real Property Tax
- most counties and cities

Personal Property Tax
- some counties and cities

Gift and Estate Tax
- U.S.

Overview

⊗ Find out about the tax laws as soon as possible—either before you arrive or right after you get here. Tax planning often saves time and money.

The information here explains the general U.S. tax rules, but each rule works differently in different situations. Get help from a tax professional, the organization that sponsors you, or your student advisor soon after you arrive in order to avoid probems (see "Getting Help" in this chapter). For example, many newcomers are surprised at the amount of taxes they owe at the end of the year. The Internal Revenue Service (IRS) forms for calculating taxes are not as accurate as the forms in other countries. A tax professisonal can help you plan ahead so you know what to expect.

You will need to calculate your income and many major expenses. During the year, save all your receipts and other documents that may affect your taxes (see section on "End-of-the-Year Taxes" in this chapter).

Kinds of Taxes

Sales tax

You probably will pay a sales tax every time you go shopping; each state and local government has different rules. The sales tax is added onto the price of taxable items such as jewelry, automobiles, certain foods, and clothing. You may not have to pay a sales tax for many items if you work for a foreign or international organization such as an embassy or the United Nations.

Income tax

⊗ Even if you pay no taxes, you probably will need to file a return; that is, you must fill out the appropriate forms and send them to the Internal Revenue Service (IRS) and state taxing agencies.

You probably will pay U.S. income tax if you have income from any U.S. sources. Most states and many counties and cities also have an income tax. Save any records of income—such as:

- your salary as an employee.
- consultant fees, or income earned as a non-employee consultant.
- some scholarships and fellowships.
- capital gains.
- dividends and interest.

You may not need to pay U.S. income tax if your country has an income tax treaty with the U.S. and you meet the conditions of this agreement.

If you are an employee, you usually pay income taxes with each paycheck; you may pay more at the end of the tax year (see section on "Your Paycheck" in this chapter).

Social Security & Medicare

If you are working in the U.S. for a U.S. employer, both you and your employer will pay Social Security and Medicare taxes under the Federal

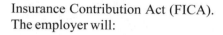

Insurance Contribution Act (FICA). The employer will:

- withhold your part of the tax amount from your paycheck.
- add the employer's part of the tax.
- make payment to the government. The money goes toward an account in your name. Your employer will send the taxes you owe directly out of your paycheck, add the employer's contribution, and send the money to the IRS.

You may not need to pay if:

- the U.S. has an agreement about the Social Security and Medicare systems with your home country. You will need a certificate stating that you will continue to be covered under that system.
- you are a student. Ask your advisor.

Property tax

 You will get a bill or form in the mail for these taxes.

Real property tax. Most city and county governments tax real property, such as land or a home. This tax is only for property owners—rather than renters (see "Buying/Finding a New Home"). Each city or county has its own rules and tax rate.

Personal property tax. Some city and county governments also tax large items such as cars, boats, fur coats, jewelry, stocks, and other investments. Each city or county has its own rules and tax rate.

You pay these taxes when you receive the bill or special form from the city or county agency (see section on "End-of-the-Year Taxes" in this chapter).

Gift and estate taxes

If you want to give a large gift (for example, more than $10,000) or leave an estate (property and/or money) following your death, ask about these taxes.

Your Paycheck

Overview

As an employee, you will pay income and Social Security taxes with each paycheck. Your paycheck shows the amount of money:

- you have earned.
- your employer has withheld, or taken out, for taxes during the year.

At the end of the tax year, you will get a W-2 form, or Wage and Tax statement, which shows the amounts earned and withheld for the year.

 Find out if your country has any agreements with the U.S. about Social Security or income taxes. If you are exempt, make sure your employer did not withhold these taxes from your paycheck.

Income taxes

Overview: At the end of the tax year, calculate all the taxes you owe for that year. Then subtract the income taxes you have already paid during the year. If you have not paid enough, you will pay more money; if you have paid too much, ask for a refund (some money back), from the government.

Employees. Employees fill out a W-4 form, or Withholding Allowance Certificate, right after they start their job. This form tells the amount of taxes the company may withhold (take out), from each paycheck.

⊗ If you use the calculation on the W-4 form to determine the amount of taxes to withhold, you may need to pay a large amount of taxes in April, when "end-of-the-year" taxes are due. To avoid problems later on, ask a tax professional to help you estimate the taxes you will owe.

Consultants. Consultants or self-employed workers may need to estimate the taxes they owe for each quarterly time period and send the money to the U.S. Government. Your state, county, or city may have rules about estimated taxes too.

Social Security (FICA) & Medicare

Both you and your employer contribute to your Social Security and Medicare taxes—up to a certain amount for each year (see "Kinds of Taxes/Social Security" in this chapter).

End-of-the-Year Taxes

The tax year

The tax year for most taxpayers is from January 1st to December 31st. The deadline for paying your Federal taxes is midnight of the next April 15th. For example, the tax deadline for income earned in 2005 is April 15th, 2006; the date and time postmarked on the envelope must be before midnight, April 15th. Many post offices stay open until midnight on April 15th so that you can file (send) your return on time. You may also file online with the IRS e-*file* program for an extra fee.

Planning ahead

Planning ahead is important—especially if you have a high income. For example, you may want to:

- plan how much to withhold. If you withhold too little, your tax bill may be much greater than the amount you have already paid. If you withhold too much, you will not have use of the money until you get your tax refund.
- look into making a tax-deductible contribution to a charity such as a church or museum.
- find out if you can save money by making certain investments—for example, buying a home or putting money in a tax-deferred retirement account (see chapter on "Retirement and Investment Plans").

🕐 If you have a high income, a tax professional may help you save time and money (see section on "Getting Help" in this chapter). Do not wait past December. In March or April, most CPAs are very busy. They may charge more or may not be able to see you.

How to file your return

1. Send a W-7 form to the IRS at least 8 weeks before April 15th.

The W-7 form is an application for the ITIN (see "Documents you need" in this chapter). You will need a separate form for each person who is applying.

 Copy and notarize all records required for the application. Do *not* send the originals.

2. Calculate the total taxes you owe.

Be sure the information on your forms is true. You may pay fines or other extra fees if your forms do not show all the taxes you should pay; you may even lose the right to work or stay longer in the U.S.

3. Copy all your records.

Save all records for 3 years; the IRS may ask to see your documents and papers if you are still in this country. Save copies of all:

- your returns.
- personal records (see section on "Documents you need").

4. File your tax return on a 1040 IRS form by midnight, April 15th.

You may pay with a check by mail or online with a credit card for an extra fee. Be sure to include your SSN and the appropriate ITIN for each dependent.

What happens if I do not have all my documents in time? You must still pay your taxes by April 15th. If you cannot fill out all the forms by that date, you may file for an extension—that is, ask for more time to file, or send in, the forms.

What happens if I do not pay my taxes on time? You will pay interest for every month you are late. In some cases, you may also pay a penalty, or other extra fees.

My partner and I have been living together for 8 years. Can we file as a married couple? No, you must be legally married.

Documents you need

The Individual Taxpayer Identification Number (ITIN). The ITIN is for all persons who are not eligible for an SSN —for example, a non-resident who has earned U.S. income or the spouse of a U.S. resident or child of a person holding an H-1 visa. Every person must have either an SSN or an ITIN—even a 1-month-old baby.

Use the W-7 form to apply for each ITIN. To apply, you will need a passport or two other forms of identification—for example, a foreign driver's license, a civil (non-military) birh certificate, or a visa. Do not apply for an ITIN for anyone who *is* eligible for an SSN, even if that person has not received it.

Note: This sheet is an overview; it is not a government tax form.

Overview of Federal Income Tax

Gross income	**Start with your total income for the year.**	$ _____
(-) Adjustments	Minus adjustments	$ _____
Adjusted gross income (AGI)	**Your new total is the adjusted income.**	$ _____
(-) Deductions	Minus deductions	$ _____
(-) Exemptions	Minus exemptions	$ _____
Taxable income	**Your new total is the amount of income that can be taxed.**	$ _____
(x) Taxable income x rate	Multiply the taxable income x the rate.	$ _____
(-) Tax credits	Minus tax credits (payments such as child care or certain foreign taxes)	$ _____
Total Federal income tax liability	**Your new total is the total amount of taxes you owe for the year.**	$ _____
(-) Taxes paid for the year	Minus taxes you have paid—such as those withheld from your paycheck	$ _____
Federal income taxes owed or a refund for taxes already paid	**Your new total is the amount you will pay or receive.**	$ _____

The names on your passport, W-7 forms, and tax returns must be *exactly* the same. For example, if your child's middle name is on the W-7 form, the middle name must also be on your tax return.

Filing forms. You may get all the filing forms you need from:

- a tax professional.
- the public library.
- an IRS office or the IRS website.

Forms showing your income. By February 1st, you should receive documents in the mail from all sources of U.S. income, showing the amount of income and any tax withheld for the previous year.

Personal records. You may need to document the information used in your filing forms with records or receipts showing:

- personal expenses proving adjustments and deductions—such as
  - some monies put in a tax-deferred retirement account.
  - some trade or business expenses.
  - contributions to some U.S. charities.
  - moving expenses—including moving expenses you paid and the income you received from your employer to pay for those expenses.
  - interest on the mortgage you paid if you own a home.
- some state and local taxes. Do not include sales taxes.

- travel in and out of the U.S., including:
  - the dates you have traveled into and out of the U.S. for this year.
  - the number of days you were in the U.S. during the last 2 years.

How Much You Pay

Status

Legal status, or visa. The type of visa is important for calculating your taxes. For example:

- students with an F, J, or M visa may pay taxes as nonresidents.
- employees of foreign governments and certain international organizations are often taxed according to special rules.

Check with a tax professional or an attorney. If you have not left your home country yet, make sure you have the best type of visa for you.

Residence status. In general, your status may be "resident alien" if you:

- have a "green card" or a "pink card."
- have been in this country for more than 183 days in one tax year.

Most resident aliens:

- pay U.S. taxes on all world-wide income earned in that year.
- can take advantage of more deductions and exemptions than nonresident aliens.

Note: Nonresident aliens pay U.S. taxes only on U.S. income sources.

The rules for residence status are especially complicated; for example, your tax status may not be the same as your immigration status. Ask a tax professional.

Filing status. When you fill out the forms, you will file as a single, married filing jointly, married filing separately, head of a household, or qualifying widow(er) with dependent children.

Taxable income

Gross income. Your gross income is the total amount of income you receive during the tax year. You lower your gross income when you subtract:

- adjustments such as
  - Individual Retirement Account (IRA) deduction.
  - moving expenses.
  - half of self-employment tax.
  - alimony.
  - student loan interest.
- business expenses you pay your-self—for example, the cost of a business trip or moving expenses.
- investments in tax-deferred retire-ment funds.
- deductions. Taxpayers who have few deductions may take the stan-dard deduction. Others itemize (list), their deductions in order to lower their taxes even more. Some deductions are

- income taxes paid to a state, county, or city in the U.S.
- interest on home mortgages.
- some contributions to charity.
- exemptions. Exemptions are a tax deduction for
  - yourself.
  - each of your dependents.

Credits. Credits lower your taxes even more than adjustments, deduc-tions, and exemptions: each credit dollar lowers your taxes by 1 dollar. Credits can be given for:

- child care expenses.
- education expenses.
- foreign taxes.

Tax bracket. In general, the greater the amount of taxable income, the higher the rate of taxation.

Getting Help

Tax professionals

A tax professional will:

- help you plan for your taxes (see section on "Planning ahead" in this chapter).
- calculate the amount you owe.
- fill out the U.S., state, and local tax forms.
- tell you when and where to send any payments.
- tell you what other papers and documents you need to save during the year.

If you plan to be in the U.S. a long time and have a high income, tax professionals can help you with a long-term plan for investments.

Look for a professional who is:

- experienced in international taxes.
- a Certified Public Accountant (CPA) or licensed attorney.
- a member of a professional association, such as the American Institute of Certified Public Accountants.

 Accountants often charge $85–$150 an hour; tax attorneys may be about $200 an hour.

Words to Know

1098: an IRS form showing payments such as mortgage interest and fees and real estate taxes

1099 form: an IRS form showing income from dividends, interest, and royalties

Accountant (see "Certified Public Accountant")

Adjustments: a type of investment or expense that lowers your taxable income

Assets: everything you own that is worth money—such as a home, stocks and other investments, a car, or jewelry

Capital gains tax: the tax on the money you earn when you sell stocks, bonds, real property, or other investments

Certified public accountant (CPA): a licensed professional who helps you keep track of your money and understand the tax rules. Some CPAs are familiar with the tax rules of both the U.S. and other countries.

Credits: expenses that reduce your taxes directly. Credits lower your taxes even more than deductions or exemptions. Each credit dollar lowers your taxes by 1 dollar.

Deductions: expenses that reduce taxable income

Dependent: a person whom you support by using your income to pay for major living expenses—such as housing, food, and clothing. Usually, your dependent is a child, spouse, or parent who lives with you.

Disabled: unable to work for a long time because of an injury or sickness

Dividends: money from company profits that is paid to stockholders

Estate tax: the tax paid when someone dies. The tax is on all the dead person's assets—such as property and money.

Estimate: calculate the approximate amount ahead of time. Estimates are not exact; for example, when you estimate income, you calculate how much you will earn within a certain time—as best you can.

Exempt: free from. If you are tax exempt, you do not have to pay U.S. taxes.

Exemptions: a tax deduction you can take for yourself and each of your dependents. In general, the number of exemptions depends on the number of your dependents—for example, a spouse or child who needs your income for major living expenses.

Federal Government: U.S. Government—rather than state or local governments

FICA: (see "Social Security tax")

Gift tax: the tax someone pays when he or she gives a gift that is worth more than the amount of money decided by the government

Gross income: the total amount of money received during the year—including your salary, scholarships, interest, and the profit from selling stocks, real property, and other investments

Income tax: the tax you pay on the money you have earned during the year

Individual Retirement Account (IRA): a type of account in which individuals invest money for their retirement

Individual Taxpayer Identification Number: a nine-digit number that the IRS uses instead of a Social Security Number (SSN). Only persons who cannot get an SSN may apply for this identification number. You may use the ITIN only for taxes; you may not use it for any other type of identification. It is not a permit to work in the U.S.

Interest: the money you pay for borrowing money, or the money paid to you for having an "interest-bearing" account—such as a savings account or money market fund.

Joint return: a filing status. With a joint return, a married couple calculates their incomes together; the filing status determines the rate you pay.

Medicare: the public health system for people who are retired

Personal property tax: a city or state tax on items such as jewelry, fur, cars, stocks, or other investments.

Real property tax: the tax you pay on real property—such as land, houses, or other buildings you own. Some city and state governments require this tax.

Refund: money you get back. You get a tax refund if you have paid more than enough taxes during the year.

Resident alien: a person who lives in the U.S. but is not a U.S. citizen

Residence status: your U.S. tax status—such as a "resident alien" or "nonresident alien." This status is for paying taxes only; you may have a different status for other purposes.

Return: see "Tax return"

Sales tax: taxes you pay when you buy something

Schedule: a filing form with information listing the sources and amounts of your income

Single return: a filing status. With a single return, you file as an unmarried person.

Standard deduction: a fixed amount you may take to lower your taxable income. You may take this deduction instead of listing expenses separately.

Social Security tax or Federal Insurance Contribution Act (FICA): the taxes you and your employer pay for the Social Security System, which provides benefits for retirement, old age, or disability.

Tax deferred: (income) on which no tax is currently paid. The tax is paid at a later time. For example, the taxes on most retirement investments are tax-deferred.

Tax return: a form used to calculate your taxes. You must complete this form and send it to the IRS and state tax agencies.

Taxable income: the total amount of your income used to calculate your taxes; your gross income minus deductions and exemptions

United States Citizenship and Immigration Services (USCIS): a division of the Department of Homeland Security. The USCIS has responsibility for immigrant and non-immigrant visas, procedures for coming into the U.S., working permits for international residents, and financial benefits for immigrants.

W-2 form: The form you get from your employer at the end of the tax year. This form shows how much money you have earned and how much has been taken out for taxes.

W-4 form: The form you fill out when you start your job. Your employer uses this form to calculate how much tax money to withhold, or take out, from each paycheck.

W-7 form: The IRS form used to apply for an Individual Tax Identification Number (ITIN). Apply at least 8 weeks before April 15th.

Retirement & _Investment Plans_

Am I eligible?

How much may I contribute?

How much will the employer contribute?

Who sets up the plan?

Who makes the investment decisions?

Which taxes will be deferred?

What are the rules for withdrawing, or taking out the money?

What happens if I leave my present employer?

Overview

Most employers offer some type of plan to help you financially when you retire. If you earn U.S. dollars, you are legally eligible to participate in your employer's plan.

The purpose of this chapter is to help you understand the general benefits of the plan or plans available to you. But these plans are only one part of your overall investments for the future. After you read the chapter, discuss the plan with your employer or financial advisor so you can make the right investment decisions.

Note: If you will be living in the U.S. for many years, you probably will benefit from some type of employee-sponsored retirement plan. If you will be here for only one or two years, consider:

- other investment options and retirement plans available to you.
- the rules and processes for withdrawing the money after you return to your home country.

Note: All of the plans described here are generally considered retirement investments—even though some plans allow you to withdraw the money while you are still working.

Why do I need a retirement plan now? Generally, retirement plans offer benefits that

other types of investments do not have. Understanding those benefits will help you:

- put together an overall investment plan that meets all your needs—now and in the future.
- get started now. Most financial analysts agree that the earlier you begin to invest in an overall plan, the more likely you are to achieve your income goals in later years.
- make the right choices about investing money in your employer's plan.

Benefits

Employer participation. With some plans, the employer invests part or all of the money that you will collect when you retire. The amount of this employer contribution varies with the plan. Often, this amount depends on the contribution of the employee; the more that you invest, the more your employer also invests—up to a specific limit.

Tax deferment in the year you invest. With some plans, the money you invest is tax-deferred (delayed); in other words, you will not pay taxes on that money until you withdraw it later on. For now, it is deducted from (taken off) your gross taxable income.

Continued tax deferment. Most plans allow you to defer your

Disclaimer: Nothing in this chapter should be construed as providing specific financial, investment, insurance, business, tax, or legal advice. *Hello! America, Inc.* obtained this information from sources it believes to be reliable, but it cannot guarantee the accuracy and completeness of such information. Consult with your financial advisor, insurance representative, accountant, tax advisor or legal counsel before making any investment decisions.

investment's earnings; because your original investment and earnings are not reduced by taxes, your investment will grow faster year after year, when compared with comparable taxed investments. The faster growth that comes from a tax-deferred investment is called tax-free compounding.

? ***When will I pay taxes on the investment?*** You will pay taxes on all tax-deferred money at the time you withdraw it or receive it as a pension – except for withdrawals from a Roth IRA (see section on "Personal IRAs" in this chapter). The tax-deferred monies may include your original investment and the earnings on that investment. The tax rate you will pay depends on your taxable income at the time of the withdrawal.

Although you pay taxes when you withdraw the money, you still have benefited because:

- your investment has grown faster than comparable taxed investments.
- your individual tax rate may be lower. Many retirees earn less than they did during their working years.

Note: The rules for retirement investment plans are complicated and constantly changing. See a tax or investment professional to find out how much you may invest and what types of investments are best for you.

⊗ Be cautious when investing money you may need in the years to come. Remember that stocks and funds that have gone up in the past may go down in the future. Also remember that you will pay taxes when you withdraw money from your

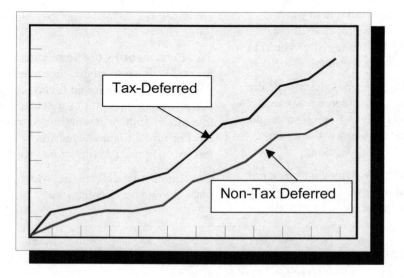

Sample growth of comparable tax-deferred and non-tax deferred investments. Notice that the difference in their value increases every year.

investment; include these taxes when planning your future finances. See an investment counselor before making any major investment decisions.

Employer-sponsored Plans

With employer-sponsored pension plans, the employer sets up the plan and contributes all or part of the money. Most large U.S. corporations and organizations contribute to one of these plans.

Defined Benefit Plan, or Pension Plan

The employer:

- sets up and manages the plan, as well as makes the investment decisions.
- contributes all of the money.
- decides the age when you may begin receiving your pension.
- decides ahead of time the amount of your monthly pension; this amount usually depends on the length of time you worked for that employer and the amount of compensation you were receiving at the end of your time there.

If you leave an employer after working there for several years, you may have "vested rights"; that is, you may be entitled to receive a pension starting at the age decided by the employer.

Benefit: *The employee receives a regular fixed pension payment paid for by the employer.*

Cash Balance Defined Benefit Plan

The employer:

- sets up and manages the plan, as well as makes the investment decisions.
- contributes all of the money to the employee's account. The amount contributed is a fixed percentage of the employee's pay.
- credits the interest to the employee's account.
- must offer an annuity option.

When you leave the employer, all the money in your account is yours. The amount in the account depends on the amount of the contributions and the later growth of the investment. To continue benefiting from a tax-advantaged plan, you may:

- "rollover" the account to an IRA.
- re-invest the money in your new employer's tax-advantaged plan, if the new employer's plan allows this option.
- receive regular (annuity) payments based on the value of the account.

Benefit: *The employee's investment is paid for by the employer.*

Defined Contribution Plan, or 401 (k)

The employer sets up the plan, and the employee has the option of contributing pre-tax money in this type of plan. The employer:

- may or may not contribute (match) a percentage of the employee's contribution.

- deducts your contribution from your salary, up to the legal limit. For tax purposes, your gross income is reduced by the amount of your contribution.
- usually offers a set of investment options – for example, a list of specific mutual funds; you decide in which of these funds to invest.

The actual amount in the employee's account, at any time, depends on the amount of the contributions and the later growth of the investment.

You may begin making withdrawals at a certain age—typically age 59½. You must begin making withdrawals at age 70½. If you leave your employer, you may:

- re-invest the money in your new employer's tax-advantaged plan if the new employer's plan allows this option.
- "rollover" some or all of the money to an IRA.
- leave the money in your current employer's plan if the plan allows this option.

Benefits:

- *The employee's contribution and earnings are tax-deferred.*
- *Some employers contribute to your account.*

Personal IRAs

You set up, manage, and contribute all the funds to the Individual Retirement Account (IRA). Ask a tax professional or investment broker if you are eligible and how much you may contribute. Below are the two types of IRAs.

Traditional

With a traditional IRA you:

- may deduct your contribution from your gross income. Any earnings from the fund (capital gains, dividends, interest) are tax deferred— that is, you pay the taxes when you withdraw the money.
- must begin to make withdrawals by age 70½.

Benefit: Your contribution and earnings are tax-deferred.

Roth

With a Roth IRA you:

- invest after-tax money in the fund.
- do not pay taxes on the money you withdraw (initial investment, earnings, and capital gains).
- may begin to withdraw from the fund immediately—up to 100% of the amounts contributed to or transferred into a Roth IRA. You may need to wait five years before withdrawing other amounts (such as earnings) tax-free.
- do not need to meet any minimum distribution requirements; that is, you may:
  - leave the money in the account as long as you wish.
  - take out as much money as you wish. The money is tax-free.

Benefit: Your contributions and earnings are not taxed, even when you withdraw from the investment.

The opportunities for having a Roth account are limited. Ask a professional whether you are eligible.

Small Businesses and the Self-Employed

Owners of small businesses may set up one of the following plans:

- Keoghs (pronounced "kee-oh").
- Simple IRAs.
- Sep IRAs.

With all the plans, the invested money and the earnings are tax-deferred. The options and regulations vary. Ask an accountant.

Note: Small business owners who are employed by their own companies often set up Simple and Sep-IRAs for themselves, as individual employees.

Words to Know

After-tax money: money on which you have paid taxes

Annuity: fixed payments you get regularly—often every month or year

Cash Balance Defined Benefit Plan: a type of employer-sponsored benefit plan that defines an employee's benefit as the amount credited to an account

Compensation: money or benefits earned

Defer payment: (to) delay paying (taxes)

Defined Benefit Plan: a type of employer-sponsored plan that provides a retirement benefit defined by a formula

Defined Contribution Plan (401(k)): a type of employer-sponsored plan in which the employee contributes and the employer may or may not contribute. The contributions are invested and the investment gains or losses are credited to the account.

Earnings: the interest or dividends you get from the investment.

Employer-sponsored Plan: see Cash Balance Plan, Defined Benefit Plan, and Defined Contribution Plan

Individual Retirement Account (IRA): a retirement plan in which an individual contributes to and invests all the money

Keogh (pronounced "kee-oh"): a plan for an employee who owns the company

Match: money employer contributes to employee's 401(k) account

Pension: money you receive regularly after you leave the company. The amount of money varies with the plan.

Pre-tax money: money on which you have not paid taxes

Rollover: reinvesting money from an existing tax-advantaged plan into a new one

Roth IRA: a type of IRA in which the withdrawals are tax-free

Simple IRA: a plan for the employees of a small business (fewer than 100 employees)

Sep-IRA: a plan for the employees of a small business

Tax-advantaged plan: a plan that allows you to delay paying taxes on specific U.S.-earned income

Tax-deferred money or earnings: money or earnings for which you do not pay taxes right away; with tax-advantaged retirement plans, the taxes are often paid when you withdraw the money.

Tax-free compounding: the increase in growth of a tax-free investment, when it is compared with a comparable taxable investment. For example, if you save $1,000 in taxes, that $1,000 will earn interest in the first year; both the $1,000 and the interest it has earned also will earn interest in the second year. The compounded growth will continue each year until you withdraw the money.

Traditional IRA: a type of IRA in which you must begin to make taxable withdrawals at a specific age

Vested: entitled to receive a benefit after working for an employer for a certain number of years. The benefit may be a pension or the employer's contribution to your retirement account—depending on the type of company's pension plan.

Settling In

Finding a
___New Home___

Apartment (condominium)

Detached house (split-level)

Detached house (colonial)

Townhouse (rowhouse)

Residential Areas

Areas

You may live in:

- an urban area. Be sure the area is safe—night and day.
- the suburbs near a big city. The homes are often larger and newer than city homes, with bigger yards. You may need a car for everyday shopping and errands. Check the time it takes to get to work.
- a rural area.

In general, prices are highest in the areas closest to a big city. Taxes and insurance costs are higher in a city, too (see sections on "Renting" and "Buying" in this chapter).

Types of homes

You may rent or buy a:

- detached home. The home is not attached to other homes.
- townhouse, or rowhouse. The home is attached to other homes. With a townhouse, you may pay a monthly fee for taking care of common grounds such as a grassy area or a swimming pool.
- condo. You own the apartment. Together, all the owners in the building own the common areas— such as the lobby, hallways, pools, and parking lot; owners pay monthly condo fees to take care of these areas.

- co-op. A corporation owns all the apartments, as well as the common areas. You pay the mortgage to the corporation; but, by law, each owner has a share in the corporation. The monthly fees are higher than condo fees, but they include real estate taxes.

In general, if you rent, you do not pay any condo fees for taking care of common areas; but you can use any facilities such as a party room or pool. You may pay extra for parking.

What to look for

Safety: Walk around and talk to people in the area; be sure to go at night and during the day. If you are concerned, call the police crime division for the county or city to find out about crimes in that area; look in the front of your local phone book for the number.

Schools. Each local county or city manages its own public schools. Find out which schools are best before you decide where to live (see chapter on "Your Older Child").

Residents/neighbors. Do you see children around? Do both husbands and wives work? If so, will you or your spouse be lonely during the day?

Transportation. If you plan to use public transportation, ask: How far is the bus or subway stop? How often do the buses run? Do they run on weekends? (see "Public Transportation/Getting Around")

If you plan to drive, ask: How far is the main road? How heavy is the traffic at the time of day I will be driving? How much time will I need to go to work or school?

Parking. Is parking available? Will it cost extra?

Stores and other services. Does the area have good restaurants, shops, beauty salons, libraries, or houses of worship? Will you walk or drive to these places?

The Fair Housing Law

By law, no homeowner or landlord can refuse to rent or sell because of your:

- race.
- sex.
- country of origin (the country you come from).
- religion.

In addition, local fair housing laws may include:

- children. Families with children have the same rights as childless families.
- sexual orientation (homosexuality).
- disability—for example, a long-term mental or physical condition.

In many cities, homeowners may refuse to rent or sell to individuals or families because they:

- have pets.
- do not have enough money.
- have too many people for the size of the home.

If you think someone is disobeying the law, call the Office of Fair Housing and Equal Opportunity; find the number under:

- "Fair Housing" or "Housing" in the city or county government section of your phone book.
- "Housing and Urban Development" in the U.S. government section of your phone book.

Who Can Help

Tip: The Chamber of Commerce official Global Locator can connect you to real estate agents, apartment managers, relocation companies, and other businesses in the area you want.

Many newcomers use a real estate agent, relocation center, or rental service (see section on "How to rent a home" in this chapter). Most homes for rent or sale are in multiple listings; that is, they are all on one list that most real estate services use.

What to look for. Pick an agent who:

- is trained. Be sure the professional is a member of an association of realtors. To be a member, the professional must be certified.
- pays attention to what you want and what you can afford.
- knows the area. If you don't know where you want to live, you may need to use several agents or a relocation service.
- has patience. Do not let an agent "talk you into" making a decision before you are ready.
- is experienced. How long has the agent been selling/renting homes? Does he or she work full-time or part-time?

 Many international visitors want agents who speak their

own language. But also ask yourself: Would I trust this person in my own country? Is this agent experienced?

Renting

Rental prices vary according to the area and the type of housing. Furnished apartments and homes cost about 20%–50% more, but you may rent furniture separately at less cost (see section on "The lease" in this chapter). Usually, you pay a fee for the rental application. This covers the cost of checking your credit status.

Many single men or women rent:

- a basement apartment in a townhouse or rowhouse.
- a room in a family home. Usually, you get
  - a private bedroom and bathroom.
  - use of a washer and dryer.
  - use of the kitchen to prepare your meals.
- a house or an apartment with a roommate. Some cities have services that help you find a roommate; all types of people use these services—including students, young professionals, and executives. You will pay a fee for the service—often, under $100. Look in the Yellow Pages directory under "Roommate." Many large corporations have a bulletin board where you can post your name.

How much you can afford

In general, do not spend more than 28%–33% of your income on monthly payments—including the rental fee,

parking and association fees, and insurance. If you owe a lot of money, your monthly payments should be less.

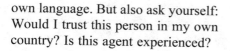 When you apply for a lease, you will show your driver's license or other photo ID. If you are a student, you may not need any more letters or documents. Others may also need information such as:

- the name of your employer or school.
- proof of income—for example, some proof of the amount you expect to earn this year.
- the address where you lived before.
- the name of your landlord, if you lived in the U.S.
- local references, if possible—for example, your employer or sponsor.
- the name of your local bank.

Some apartments in many large cities are rent-stabilized or rent-controlled; that is, the landlord cannot raise the rent more than a certain amount every year. In general, these apartments are less expensive. The laws are different in every city. For example, in New York City, apartments built before 1974 may be rent-stabilized or rent-controlled.

How to rent a home

1. Begin your search.

You may get information from:

- real estate agents. Many real estate agents both sell and rent homes. Most prefer to sell, but a few housing professionals specialize in rentals.

- newspaper advertisements.
- housing magazines. Often, you can find these free magazines near a bank machine (ATM) or in special boxes on the street.
- apartment search companies. These companies have offices in many metropolitan areas. The services are free.

2. Meet with the housing professional helping you.

The agent will:

- ask what kind of home and community you want.
- ask about your salary and the money in your bank account. Then the agent will tell you how much you are "qualified for," or able to pay.
- give you listings of homes you might like.

3. Visit the places you have chosen.

Most agents will drive you to the homes; rental services may give directions but not drive you there. The owner will probably not be there. Call the agent or rental office if you have questions.

4. Try to negotiate the price.

Apartments owned by a business often have a fixed price, but private owners may be willing to negotiate.

For example, you may be able to negotiate a month of free parking or a lower rental rate.

5. Read the lease; be sure you understand it.

Everything you expect to get should be in the lease. For example, if the agent told you the rent includes parking, the lease should say so.

6. Fill out the application form and pay the application fee.

7. Sign the lease.

8. Take photos of any damage in your home before you move in.

You may need proof of this damage in order to get your deposit returned.

9. Make your first payment.

This payment includes the security (or damage) deposit—usually equal to one month's rent (see "International Transactions/Money Matters"). If you have not damaged the house, you will get this money back when you leave.

Find out if you can "break the lease," or leave early, if necessary. Usually you will pay one or two months' rent or more. You may also have to give notice (tell the landlord that you are leaving ahead of time).

The lease

The lease should include:

- the amount of the deposit.
- the amount of the rent.
- the day you must pay the rent.
- a list of any other payments you must make.
- a list of any extras, such as the use of a washer and dryer.
- the rules for breaking a lease or moving out early.
- any other rules you must follow— such as not having pets.
- any fees or costs the landlord pays—such as utilities, lawn services, pest control, or repairs.

Monthly payments

Rent. This is the largest payment.

Insurance. (See "Renters Insurance/ Insurance You Need")

Utilities. Rental payments sometimes include utility costs. Check with the real estate agent for average costs.

Parking fees.

Water and sewer.

Telephone. You will pay a monthly fee for basic telephone service; extra features and long-distance calls add to the cost (see chapters on "Moving In" and "Communications at Home").

? *What furniture and appliances can I expect?*
Most furnished and unfurnished apartments come with:

- kitchen appliances such as a refrigerator, oven, and stove.
- overhead lights for the kitchen and bathrooms.

Most houses have a washer and dryer inside the home. With apartments, the washer and dryer may be in a separate room for several families to share.

Furnished apartments vary. Most come with:

- draperies or curtains for windows.
- a table and chairs for the dining room and kitchen.
- a couch and chairs for the living room.
- at least one light in every room.
- a bed in every bedroom.

Corporate furnished apartments (apartments that companies use just for their own employees and guests) usually have more. For example, you may find:

- housewares (plates; glasses; coffee cups; and utensils such as knives, forks, and spoons).
- pillowcases, sheets, and blankets for each bed.

? *What if the landlord does not follow the terms of the lease—for example, if he does not fix a broken pipe?* If necessary, call the local office of Landlord-Tenant Relations for your county or city. Look in the county or city government section of your phone book under "Housing." If the number is not listed, call the general number and ask.

Buying

When to buy

In most areas, you will lose money if you buy a home and then sell it in 1–2 years. Check:

- the price of homes. Are they rising, falling, or staying the same?
- the cost of selling. You will pay fees to the real estate agent and for closing costs.

How much can you afford

In general, do not spend more than 28%–33% of your salary on the monthly payments—mortgage principal, interest, property taxes, and insurance. As with rentals, this percentage can change according to your debts or taxes.

 When buying a home, remember the closing costs and other fees you pay right away. These fees include the cost of a lawyer, points (special loan fees), homeowner's insurance, and the loan application fee. For example, closing costs for a $200,000 home may be $2,000 or more. Often, the bank or the seller will agree to pay some of these costs. Negotiate.

Types of agents

The two types of real estate agents are:

- a seller's agent, who works for the seller, not the buyer. In many areas, they must tell the seller your "highest price," or the most you will pay—information you probably don't want the seller to know.
- a buyer's agent, who works only for the buyer, not the seller. You may need to pay the buyer's agent a fee, but most agents will return the fee when you buy a home.

Most agents work as seller's agents for homeowners and buyer's agents for people looking for a home. By law, an agent must tell you if he or she has a contract with the owner of any home you are looking at.

Ask if the agent will help you:

- negotiate the best deal.
- find out everything—both good and bad—about the home and the area.

Monthly expenses

Principal and interest. This mortgage payment is usually the largest expense of owning a home.

Taxes. The amount depends on the location and the cost of the home.

Insurance. The cost depends on your home's:

- cost, or the price you paid.
- age.
- location; insurance for homes in a big city usually costs more.
- construction.
- safety devices—such as a burglar alarm system.

Tip: You may be asked to set up an escrow account. The bank will collect a portion of your real estate tax and sometimes an insurance premium as part of your monthly payment. The bank will pay these bills from your escrow account.

Condominium or homeowner's association fees. If you buy a townhouse or condominium, you will pay a monthly maintenance fee. The fee for some condos may be $400 a month for keeping the building clean. For other condos, the fee may be $800–$1,500 a month; this fee usually includes a 24-hour person near the door, swimming pool, health club, and tennis courts.

Words to Know

Application fee: money you pay for someone to process your application

Buyer's agent: a real estate professional who helps a buyer find a home. This agent works for the buyer, not the seller.

Closing costs: fees you pay when you finalize, or "close on," the purchase of the house.

Abbreviations

You will see these abbreviations in the classified ads for places to rent or buy.

Appt:	Appointment	**Ht:**	Heat
Apt:	Apartment	**Immed:**	Immediate
Balc:	Balcony	**Incl:**	Included
Bdrm (or BR):	Bedroom	**Kit:**	Kitchen
Bsmt:	Basement	**Lbr:**	Library
CAC:	Central air conditioning	**Prkg avail:**	Parking available
CATV:	Cable television	**Redec:**	Redecorated
DR:	Dining room	**Refs req:**	References requested
D/W:	Dishwasher	**TH:**	Townhouse
Effcy:	Efficiency	**Utils:**	Utilities
Elec:	Electricity	**W/D:**	Washer and dryer
Hdwd flrs:	Hardwood floors	**W/W:**	Wall-to-wall carpeting

Condominium (condo): one of many homes in a building. Usually, each condo is owned by the person who lives in it. All the owners together own the common areas—such as the hallways, pool, or party room.

Condominium association fees: money you pay for the care of the condo building

Co-op: one of many homes in a building. Each landlord or resident pays a separate mortgage; but all the owners together are part of a corporation that owns each of the homes and the common areas.

Detached house: a home that is not attached to another house

Efficiency: a small apartment—usually with one main room, a kitchen, and a bathroom (see "Studio" below)

Escrow account: a bank account that sets aside money for your real estate taxes and insurance.

Homeowner's association fees: money you pay for common services such as swimming pool and upkeep of community property

Insurance: a way to protect your belongings and property

Lease: a written agreement between a tenant and landlord

Mortgage: the monthly payment a homeowner makes to the bank. This payment usually includes the principal and interest of the loan.

Points: the fee you pay for a loan

Principal: money a bank lends you

Qualified: able to afford, or to pay

Real estate agent (realtor): a housing professional who can help you find a home to buy or rent

References: your employer or another person who can give the bank information about your job, income, or ability to pay

Relocation center: a place with professionals who help you find a home and learn about the area

Rentals: rooms, apartments, or houses you rent rather than buy

Rent-controlled or rent-stabilized: an apartment with rent that the city regulates. The rent may go up only a certain percentage every year.

Rowhouses: city houses that are attached to each other on the sides

Rural: an area not near a city

Security deposit: money paid to a landlord before a place can be rented. You get all this money back if you do not damage the house.

Seller's agent: a real estate professional who helps someone sell a house. The agent works for the seller, not the buyer.

Studio: a one-room residence with a kitchen and bath

Suburb: an area where people live just outside a city.

Townhouses: homes that are attached to each other at the sides

Utilities: services such as electricity, gas, water, and sewer

Moving In

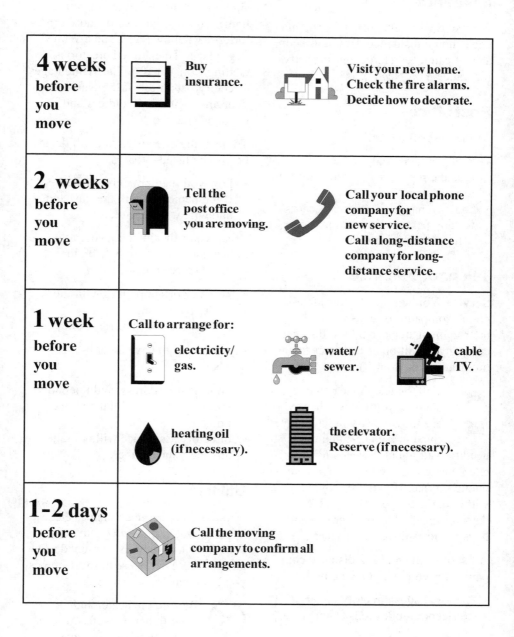

4 weeks before you move	Buy insurance.	Visit your new home. Check the fire alarms. Decide how to decorate.
2 weeks before you move	Tell the post office you are moving.	Call your local phone company for new service. Call a long-distance company for long-distance service.
1 week before you move	Call to arrange for: electricity/gas. water/sewer. cable TV. heating oil (if necessary). the elevator. Reserve (if necessary).	
1-2 days before you move	Call the moving company to confirm all arrangements.	

Before You Move

Insurance

Everyone who rents or owns a home needs home insurance. Buy it as soon as you can (see "Home and Property/ Insurance You Need").

Post office

At the post office, get:

- a "Change of Address" card that tells the post office to send any mail to your new home.
- some "Change of Address" cards for any person, publication, or office that sends you mail.

Telephone service

Service. You will need a local telephone company for calls in your metropolitan area and a long-distance company for all other calls (see "Communications at Home").

 Call the telephone company as soon as you know where you are moving. If you have never lived in the U.S., you may need to wait about 2 weeks for the telephone company to approve your phone service. If you are moving within the U.S., you may wait 2–3 days for local telephone service and 7 days for long-distance service.

A list of local and long-distance companies for your area may be in the:

- Yellow Pages directory under "Telecommunications Companies."

- front pages of the White Pages directory.

Telephone directories. When you sign up for phone service in your home, you will get two or more directories—a Yellow Pages and a White Pages (see "Telephone Directories/ Getting Connected"). The White Pages directory lists most of the residents for your area, with their address and telephone number.

To be in the directory, you will decide how to be listed—that is:

- how your name will be spelled.
- if the names of both the husband and wife will be listed.

When you call someone, your telephone number also will be on the Caller ID screen of all:

- home or office phones with the Caller ID option.
- cellular (cell or mobile) phones.

If you decide to have an unlisted number:

- your name, address, and telephone number will not be in the phone book.
- directory assistance will not tell anyone your number.

Utilities

"Utilities" are services such as electricity, gas, water, and sewer. In some condos or townhouses, the condo fees pay for these services. In most homes, you must pay.

 Be sure the heater and air conditioner are safe. In some cities, homes often have heaters in the attic; these heaters may be unsafe. Ask a professional to inspect the heater for safety. If you are renting, your landlord usually will hire someone. If you are buying, hire an inspector to look over the whole house—including the heater and air conditioner.

 Most utility companies need to know 3–7 days ahead of time. Find the number for the local utilities company in the city or county government section of your Yellow Pages directory under "Public Utilities," "Electric Services," "Gas," or "Utilities."

 How do I pay for utilities? You get a bill each month. Some services may be free.

 You may need to pay a deposit for each utility. You will get this deposit back at the end of the year or when you move again.

Electricity. Ask the utility company about its energy-saving programs. If you use one of these programs, you may get a discount on your monthly bill.

Heating oil and gas. If you have an oil-burning furnace, contact a local oil supply company. Find the number in the Yellow Pages directory under "Gas Companies."

Before you move, ask the person who used to live there about the cost. Many gas companies offer plans for saving heat and lowering costs; if you like, your gas company will visit your home to explain these plans.

Water and sewer. Find the number under "Water and Sewer Service" in the Yellow Pages directory. Make sure your water is turned on and your house is connected to a sewer.

Furniture

Find furniture stores in the Yellow Pages directory under:

- "Furniture-New."
- "Furniture-Rental."
- "Furniture-Used."

For used furniture, also check:

- the classified advertisements in the newspaper under listings such as "Merchandise Mart," "Apartment & Moving Sales," "Garage Sales," and "Estate Sales."
- flea markets. Some have the same hours each week. Others come for 1–2 days every once in a while.
- yard sale signs in your neighborhood. Friday, Saturday, and Sunday are the best days. You may try to bargain at these sales.

If you are renting, find out what comes with the rental fee before you buy or rent your own furniture (see "Renting/Finding a New Home").

Cable TV service

The cable gives you:

- more channels to watch (see "Radio and TV/News, Sports, and Entertainment").
- better video and sound if your channels are not coming in clearly.

You may get cable TV in most areas.

If you live in an apartment building, first ask the building manager if the building is wired for cable TV.

To have cable TV installed in your home, call the cable company for your area.

Ask the company for:

- booklets that explain the kind of programs on each cable channel.
- a sample cable guide.
- a price list for each service; also ask about discounts or "specials."

Your Pet

Ask your local Department of Animal Control about:

- licensing. Most dogs and some cats must have a license.
- neutering laws. In some cities or counties, you may get a discount if your pet has had surgery so it cannot reproduce.
- leash laws.
- vaccinations against certain diseases. For example, in most cities, dogs and outdoor cats must wear tags with the date of their last rabies vaccination; otherwise, Animal Control will pick them up.

Fines, or penalty fees, for unlicensed pets may be as high as $100.

Moving Inside the U.S.

 Keep everything safe from thieves—especially if you are moving yourself. If the move takes more than 1 day:

- Do not keep your furniture and other things in the truck overnight.
- Buy a time-activated light for the empty house.

The cheapest way to move is to rent a van or a truck and move yourself. To hire a moving company, call 3 weeks or more before you move (see "International Movers/Before You Come"). If you need to move soon, try to move:

- between the 7th and 10th days of the month; you may be able to get a mover in 1–3 days.
- in the middle of the month; you may be able to get a mover in about 1 week.

 Start early in the morning; some movers charge more after 5 pm. The cost usually depends on the:

- number of hours worked.
- number of people working.
- weight of the furniture and boxes.
- driving time from one home to another.

Tip the movers about $10 for each worker for a move that takes 1–2 days.

After You Move

Trash collection

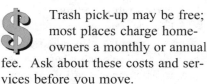 Trash pick-up may be free; most places charge home-owners a monthly or annual fee. Ask about these costs and services before you move.

If the local government does not pick up the garbage on your street, you must buy the service from the company in your area.

Street pick-up. Put your trash in plastic bags, tightly tied at the top. Put the bags in a plastic or metal can with a lid on top. Leave the cans or bags near the street curb the night before or early in the morning (by 7 am) on pick-up day. Make sure that raccoons or other animals cannot get into the trash; if the trash is spilled on the street, the garbage service will not pick it up.

Large items. The regular service probably does not pick up large items—such as sofas, refrigerators, or mattresses. Most communities have two or three "major clean-up" days a year when you can throw away large items.

To throw out the items right away, call your trash service. Find the number in the city or county government section of your phone book under "Trash Collection Services." If it isn't listed, call "General Information" for your city or county.

Recycling. In most communities, you put newspapers, glass and plastic bottles, aluminum cans, and other items in a separate box for recycling. Other communities have centers where you take these items. To call, find the number in the county or city government section of your phone book under "Recycling" or "General Information."

Apartment buildings and condominiums. Most have a trash room on each floor. Ask the building manager about recycling.

Fire alarm systems

In most communities, by law, every home must have a smoke detector on each floor or level of the building. The detector makes a loud noise if smoke is in the air. If your smoke detector runs on batteries, it will make a noise when it needs new batteries. Some people replace these batteries every year—just to be safe.

You also should have a fire extinguisher in each level of your home—especially the kitchen. You can buy extinguishers at a hardware store.

Home Services

Home decorating

You may hire a private decorator or you may use a personal decorator from a store (see "Special Services/ Shops & Malls").

Lawn care

If your new home has a lawn, ask if your landlord hires someone to take care of it. If not, you are responsible. You may hire a lawn-care company to do all the yard work. Some companies give discounts if many people on the same street use them.

Housekeeping

You may get a housecleaning company or an individual housekeeper. With a company, one or more people come at the same time. Most cleaning companies are bonded; that is, they will pay if anything is damaged or stolen.

Individual housekeepers often cost less than the companies and will do more types of jobs. You may need to pay Social Security taxes; ask an accountant.

Extermination

In some areas, you need an exterminator to keep out mice or bugs–for example, termites (bugs that eat wood and may harm your home). If you are renting, the landlord may hire an exterminator to come in once a month.

Snow Plowing

If your area gets snow in the winter, you may hire someone for the season. The contractor will plow your sidewalk, driveway, and the paths around the house. In some places, you also may hire a young person to do the shoveling or plowing for you.

 If you live in an area with freezing temperatures in the winter, ask how to take care of the home. For example, you may cause much damage if you do not keep the pipes from freezing.

Alarm Security System

Alarm security systems let you know if a robber is trying to get into your house. If your home already has a system, you pay every month to keep the service. Installing a new system may cost $1,000 or more; ask your neighbors if you need one.

Words to Know

Alarm security system: a system in your house that warns you if someone is trying to get in

Appraisal: a professional estimate that tells how much something is worth. You ask a professional appraiser to tell you how much items such as jewelry or furniture are worth so you can take out the right amount of insurance.

Deposit: money you pay before a service starts

Extermination service: a service that gets rid of mice, rats, and bugs

Flea market: an open area where people sell items on tables or in tents. Flea markets are good for items such as antiques, furniture, jewelry, audio and video cassettes, and clothing such as jackets and hats.

Hardware store: a store that sells many items for the home—such as tools, light bulbs, door knobs, and wooden shelves

Leash laws: laws about keeping your pet on a leash, attached to you, or tied up

License tag: a small metal tag to put on your pet's collar to show it is registered with the city

Listed telephone number: a number that is in the White Pages of the telephone directory, along with your address

Neutering: "fixing" your pet so that it doesn't reproduce

Recycling: to make new products from old cans, bottles, plastic, and paper

Sewer: the pipes that take water and waste out of your house

Smoke detector: an alarm in your home. It makes a loud sound if smoke is in the air.

Snow plowing: clearing the road, driveway, or path of snow. The city or town plows the streets; you shovel or plow your sidewalk, driveway, and the paths around the house.

Unlisted telephone number: a number that is not in the White Pages of the telephone directory

Utilities: services such as electricity, gas, water, and sewer

Communications

at Home

"You have reached…"

Leaving a message

Answering machine: "You have reached the office of Henry Marvin. I'm either on the phone or away from my desk. Please leave your name, number, and a brief message. I'll get back to you as soon as possible."

Sophia (hears a long beep sound on the phone): Hello, this is Sophia Césare. I'm calling to confirm my interview with you for tomorrow, June 25th at 2 pm. If you have a problem with this date or time, please call me back to reschedule. I'll be in my office all day until 5 pm. My number is 710-9999.

Note: Sophia gives the reason she is calling. She leaves her number and gives a good time to call back.

Overview

Communication technology is changing all the time; many companies will try to get your business. Choosing what is best is often confusing.

How to Set Up Your Home Communications

1. Decide on general needs for your home—including:

- telephone equipment, such as a computer, fax machine, and answering machine.
- communication lines.Many families want a separate line for:
  - their children—especially if they are teenagers and like to talk on the phone a lot.

  - each communications service—for example, the telephone and the computer. With a separate line, you can talk on the phone and access the Internet at the same time.

Note: If you have Digital Subscriber Line (DSL) service, you may access the Internet and use the telephone at the same time.

If your new home does not have the lines you want, ask the telephone company for the cost of installing and using new lines.

2. Decide which options you want for your telephone and telephone service (see "Words to Know/Options & Features" at the end of this chapter). One option is voice mail. Ask about the monthly fee and decide if an answering machine is better for you. Voice mail is usually more expensive, but it lets callers leave a message when the line is busy.

3. Decide if you want an unlimited or per-call plan (see "local service/home phones" in this chapter).

4. Call your local telephone company as soon as you know where you will be moving. Look over the options ahead of time (see "Words to Know/Options and Features"). If you have questions, ask when you sign up for service. Be sure the service has a low cancellation fee.

If you do not have time, say that you just want "basic service" now and you will sign up for options later.

5. Sign up for long-distance services, or U.S. services that are outside your local area. You should have a long-distance company by the time you move. If you are not moving for a month or more, you may investigate long-distance services if you like; if you have little time, sign up with a large telephone company with a low cancellation fee and investigate later.

6. **Sign up for Internet services, if you need them right away.** You can get a disk for an Internet service provider (ISP), such as AOL, in the post office and many shops and drug stores (see "Accessing the Internet/ Getting Connected").

7. **Buy the telephones you need.** Remember: Some features, such as conference calling, caller ID, and redialing, need special phones. Ask about costs.

8. **Find out about special services for international calls.** See "Home Phones/International" in this chapter.

9. **Review your home phone services when you have time.** The section on "Choosing a Plan" in this chapter explains how to choose phone, computer, or fax services.

Home Phones

In general, phone services for your home are faster to get and more reliable than you may expect. Calls to places within the U.S. generally cost less from your home phone than from a cell or any other phone.

Local service

Home phone services let you make local calls. You pay a monthly fee, plus at least $3-$7 a month for each common option—such as voice mail, call waiting, or call forwarding.

Often, companies "bundle" popular options; that is, you may pay one, lower price for two or more options.

For all local calls, you will choose between:

- unlimited (flat rate) plans. All local calls are free. Most people use this plan.
- per-call (measured or message rate) plans. The monthly price is less than the flat rate plan, but your total bill may be more if you make a lot of calls. Usually, this plan is good for a person who makes only 2-3 calls per day.

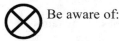 Be aware of:

- cramming (adding false charges or fees to a telephone bill).
- slamming (changing long-distance companies without asking you). You have the right to choose your own company.

If you have a complaint, first call the phone company and ask about the charges. If you are not satisfied, then call the Federal Communications Commission (FCC), the U.S. government agency in charge of telephone communications.

Tip: The front part of the White Pages has information about:
- which telephone companies are offering service in your area.
- how to pay your bill.
- whom to call if your phone service isn't working well.

Tip: See "Telephone Directories/ Getting Connected" for more information on using telephone directories.

Long distance

Sign up for a home long-distance service, even if you will be using a calling-card or cellular (cell) phone much of the time. Shop around. You may want one service for your local calls and a different service for long-distance calls (see "Choosing a Plan" in this chapter).

 You may want a separate service for long-distance calls you make from a hotel room or other land-based phones outside your home. Some of these services offer rates as low as 3¢ or 4¢ a minute for any U.S. location (see "Choosing a Plan" in this chapter).

International

You may want a different service for all international calls—whether you are calling from your home or from a hotel room. The per-minute rates vary with the country you are calling. Explore all possibilities; also check the cost of calling the U.S. from the international places you visit often. To find the best rates for your home country, search on the Internet with the name of the country and the word "calling card." Also look in travel and business magazines.

 The services for long-distance and international calls usually cost less than the phone cards you buy from the store. You pay with your credit card or through your home telephone bill. Usually, the service has no time limit; also, you may just call up and pay for more money on your

account with a credit card. Usually, these services have lower surcharges and rates than the telephone services you buy from a gas station or convenience store.

Cellular Phones

Overview: Cell phone service is different from the service in most other countries. For example:

- You may not use most U.S. cell phones in other countries. The cell phone from your home country probably will not work here.
- Cell phones may fade in and out— especially if you are talking inside a building or in a hilly area.
- Some cell phone service is regional; that is, you will pay a lower cost for areas right near you and a higher, long-distance cost for service in other parts of the country.
- A few areas of the country have no cell phone service.

 Common monthly fees are $19.99 to $199.99—depending on the number of free minutes, the cost of the calls, and the options you use. Cell phone rates also may be lower for incoming calls than for outgoing calls.

Local. If you will not travel outside your local area, consider a local plan; you will pay more for long distance but less for local calls.

Long distance. Most companies offer a one-rate plan for all areas in their network; you will not pay long-distance charges for calls anywhere inside that network. If you often travel within the U.S., look for a plan that includes the locations you may visit.

International. Only a few U.S. cellular phone services provide international service; generally, these have higher monthly fees than domestic-only services.

Tip: If you need a cell phone for international travel, rent a phone that works in the countries you are visiting. With some rental phones, you will have a U.S. local telephone number, so people may call you easily. You must sign up before you leave.

You may also want a calling card for:

- any long-distance call from a land-based phone outside your home—for example, from a phone booth or from a friend's home.
- all international calls—even if you are calling from your own phone.

Tip: If you like, you may get a plan with billing through your local telephone company.

Computers

Overview

You may find computers in electronic and office-supply stores, catalogs, or on-line. Prices vary; shop around or wait for special sales. Many public libraries, office-supply stores, and printing shops let you use a computer for an hourly fee. The public library near your new home may offer free access, but the time you can use the computer may be limited.

To set up the computer you brought from home, see "Accessing the Internet/Getting Connected."

Common computer prices range from $500-$1500 for a new computer—with a large screen, printer, and popular software installed. Some computers also have a modem—commonly with a speed of 56K.

Internet Service Provider (ISP)

With some plans, you pay a monthly fee, in addition to a fee for each minute you are on the Internet. With other plans, you pay only the monthly fee; you may spend as much time as you like on the Internet.

Tip: Many families sign up with a free e-mail service. Usually these services are reliable and convenient. However, they often have some limitations—for example, smaller limits on the size of the attachments you send or receive.

You may get good advice on choosing an ISP from the Internet. In general, look for the following characteristics:

Local access. Check to be sure you will not pay long-distance rates each time you access the Internet. Ask the ISP for a list of its access telephone numbers; then check to be sure the number is toll-free in your new location. Also be sure the service has an "800" number you can use when traveling.

Technical support. Find out if technical support (help with problems) is available 24 hours, 7 days a week.

Software. Most ISPs offer:

- e-mail. Find out if you may use the language(s) in which you want to communicate.
- a web browser.

Speed. Ask about high speeds such as DSL if speed is important.
Many services are so busy during peak hours that you can use them only at certain times of the day. Ask others who have used the service if they have had problems accessing the Internet during the start or end of the business day.

Free trial. If possible, get an ISP that offers a free "trial" period (free service for a limited time).

Fax Machines

A fax machine is useful for sending messages to business contacts such as banks, accountants, and investment firms—particularly for international families. Many international banks accept faxed signatures to authorize wire transfers. It is also useful for copying documents.

You may find fax machines in office-supply and electronic stores, catalogs, or on-line. Many computers come with modems and software that let you send and receive faxes. This is the least expensive option if you do not send or receive many faxes.

A typical fax machine costs $99-$300.

Common features to look for are:

- an all-purpose printer. Many fax machines also can serve as your computer printer; that is, you may print documents from word processing and other programs.
- a plain paper printer. The message is printed on regular paper. "Thermal" fax paper is harder to read and handle.
- call forwarding. When you are traveling, you may forward all your faxes to a machine in your temporary location.
- re-dialing. If the number you are faxing is busy or out-of-service, your fax machine will keep trying the number regularly.
- message storing. This feature is useful when your fax machine is out of paper. The machine will store messages and print them out at a later time.

Choosing a Plan

Below is a list of what you may want to consider when looking over your plans.

Options and features. Review your telephone bills for the last 3-6 months. What areas do you call often? At what time of day do you make calls? Do you make many calls—or just a few? The answers to these questions will help you choose the options and features that are best for you (see "Words to Know/Options & Features" at the end of this chapter).

Tip: Search for some Internet sites that help you assess your needs and then suggest the best plan (see

"Chapter Information" in the Appendix).

Rates. Check the monthly fees and per-minute rates for places you call frequently. For example, some local plans have a wider "local" area; that is, you may call many more places without an extra charge.

Tip: The cost for a long-distance call may depend on the time or day of the week you call.

Surcharges and taxes. Compare the surcharges for each plan.

Discounts. One common discount is for bundling—that is, buying two or more services from the same company. For example, you may get a discount for buying both your Internet and long-distance telephone services from Verizon, AT&T, or AOL. You may also get a discount for buying cell-phone services for two people— for example, for you and your spouse.

Foreign languages. Many companies have someone who speaks Spanish or another foreign language.

Quality of service. If possible, try to find out if customers are satisfied— particularly for cell-phone and Internet services.

Added benefits. For example, you may be able to get frequent flyer miles.

Billing increments. Billing increments can be important for calling card and cell phone service— particularly if you make many short calls to faraway places. The shorter the billing increment (time period used to calculate the cost of the call), the less you will probably pay for the call.

Tip: Telephone companies change discounts often—sometimes every month. After you have been here a few months, several companies may call you again and again to explain their discounts. You may listen if you have the time; if you are busy, just say "I'm not interested" and hang up.

⊗ Be aware of the following items:

- Information" or contest" forms. By signing some of them, you may authorize a company to change your local or long-distance service.
- Huge discounts. Some companies compare their rates with only the highest rates of well-known services
- Hidden monthly access fees, or fees you pay each time you make a call.
- Introductory offers. Some plans may give you service at a discounted rate for just a limited time. When you have used the service for a while, the rate may be much higher.
- Cancellation policies. Be sure you can cancel if you want to change services. Ask about the fees for changing.

Words to Know

General

Access number: a telephone number you call in order to use your service. Usually, the number is toll-free.

Answering machines: a machine that records a message when you are away from the phone. (see "Voice Mail")

Billing increments: units of time used to calculate the cost of a call. For example, with a 1-minute increment, you will pay for a whole minute, even if you talk for only 30 seconds. Common billing increments are 3 minutes, 1 minute, 30 seconds, or 6 seconds

Calling card: a card that lets you make local, long-distance, or international calls. Usually you call a toll-free number and enter a personal code that identifies your account.

Cancellation fee: (see "Termination fee")

Carrier: a company that provides communications services—for example, American Telephone & Telegraph (AT&T), Nextel, Sprint, WorldCom, or Verizon

Cellular phone (cell phone): a wireless phone

Communications plan: a plan, or agreement, for any kind of telephone, e-mail, or Internet service

Conference call: a call in which three or more people can talk to each other on the phone

Connection fee: a fee you pay for starting, or connecting to, the service

Flat rate: a kind of basic service. The price for this service is the same every month; you can make as many local calls as you want at no extra cost.

Hold: to wait on the phone. To put someone on "hold" is to have that person wait on the phone while you talk to someone else.

Land-based phone: a phone that uses a line in a home, office, or other building. A phone that is not a mobile or cell phone.

Measured rate: a basic phone service. Each month, you can make a certain number of local calls for "free." After that you pay extra for each call.

Mobile phone: (see "Cellular phone")

Per-call service: (see "Measured rate")

Personal code (for phone or Internet service): the code or group of numbers that identifies your account. You will pay for any calls charged to this account.

Phone card: (see "Calling card")

Pre-paid calling card: a calling card with a set amount of service. You pay for the card and the service when you buy it.

Roaming charges: Charges you pay for connecting to an area that is not served by your provider. The roaming charge is often added to the long-distance rate for each minute of the call.

Service provider: company providing, or giving you, the telephone or Internet service

Standard calling card: a calling card that bills you monthly, through your credit card or telephone service provider. You are not limited to a specific amount of service.

Surcharge: any charge you pay in addition to the service unit, or per-minute rate

Termination fee: a fee you pay for canceling, or stopping, a service before the time specified in the agreement

Thermal fax paper: paper used only for receiving faxes—rather than plain paper. Faxes on thermal paper are harder to read and handle.

Unlimited rate: (see "Flat rate")

Voltage converter: a device, usually a transformer, for changing the U.S. voltage to the voltage needed by your equipment

White Pages: the telephone directory that lists people's names and home phone numbers
Yellow Pages: the telephone directory that lists business phone numbers and advertisements

Words to Know

Kinds of Calls

"800" numbers: toll-free calls. You do not pay long-distance charges (see "Toll-free number"). "800" numbers have an area code that begins with "8."

"900" numbers: a telephone call that has a per-minute cost–often more than $4 per minute. "900" numbers have an area code that begins with "9".

Access number or code: a telephone number or code you dial to access a long distance or Internet service. You will pay for any calls made with this code. Usually, the number is toll-free.

Domestic: (calls) made to a place inside the U.S.

Incoming: (calls) you receive; calls someone else makes to you

Local: (call) inside your toll-free area, or the general area where you are staying. You will not pay long-distance charges.

Local toll (calls): (see "IntraLATA")

IntraLATA: (calls) to places that are outside your toll-free area—but closer than long-distance calls. Usually, IntraLATA calls are about 15-30 miles away; you will pay a small extra charge.

Long-distance: (calls) made to places that are not in the "free" area for your phone service. Investigate long-distance plans for your home phone and cell phone.

Outgoing: (calls) you make to someone else

Toll-free number. A number you may call without paying long-distance charges; usually the number begins with prefixes such as "800." "900" numbers are not free; do not call until you know the cost (see chapter on "Getting Connected").

Words to Know

Options & Features
The options below are for both home phones and cellular phones, unless they state otherwise. * Options may need a special phone.

Answer Call: (see "Voice Mail")

Call Waiting: lets you get a second call while you are already on the phone. You may put the first caller on "hold;" that is, the first caller waits while you answer another call.

Call Forwarding: lets you receive calls while you are on another phone. For example, you may forward your calls to an answering service or to your office.

*Caller ID: shows the telephone number of the person calling you

*3-way Calling: lets three people talk to each other, on two separate lines, at the same time

*Cordless (portable) phone: a home-phone option. The receiver has no wires; so you do not have to stay in one place while you are on the phone.

Digital Subscriber Line (DSL): a high-speed service that has a direct connection to the Internet. With DSL, you may use the telephone and access the Internet at the same time

*E-mail access: a cell-phone option that lets you send and receive e-mail messages.

Foreign language: Some cell phones and long-distance services give instructions in one or more foreign languages. Spanish is the most common foreign language available.

*Headset plug-ins: a microphone and set of ear phones. The headset sends the sound of the other person's voice through the earphones; you talk through the microphone. Choose this option if you do not want others to hear the conversation.

*Internet access: a cell-phone option that lets you access the Internet

*Multiple lines: an option that lets you have different telephone numbers and services on one phone

*Redial: a fast way to dial the last number you called. You just press a button and the telephone redials for you.

*Speaker phone: a phone that transmits the caller's voice through a speaker. You do not need to hold the phone. A speaker phone is convenient when calling doctors, theaters, or any large organization that may put you on "hold" for a long time. With a speaker phone, you do not need to hold the phone while waiting. (see "Headset plug-ins")

*Speed dialing: lets you store several numbers in the phone. To call one of the numbers on your list, press only one button.

Voice Mail: gives the caller a message when no one answers the phone. Usually, you can record your own message. You may also leave a message if the line is busy—but you may need to pay extra for this option.

Insurance You _Need_

Medical

Medical: visits to the doctor, lab tests, hospital stays, surgery, ambulance, treatment (medicine, therapy)*
Dental: visits to the dentist, x-rays, and treatments such as fillings, oral surgery
Medical evacuation:* transportation to your home country if you get sick and cannot continue your studies or work here
Repatriation of mortal remains:* transportation of your body to your home country if you die

Home and Property

Personal property: the value of personal property such as furniture, electronic equipment, and jewelry if damaged, lost, or stolen
Liability: medical costs of an injury to a visitor on your property or in your home
Your home (only for people who own their own home): repairs to your home property—that is, the building itself and surrounding property, such as a garden. The insurance will pay for the repairs if your home is damaged or for the value of your home if it is destroyed

 Auto

Collision: repairs to a car if it is damaged or the value of your car if it is destroyed
Liability:* * injuries to people hurt in an accident when you are the driver
Comprehensive: repairs to your car or the value of your car if it is damaged or destroyed when no one is driving it.

* required by the U.S. government for several types of visas
** required by most states in order to drive a car

Note: This page lists only the major types of insurance; ask your insurance agent if you need other types of policies. Also note that you may not need all the types here. For example, you may not need collision for an old car; again, ask your agent.

Overview

Why you need it

While you are in the U.S., you need insurance in case:

- you become sick or injured.
- you cause someone else to become sick or injured.
- any property you own is damaged or stolen
- you cause someone else's property to be damaged.

Note: If you become injured at work, most likely your employer's insurance will pay for your medical expenses. Notify your employer right away.

How the system works

When you buy insurance, you pay a premium regularly—for example:

- monthly (every month).
- quarterly (every 3 months).
- semi-annually (twice a year).
- annually (every year).

The insurance company puts all the premiums together into a "pool." When you have an expense for which you are insured, you make a claim to the company; that is, you or your doctor sends the bill to the insurance company. The company then pays you from the "pool."

Pay your premiums on time. If you do not, you may lose your insurance.

Choosing a company

Agents. Choose an agent who:

- is experienced with newcomers to the U.S.
- takes the time to explain the different policies.
- does not try to sell you more than you need. You may want to ask a few agents how much to buy.

Tip: Some agents work for only one company; they choose the best plan offered by that company. Other agents sell plans for four or five companies, so you have a wider choice.

To compare the plans of different insurance companies, look up insurance websites on the Internet.

Reputation. Ask people you know about companies they use. Are they happy with the service? Were they satisfied with the way the company paid their claims?

Financial rating. If a company goes out of business, you may lose your coverage. Ask an insurance agent for the *A.M. Best* or *Weiss* rating to find out about the company's financial status. Try to use a company with the highest rating. Do not use a company with a rating lower than B.

You may get a discount if you buy more than one type of insurance from the same company.

In general the amount of the premium depends on:

- the type of insurance.
- the policy maximum, or the largest amount of money you are insured for. For example, a medical policy with a maximum of $50,000 for a single illness costs more than a policy with a maximum of $25,000.

- the amount of your deductible (see section on "Lowering the premium" in this chapter).
- your gender (male or female) and age
- the area you live in. For example, if you live in an area with little crime, your payments for home and car insurance probably will be lower.

Saving money

Different prices. Compare prices for similar amounts of coverage.

Tip: You may have more choice from an agent who sells insurance from several different companies.

Higher deductible. Your premium will be less if you pay a higher deductible; but you will pay more out-of-pocket money if you have a claim.

Discounts. You may get discounts for different types of insurance—for example if you have:

- safety devices in your home or car. Some safety devices are
  - burglar alarms.

- extra fire extinguishers and smoke detectors in your home.
- air bags that protect your body in case of a car accident.
- a club or boot that locks your steering wheel or tires.
- healthy personal habits. For example, you may pay less for medical insurance if you do not smoke.

Medical

Overview

In many countries, the government pays for the medical care of its citizens. In the U.S., most individuals and families are responsible for their own medical care. This care is expensive; for example, one night in a hospital usually costs $1,000 or more. Also, some hospitals or doctors may not treat you.

Injury and illness. If you are just visiting here for a short time:

- Your medical insurance from home may still protect you.

Your insurance company should have a license from the Department of Insurance for your state. Many state departments also have information you can get for free or for a low price. For example, the Department of Insurance in California has information about:

- the financial ratings of different companies.
- the cost for each type of insurance. This information helps you compare the costs of different companies.
- insurance costs for each region. This information helps you find out the difference between insurance costs for different areas of the city.
- the number of complaints about the company.

Find the telephone number in the state government section of your phone book under "Insurance."

- You may get special travel insurance. You will need more insurance if you live or stay here more than a few months.

Most U.S. employers pay for a medical insurance plan. If you have a medical condition that requires a lot of care or medication, be sure that the insurance will pay for any care and medication you will need.

U.S. requirements. To get a "J" or "F" visa, the U.S. requires that you have a minimum benefit of $50,000. This insurance covers you for

- illnesses and injuries.
- medical evacuation, or your return to your home country for medical treatment.
- repatriation of remains, or the return of you body to your home country if you die.

This minimum is a good guide for all newcomers to the U.S.

Dental insurance. With some plans, you may buy dental insurance as an extra part of your plan. Dental insurance may help pay for:

- routine care (cleanings, x-rays, fillings).
- emergency care.
- oral surgery.
- orthodontic care.

Always carry your health insurance card with you. If you are in an accident or need to see a doctor while you are away, you will need the card in order to get treatment. If you need a doctor while you are traveling, call your insurance company before you go; ask if you need to go to a specific doctor, clinic, or hospital. In an emergency, just go to the hospital or doctor; your insurance probably pays for all emergency care—wherever you go.

Where to go

Group plan. You and your family probably can get group insurance through an organization—such as:

- the company that employs you.
- your university (if you are a student or professor).
- a professional association (if you are a member).

A group plan is usually better because:

- it costs less.
- you will be able to get insurance more easily if you have a pre-existing condition.

Individual plans. Only a few insurance companies give individual coverage if you do not have a "green" or "pink" card," if you are not a U.S. citizen, or if you have not lived in the U.S. for the last 6 months.

Health insurance costs vary. If you are an employee, your company will probably pay for part of the insurance.

The cost of health insurance depends on:

- the type of plan.
- the kind of coverage, or what it pays for.
- your gender (male or female).
- your age.
- your health.

What it pays for

Basic coverage. This coverage should include any care caused by the illness or accident—including:

- visits to the doctor.
- hospital visits.
- lab tests.
- surgery.

Many companies have a ceiling, or maximum payment for a single accident or illness. Make sure this ceiling is high enough to pay your medical bills for this illness; if they are not, you will pay these bills yourself. Also, you may not be eligible to collect insurance for any pre-existing conditions (see "Limitations").

Most plans also have a "cap," or a maximum amount you pay for medical expenses in a year; if the expenses go above that amount, the insurance covers 100%.

Other benefits. Some insurance plans help pay the costs for:

- regular check-ups.
- prescription drugs.
- maternity care.
- eyeglasses.

Limitations. Find out when the insurance policy does *not* pay. For example, ask if the insurance pays for:

- any care you need right away; with many policies you must wait a certain period.
- medical care when you are out of town.
- certain types of medical care—such as acupuncture, mental illness, or physical therapy.

- pre-existing conditions. For example, suppose you have had a heart attack in the past; make sure the insurance covers any expenses for another attack.

In addition to the premium, you pay a:

- deductible. The deductible varies— but may cost more than $500 or $100 a year, per person. Ask.
- co-payment, or specific amount you pay each time you use the insurance—for example, when you visit a doctor or buy prescription medicine.

Types of plans

Indemnity. With an indemnity plan, you choose your own doctor; the insurance plan pays for some of the expenses. The doctors are private; that is, they do not work for an insurance or health-maintenance organization (HMO).

Two advantages are:

- You may choose any qualified doctor.
- You do not need to go to a primary-care doctor before you see a specialist.

Two disadvantages are:

- The indemnity plan usually costs more than managed care or an HMO (see next page). Many sponsors and employers do not offer this plan because it costs a lot more than the other types of plans.
- You may need to pay the doctor at the end of your visit. Then you wait until the insurance company sends you the money.

Managed care, or Preferred Provider Option (PPO), and Health Maintenance Organization (HMO). With managed care or a PPO, you choose from a list of doctors or dentists who work with your plan. These doctors are usually private; that is, they do not work for an insurance or health-care company. With a Health Maintenance Organization (HMO, the doctors usually work for the health-care company.

Note: With most plans, you are permitted to see a doctor who is not part of the insurance company's network. You will pay extra for this option.

Also, with most plans you must see a primary-care doctor first. To see a specialist, you get a referral from your primary-care physician. For example, if you have a "bad back," the primary-care physician may send you to an orthopedist, or bone doctor; if you go to the orthopedist without this referral, the insurance will not pay. A few plans let you go directly to some or all specialists.

Ask:

- Who are the primary-care doctors and dentists on the list? Where are their offices? Does someone you know use and like these doctors? Do the doctors have the services you need?
- Which specialists will you be able to see without a referral from your primary-care physician?
- Who are the specialists? Will you be able to see a specialist who is not on the list? How much extra will you pay for this option?
- Which hospital will you use? Is it close by? Is it a good hospital?

In addition to the premium, you probably will pay a co-payment; that is, you pay $10 or $15 for each visit to a doctor or dentist or each time you buy medicine.

Health Maintenance Organization (HMO). Like the PPO, the HMO has a list of doctors or dentists who work with the plan. With an HMO, the doctors usually work for the health-care company. In most cases, you must also see the primary care physician before you visit a specialist for the first time. Ask the same questions about the doctors and the hospital as you would with a PPO.

The advantage of an HMO is the cost. Usually, the cost to your employer and also to you is much less. The disadvantages are:

- With HMOs, you may not be able to see the same doctor or dentist when you visit; ask the company.
- The doctor or dentist may spend less time with you than a private doctor; ask other patients.

What do I do if I am not getting good care with my plan? If your health has suffered because of poor care, complain to the health-care company. Write a letter describing your complaint; make the letter as brief as you can. Call the company and ask where to send the letter; use certified mail with return receipt requested, so you can prove the office received it.

My 13-year-old son brought home an insurance form from school. Do I need this extra insurance? If you already have a

181

family plan, you may not need any more insurance; but your child may need extra insurance if he regularly takes part in an activity that might cause injury—such as playing football.

 My daughter is going to college. Do I need extra insurance for her? Your plan may still cover a child who is:

- 18–23 years of age.
- a full-time student.

If your insurance plan does not cover your child, you probably can buy:

- insurance through the college.
- extra insurance added on to your family plan.

Home and Property

Renters Insurance

Renters insurance pays for both personal property and liability insurance.

Personal property. Personal property insurance pays for articles in your home if something of value is damaged, destroyed, or stolen. It also will pay your expenses if you need to find another place to live because the home you are renting is destroyed or damaged.

Before you get this insurance:

- make a list of valuable items—such as jewelry, furs, rugs, art, computers, and antique furniture.
- get a written appraisal, or value estimate, for each item.
- write down the serial numbers of cameras, computers, TVs, and stereos.
- give the list of your valuables, with the serial numbers, to your insurance agent.

Some policies pay for items that are lost, stolen, or damaged outside the home. For example, this type of policy pays if:

- you lose a diamond ring.
- you damage your computer while traveling.
- someone steals your wallet from a hotel room.

The average cost of renters insurance for newcomers is $150–$200 per year. You may not need this insurance if you:

- do not have valuable items.
- are staying here a short time and have this insurance from home.

Liability insurance. If a visitor is injured in your home, you may be legally responsible. For example, you may be liable if:

Be sure you understand the difference between the replacement value and the depreciated value. For example, suppose you paid $500 for a sofa 5 years ago. You might need $600 to replace that sofa, or to buy one like it. If your policy covers you for the replacement value, you get $600.

The depreciated value is probably lower, because the couch is older; this value may be around $200. If your insurance policy covers only the depreciated value, you get $200.

- someone slips and falls on your front steps or inside your home.
- your dog bites your neighbor.

According to U.S. law, you may be responsible for the medical costs for these injuries—even if you are renting the home. Liability insurance pays for any legal and medical expenses you owe.

Homeowners insurance

If you own a home, you will need insurance for:

- personal property.
- liability.
- the house, or building, itself. This insurance pays if your home is destroyed or damaged. You may need to get additional insurance for special problems in your area—for example, earthquakes, floods, hurricanes, or tornadoes.

Auto

Overview

By law, you must have auto insurance if you own or rent the car you drive. If you own the car, your liability insurance must cover you and anyone else who drives your car regularly (see "Liability insurance" in this section).

If you are renting, you may buy insurance from the rental company. Make sure you need this policy. If you own a car in the U.S., your auto insurance may also cover you when you rent a car.

A copy of your car registration should be in the glove compartment of the car— along with a card showing the type of insurance you have. Keep the originals in a safe place. Carry your AAA card with you at all times (see "American Automobile Association/Getting Around").

Insurance may be expensive— especially for newcomers to the U.S. For example, liability insurance alone may be $700–$800 a year. Check with a few insurance agents to see how much coverage you should get. Also call the National Automobile Consumer Hotline.

See section on "Saving money" in this chapter. The cost for your car insurance also depends on:

- your driving record—for example, the number of car accidents you have had in the past.
- the type of car. You will pay more for a popular, expensive car.
- the condition of the car. In general, you pay less for a car that is old or in poor condition. You will also get less money back if you have an accident, so check to be sure you want collision insurance for this car.
- the age and gender of the driver(s). If you or a driver in your family is under 25, your cost will be much higher.
- the number of expected miles you will drive the car. For example, your premium may be less if you drive the car only to and from a nearby office.

If you have been here less than 2 years, you may not be able to prove that you are a safe driver; your insurance cost probably will be high. Sometimes, a letter from your insurance company at home will lower the premium; more often, it does not help.

 Every person who drives your car regularly must be insured.

? *What if a friend drives my car and has an accident? Am I still insured?* Yes—as long as this person is a licensed driver and does not drive your car regularly.

Collision insurance

If two cars bump into each other, your collision insurance pays:

- the damage to your car—if the car can be repaired.
- the value of your car—if you need to buy a new one.

In some states, only the insurance of the driver responsible for the accident, or the driver "at fault," pays. The insurance pays the cost of the repairs or of a new car for anyone in the accident.

You may need to rent a car while your own is being fixed. Ask if the insurance pays for this cost.

Liability insurance

Suppose you are driving a car and your friend is in the seat next to you. If you bump into another car, you may be legally responsible for the cost of the:

- injuries to your friend.
- injuries to anyone hurt in the other car.
- damage to the other car.

By law, you must have liability insurance to cover the other person's costs. Each state has its own minimum—that is, the least amount of liability insurance you may have. In some states, the driver "at fault" pays all the costs; in states with "no-fault" systems, your insurer pays only for your injuries— even if you caused the accident.

Comprehensive insurance

This covers damage done to your car when no one is driving it—for example if:

- someone steals your car.
- a tree falls on your car.
- another car bumps into your car.

Life and Disability

 You may have trouble getting life or disability insurance if you are not a U.S. citizen or a permanent resident.

Life

Many Americans buy this insurance to protect family members in case the person who supports them dies. Some kinds of life insurance are also an investment, or a way of saving money. If an agent tries to sell you insurance as an investment, be careful. In most cases, other investments are better—if you do not need the insurance.

Disability

Disability insurance pays certain expenses if you cannot work for a long period of time. Your health insurance may pay your medical costs; you may need disability insurance to pay for your living expenses if you are not earning any money.

Words to Know

A.M. Best Rating: a rating that gives the company's finances. An insurance company with a high rating (A or A-) will probably pay its claims and probably will not go out of business.

Acupuncture: a Chinese type of medicine that uses needles

Ceiling: the highest amount insurance companies will pay for a medical service in 1 year

Check-ups: visits to make sure you are well. Usually, you go every year.

Claim: a right to collect money from an insurance company—for example, when you are injured

Co-insurance: the portion (%) of the medical bill that you pay after the deductible

Co-payment: a small amount of money that you pay for each doctor or hospital visit. Your insurance company or HMO pays the rest.

Collision insurance: insurance for damage to your car because of an accident

Comprehensive auto insurance: insurance that covers damage to your car when no one is driving it—for example, damage from a falling tree

Coverage: the kind or amount of insurance you have

Deductible: an amount of money the insurance company *does not* pay. For example, with a $500 deductible, you pay the first $500 of the expenses; then the insurance company pays most of the rest.

Disability insurance: insurance in case you are sick or injured and cannot work. This insurance helps to pay for your living expenses.

Evacuation: transportation to the nearest medical facility or to your home country

Financial rating: (see "A.M. Best")

Group plan: an insurance plan you get as part of a group

Health Maintenance Organization (HMO): a kind of managed-care medical insurance. With an HMO, the doctors and other providers are employees of the HMO.

Homeowners' policy: insurance you get when you own a home. The insurance covers damage to your home. It also covers liability and personal property insurance.

Indemnity medical insurance: a type of medical insurance. You may choose any doctor you like; the insurance company pays a specific amount toward the bill. Indemnity medical insurance is different from a simple payment, or indemnity, for an injury.

Individual plan: a plan you get by yourself—not as part of a group. You pay the full cost of your own medical insurance.

Insurance agent: a person who sells insurance

Liable: legally responsible for injury or property damage to someone else. You or your insurance company must pay the person you have harmed.

Liability insurance: insurance that pays if you have caused someone else or their property to be harmed. For example, you may be liable if someone falls and is hurt on your front steps.

Life insurance: insurance that pays when you die

Limitations: conditions that limit what the insurance company will do. For example, with a 6-month time limit, the insurance will not pay until 6 months have passed.

Managed care: a kind of medical insurance. With managed care, you choose a doctor from a list approved by the insurance company.

Orthodontic care: a dental service that straightens your teeth

Personal property insurance: insurance that protects the contents of your home

Physical therapy: a type of treatment that uses exercises and massage

Policy: a written agreement with an insurance company. You get a separate policy for each type of insurance—for example, health, home and property, and auto.

Policy maximum: the most amount of money you can get from the insurance company. For example, the maximum amount for some medical insurance policies is $50,000—even if the medical costs are higher.

Pre-existing condition: an illness or injury for which you have been treated before you bought the insurance. Some insurance companies will not pay for these illnesses or injuries—especially with an individual plan.

Preferred Provider Option (PP0): a kind of health care plan. With a PPO, you choose a doctor from the insurance company's list. The doctors are private. Usually you may use another doctor, but you will pay more.

Premium: the yearly amount of money you pay for insurance on a monthly, quarterly, semi-annual, or annual basis

Primary-care physician: a doctor who gives general care. With most managed care plans and HMOs, you must see a primary-care physician before you go to a specialist.

Quarterly: every 3 months

Repatriation: transportation to your home country because you are too sick or injured to continue working or studying here

Repatriation of mortal remains: transportation of your body to your home country

Semi-annually: twice a year

Serial number: the number stamped on items such as computers and TV's. If the item is stolen, the serial number may help the police find the item.

Medical Care

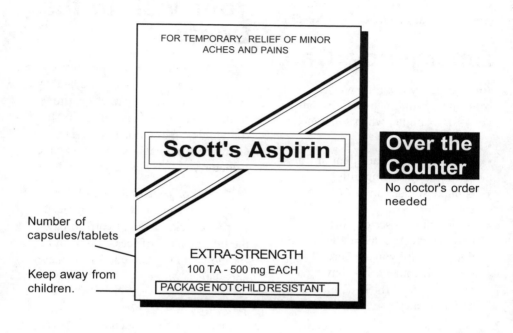

FOR TEMPORARY RELIEF OF MINOR
ACHES AND PAINS

Scott's Aspirin

**Over the
Counter**

No doctor's order
needed

Number of
capsules/tablets

Keep away from
children.

EXTRA-STRENGTH
100 TA - 500 mg EACH

PACKAGE NOT CHILD RESISTANT

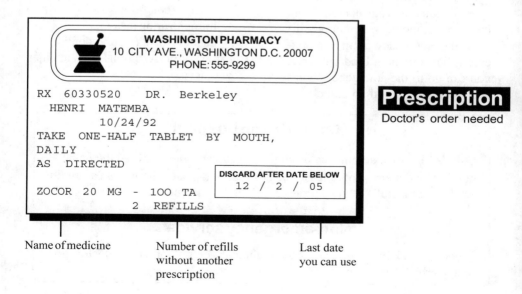

WASHINGTON PHARMACY
10 CITY AVE., WASHINGTON D.C. 20007
PHONE: 555-9299

RX 60330520   DR. Berkeley
  HENRI MATEMBA
       10/24/92
TAKE ONE-HALF TABLET BY MOUTH,
DAILY
AS DIRECTED

Prescription
Doctor's order needed

DISCARD AFTER DATE BELOW
12 / 2 / 05

ZOCOR 20 MG - 100 TA
          2 REFILLS

Name of medicine

Number of refills
without another
prescription

Last date
you can use

You need insurance to get medical care. Be sure you understand the American system of medical insurance before you make any medical appointments (see "Medical/Insurance You Need").

Emergency Care

An emergency is a time when someone's health is in serious danger—for example, when someone:

- has broken a leg.
- may die from an accident or illness, or from swallowing pills.
- is unconscious, or can't be awakened.
- is burned by a serious fire.
- may be having a heart attack. Do not wait until you are sure; if you *think* someone *may* be having a heart attack, call "911" and ask for an ambulance.

Emergency care is expensive—more expensive than going to your doctor. Your insurance company may not pay if you go to the emergency room in a non-emergency situation. Find out when you can go to the emergency room and when you should go to a clinic or a doctor. If you plan to travel, ask where you should go for medical care if you get sick on your trip.

Your Visit to the Doctor

Visit the doctor soon after you arrive—even if you are healthy. Most doctors expect you to come for an "initial consultation." In some cities, many doctors are not taking new patients; be sure you have a doctor you like *before* you need one.

For your first visit to the doctor or dentist, you need cash, a check, or credit card to pay the bill; in some offices, you must pay for the visit and then collect the insurance later.

You will also need:

- medical records such as
  - medical history if you have a pre-existing condition.
  - immunization history.
  - dental x-rays (for the dentist).
- names or prescriptions of medicines you need.

Getting to the hospital

Call **911** for an ambulance or go to the nearest hospital. Keep the name, number, and address of at least one hospital in a place where you can find it easily (see "Help!"—"In an Emergency" in the Appendix).

Non-emergency service

If you get sick in the middle of the night and you do not have a doctor, go to a nearby 24-hour clinic.

- your insurance card, which should include
  - the name of your insurance company.
  - your policy or group number.
- insurance forms for your doctor or dentist to sign.

Medicine

Choose a pharmacy that is close to your home or office. The pharmacy will keep records of your medications.

 Read the label on all medicine packages for instructions. Look for warnings—such as "Take with food" or "May cause drowsiness." If you have small children, look for "child-safety caps."

Overview

Over-the-counter or non-prescription drugs. These are for minor problems—such as common colds, headaches, and allergies. You can get these drugs at most pharmacies, supermarkets, and groceries.

Prescription drugs. Common prescription drugs are antibiotics, codeine, and birth control pills. You will need a prescription from your doctor. Some insurance plans pay for prescription drugs—but not over-the-counter drugs.

When you need a prescription drug, call the doctor; have the telephone number of your pharmacy ready in case the doctor wants to order the medicine on the phone. If your insurance pays for the medicine, bring your health insurance card to the pharmacy when you go.

Ask your doctor if you may buy a generic drug (one that does not use the manufacturer's brand name); generic drugs cost 10%–75% less; but not all generic drugs are exactly the same as the medicine your doctor prescribed.

You can get a lot of good information on medical conditions and medicines on the Internet. For example, you may read articles about the side effects of popular medicines or about treatments for certain conditions.

Abbreviations

ACU:	Acupuncture		**GYN:**	Gynecology
CD:	Cardiovascular diseases		**IM:**	Internal medicine
DR:	Doctor (may be a doctor or a dentist)		**MD:**	Medical doctor
			OBS:	Obstetrics
DDS:	Dentistry		**OBG:**	Obstetrics/gynecology
D:	Dermatology		**PED:**	Pediatrician
GP:	General practice		**RN:**	Registered Nurse (a nurse with a license to practice)
GER:	Geriatrics			

⊗ When getting information from the Internet, use only organizations with a good reputation; these are generally free. Do not follow advice on websites that charge for information or try to sell you medications. Check any information you get with your own doctor.

You may also find support groups, or groups of people with a specific medical condition. Sometimes these groups are helpful. Remember, though, that the people in the groups are often unhappy about their treatment or have severe cases. Your own experiences may not be as bad as theirs.

Tip: If you want to find help or information about a specific condition, search on the Internet with the name of the condition. To talk to a specialist in person, ask your primary care physician for a referral, or the name of a specialist you can visit.

Tip: Your primary care physician should get a copy of all your medical test results. Also, keep a copy for yourself. You will save time if you have copies of all medical records when you see a new doctor or you move back home again.

Eyeglasses/ Contacts

Who can help

Ophthalmologists are trained medical doctors who treat eye diseases. Most also prescribe lenses for eyeglasses; a few fit you for contact lenses.

Optometrists are trained eye specialists. They mainly prescribe eyeglasses and contact lenses.

Optical shops

Many optometrists work in optical shops (eye centers). When you go to the shop, you can get an exam and pick out your eyeglass frames. Often you may get the glasses in an hour; if you have a special type of lens, you may have to wait a week or more.

🕐 Most optical shops are open 6 days a week, from about 9 am–6 or 7 pm. Often, you do not need an appointment. Call ahead for an appointment with an optometrist in a private office or for an ophthalmologist.

Alternative Medical Care

Overview. To find a trained practitioner of "alternative medicines," look for specific letters after the person's name. These letters show that the practitioner has completed a certain training or passed a certain test in the U.S. Some types of alternative medicines you may find are:

Acupuncture. Look for the following letters: Dipl.Ac. (Diplomate in Acupuncture); M.Ac (Master of Acupuncture); O.M.D./D.O.M. (Oriental Medical Doctor/Doctor of Oriental Medicine).

Chiropractic. Chiropractors heal many types of pain and illnesses; but they are particularly popular for back pain. The U.S. has about 45,000 chiropractors. Look for the letters D.C. (Doctor of Chiropractic).

Homeopathy. The U.S. has only about 3,000 accredited homeopathists. Look for the following initials: D.Ht (Diplomate in Homotherapeutics); C.C.H. (Certified in Classical Homeopathy); D.H.A.N.P. (Diplomate of the Homeopathic Academy of Naturopathic Physicians).

Massage. Call and ask what type of massage you will get. If the person on the phone will not tell you, do not go; many "massage parlors" provide illegal services. Look for the letters N.C.T.B. (granted by the National Certification Board for Therapeutic Massage & Bodywork).

Nutritional therapy. Every city has many "health food stores" where you can get minerals, vitamins, and natural foods. Also, most doctors often send patients to nutritionists for specific types of problems—for example, high blood pressure. Look for the letters R.D. (Registered Dietitian); D.T.R. (Dietetic Technician); C.N.C. (Certified Nutritional Consultant).

Osteopathic medicine. Osteopaths are particularly popular for lower back pain. Look for the letters D.O. (Doctor of Osteopathy).

Note: U.S. certified doctors have the initials M.D. (Medical Doctor) after their name. Many also practice alternative medicine.

 Before you visit a practitioner of alternative medicine, make sure:

- your insurance covers this type of medicine.
- the person who practices the medicine is
  - accredited.
  - licensed to practice in your area.

Words to Know

Acupuncture: a Chinese way of healing using needles

Cardiology: the treatment and study of heart disease

Child Safety Cap: on medicine bottles, makes it very difficult for children to open

Chiropractic: a type of alternative medicine that moves the vertebrae, or parts of the spine

Clinic: a place that treats sick or injured people. Some clinics are open all day and night.

Convenience store: a small store that sells different items—such as over-the-counter drugs, food, hot coffee, newspapers, and magazines. Many are open all night.

Dermatology: care of the skin

Emergency: a time when someone may die or may lose a part of their body—such as an arm or an eye

Filling: the material that the dentist puts in any holes in your teeth

General practitioner: a doctor that handles common medical problems

Generic drug: a drug that does not use a manufacturer's brand name

Geriatrics: care of older people

Gynecologist: a doctor for women

Homeopathy: a type of alternative medicine that heals with very small amounts of certain herbs, minerals, or animal substances

Initial consultation: first visit to a doctor, or any other professional. Most doctors expect you to come in for an initial consultation *before* you get sick.

Internist: a doctor of internal medicine

Lab test: a test of your blood, urine, or other body fluids

Massage: a type of healing that uses rubbing or touching

Maternity care: medical services for pregnant women

Nutritional therapy: a type of healing that uses diet, vitamins, and minerals

Obstetrician: a doctor for pregnant women

Ophthalmologist: a physician who specializes in eye care

Optometrist: a specialist in fitting and prescribing contact lenses and eyeglasses

Osteopathic medicine: a type of healing that moves muscles and bones to heal

Oral surgery: surgery of the mouth, teeth, gums, and jaw

Orthodontic care: dental services to straighten teeth

Out-of-area coverage: for service you get far from home

Over-the-counter drug: medicine that you can get without a prescription

Pediatrician: a doctor for children

Pharmacy: a place that sells medicine

Prescription: a note from your doctor that allows you to get special medicine from a pharmacy

Referral: the specialist your primary care physician recommends that you see. With most insurance companies, you must get a referral from your primary care physician in order to see the specialist.

Refill: a prescription medicine that the pharmacy may fill again without contacting your doctor for permission

Rx: a symbol for a medical prescription

Side effects: extra changes in your body because of the medicine you are taking. For example, a medicine may help clear up your cold—but it may also make you sleepy. Sleepiness is a side effect of the medicine.

Support groups: groups of people, with the same specific condition or disease, such as alcoholism or diabetes. The members of the group give each other advice at meetings or using e-mail.

X-ray: a photograph of the inside of your body

Credit Cards & Loans

Ms. Connally: Hello, I'm Beth Connally. How can I help you?

Mr. Tanaka: My name is Hiroshi Tanaka. I have a savings and checking account with this bank. I came to find out about getting a loan.

Ms. Connally: I see…Please sit down, Mr. Tanaka…What is the reason for the loan?

Mr. Tanaka: I want to buy a new car. The dealer will finance the car for me, but I want to see what terms this bank can offer.

Ms. Connally: I see…Let's talk this over…I'll need to know how much you are paying for the car…how much you want to put down…and how much you want to borrow… First, let me look up the account you have with us.

Note: Ms. Connally will ask Mr. Tanaka many questions about the loan and about his personal finances.

Credit History

What it is

Credit history is a record of the payments a person has made in the past and the amount of money that person still owes. This record is important for getting a credit card or loan and for doing many other kinds of business—for example, renting a home.

In the U.S., credit bureaus, or companies, keep individual records. Whenever you apply for a bank loan or a credit card, the lender or card company checks with the credit company or bureau. You will get the loan or card only if you have good credit history—that is, if your record shows that you pay your bills on time.

Unfortunately, the U.S. credit companies do not look at the payment records from other countries. According to the U.S. credit bureau, newcomers have no credit history. Without credit history, a card company or lender may not accept your application for a credit card or a loan.

How to get it

To get credit history:

- apply for a credit card or loan from a bank. If the bank refuses, ask about secured credit. (See sections on "Getting a Credit Card" and "Getting a Loan" in this chapter.)
- get an American Express® card in your home country—as soon as you can; use the card. After you arrive in the U.S., call an American Express office and ask for a U.S. account.
- apply for a charge or credit card at a department store or gas station you use. If the store does not accept your application, ask for the manager at the Customer Service desk and explain your problem.

You may need to "shop around"—that is, go to a few banks or stores. Bring a letter from your:

- employer giving your salary and position.
- bank at home (see chapter "Before You Come"). The letter should give your financial history.

If you borrow money or get a credit card, be sure to pay on time. After about 6 months, your payments will be reported to the credit bureaus, and you will have a good credit history. In fact, you probably will get ads in the mail from credit card companies asking you to apply!

Note: Call your local credit bureau to review your credit history if:

- you will be applying for a large loan—for example, a home mortgage or car loan.
- you cannot get a credit card or loan and you don't know why.

If a mistake was made or a bill is unpaid, you may be able to fix the problem. You may find the number of your local credit bureau in the front part of the White Pages directory; you probably will pay a small fee.

 You may get a credit card from a credit union in 2–3 weeks. If you have a foreign

American Express® card, you may get a U.S. card in about 2 weeks. For any other card, you may wait 4–6 weeks for approval.

Credit & Debit Cards

Overview

Many Americans use credit and debit cards to pay for bills over $5–$10. The two main advantages are:

- paying for most purchases with a card is simple and quick.
- you do not need to carry around a lot of cash.

Most cards give bonuses—such as "frequent flyer" miles for airline or hotel discounts (see section on "Getting a Credit Card" in this chapter).

With most cards, you may get cash from an ATM; this cash is good for emergencies or travel expenses.

If you have a card, find the "800" telephone number on the back; write it down on a piece of paper and keep it separate from the card. If you lose your card, you will need this number.

If I have a card from home, why do I need an American one? The two disadvantages of a foreign card are:

- The bill goes to your bank at home and is converted to the non-American currency—at a cost to you.
- You must keep a bank account in your home country to pay the bills.

What should I do if my card is stolen? Report the theft right away—even at night or on weekends. First call the 800 number on the back of your card; if you did not save the number, call the bank issuing the card. You may pay the first $50 charged on your card; the credit card company will be responsible for charges made after your call.

Also call the national credit reporting organizations. Many thieves use the information on the card to apply for credit in your name. Tell the credit agencies about the theft and ask them not to give credit to anyone unless you tell them to do so.

What to get

Credit cards. You get a credit card from a bank or charge card company such as American Express®. At the end of the month, you get one bill for all your purchases. On the bill you see the:

- total amount you owe. You do not pay interest if you pay this amount within the set time—usually about 10–15 days. Look for the words "current balance" for the amount you owe.
- the minimum amount you must pay for the month. This is not the whole bill. If you pay only the minimum, you will pay interest; usually, the interest rate is much higher than the rate for a bank loan.

You may use VISA and Mastercard in most stores, the post office, restaurants, gas stations, movies and theaters, travel offices, doctors' offices, and airports—almost everywhere. Most merchants also take American Express®.

Many large department stores and gas stations also offer credit cards. Store cards have some advantages:

- You get a notice of special sales ahead of time.
- You may get a discount for opening up an account.
- Store cards are sometimes easier to get than a credit card from a bank.

 Paying with a credit card is so easy that you may forget how much you are spending. Some Americans have stopped using cards because they had trouble paying their bills at the end of the month.

Note: With a few department stores or charge cards such as American Express®, you must pay all the money you owe each month.

Debit cards. Some banks offer VISA or MasterCard debit cards—rather than credit cards. These cards look just like credit cards; but the payment comes out of your bank account right away. For example, if you buy $10 of gas with a debit card, the machine transfers $10 from your bank account and deposits it in the gas station's account. At the end of the month, you get a bank statement with the date and the amount of each sale.

A debit card is like a check—only faster. You must have enough money in your checking account to cover the payment.

Getting a Credit Card

Where to apply

Your credit union or employer's preferred bank. If you belong to a credit union, your application probably will be approved. Most embassies and many businesses can get cards for their employees from a preferred bank.

Your university. Many banks give credit cards to students. Often, you may sign up at the orientation fair.

The bank or savings and loan (S&L) where you have an account. Ask about a credit card. If possible, bring a letter from your employer stating your position, salary, and income; but do not be surprised if you do not get the card.

The bank that has a correspondent relationship with your bank at home (see "What to Find Out/Before You Come").

Banks that offer secured cards. A few banks give secured credit cards to people with no credit history. With a secured credit card, you deposit money in an account; then you can charge up to that amount. If you pay the loan on time, every month, you may get good credit history.

What to look for

For help in choosing a bank that offers credit cards, call Bankcard Holders of America.

Credit limit. The credit limit is the maximum amount you may charge to your account at any time. For example, if your credit limit is $2,000, you may not owe more than $2,000 at any one time.

Interest rates. Ask about interest rates if you plan to pay only part of the bill each month or if you may need a cash advance.

Bonuses. Many cards give bonuses—such as:

- frequent flyer miles for a specific airline. A few cards let you apply the bonus miles to any airline you want; compare the number of miles you get for the same amount of money.
- cash rebates, or money you get back for charging more than a specific amount.
- discounts for hotels, cruises, car rentals, long-distance calls, and other services.

Time. When must you pay the bill? The grace period is the time between the date when the bill is mailed and the due date. "No grace period" means you pay interest from the date when the bill is mailed.

Fees. You may pay:

- an annual fee for using the card. These may be as high as $50–$150.
- a fee for late payments.
- fees for spending more than the credit limit.

Getting a Loan

Where to go

Loans may be even harder to get than credit cards. Again, the best place to get a loan is at a credit union, your employer's preferred bank, or a correspondent bank.

When you buy an expensive item, such as a car, the dealer may be able to get you a loan; compare the terms with those banking institutions.

The time you wait for a loan approval depends on the type of loan. For instance, approval for a home mortgage may take much longer than a car loan.

If you are thinking about borrowing from a finance company, be sure the company is reliable. Also check interest rates.

Kinds of loans

Installment loans. This loan is usually for expenses such as buying a car, paying for college, or fixing up your home; most often, the term is for 2–5 years.

Mortgage. This loan is for buying a home. Usually, the term is for 15–30 years.

What to look for

Down payment. The required amount is often 10%–30% of the loan; you can put down more if you want to.

Monthly payments. The monthly payment depends on:

- the interest rate.
- the amount of the loan, or principal.
- the time period of the loan.

Interest. Rates vary. Adjustable rates are usually less than fixed rates.

Term. The term is the number of months or years you have to pay back the loan.

Prepayment option. This option lets you pay back the loan ahead of time.

You will need a Social Security card. Diplomats and students will need a letter confirming their foreign status from their employer or educational institution. If you are still waiting for your Social Security card, see "Social Security/Your Legal Status."

These documents also may be useful:

- financial reports. Bring a financial report from your home country (see "What to Bring/Before You Come"). Some lending institutions will consider this; others will not.
- letter of recommendation. Get a letter from your employer stating
  - your salary.
  - your position.
  - the time you are expected to stay.
  - your visa type.
- co-signature. If you need a co-signature, the lending institution will have a form for your co-signer or guarantor; the form states that the signer will pay your loan if you do not.

Words to Know

Cash advance: money you get as a loan from your credit card company

Charge card: a card that is like a credit card, but you must pay the whole bill every month. With a credit card, you may pay only part of the bill if you like, but you will pay interest.

Correspondent (bank): having a special relationship with a bank from another country. For example, a bank in France may have a correspondent bank in the U.S.; if you are a customer of the French bank, you may be able to get faster and better service from the correspondent bank in the U.S.

Co-signature: a signature from someone else. The other person promises to pay if you cannot.

Credit: The word "credit" has several meanings: 1) the amount of money that you deposit or pay into an account; 2) the amount of money you can borrow (see "credit limit")

Credit card: a plastic card used to buy things. With a credit card, you get one bill for all the charges you made in the month; you may pay the whole amount right away—or just part of it, with interest.

Credit history: a record of your past payments. Your credit history tells whether you have paid your bills on time.

Credit limit: the maximum amount you can charge each month

Credit union: a type of banking institution. You can join only if you belong to a certain group, such as a group of employees.

Debit card: a card you use to pay your bills. With a debit card, the bank takes the money out of your account right away.

Deposit: to place money in an account; the money placed in an account

Down payment: the portion of the cost that you pay when you buy a house, car, or other item; a deposit

Due date: the date when you owe the money. The bank or card company must receive your payment by that date. You must pay at least the minimum amount stated on the bill. If you pay after the due date, you will also pay a late charge.

Finance company: a company set up to lend money

Grace period: the time you have to pay your bill—that is, the time between the date when the bill was mailed and the date when your payment is due

Interest: money the bank pays you for keeping money in its account(s); money you pay for borrowing

Interest rate: a percentage paid for the use of money

Savings and loan (S&L): a banking institution

Term: time period in which you pay back a loan

Buying or Leasing
a Car

Minivan

Convertible

Cargo van

Sports car

Sport utility vehicle (SUV)

Sedan

___Parts of a Car___

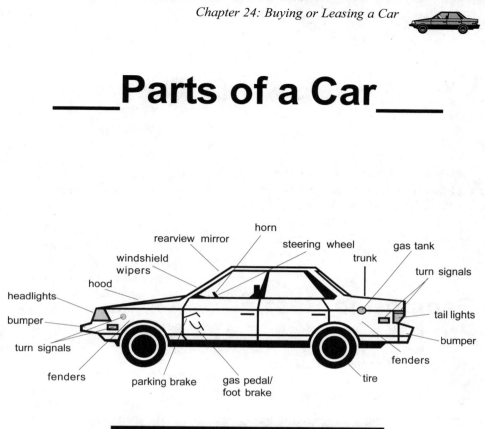

WORDS YOU MIGHT HEAR

2-door: a car with two front doors

4-door: a car with four doors. Two doors are in the front and two in the back

4-wheel drive: a car that stays on the road better because all four wheels have power. These cars are good for muddy roads and high hills.

ABS: a safety feature that keeps the brakes from "locking," or sliding, when you stop suddenly.

Air Bags: a safety feature that protects the passengers in an accident

Automatic transmission: gears that change automatically; the gears change along with the car's speed

Convertible: a car with a roof made of heavy cloth. The top can be folded back so you ride without a roof.

Hatchback: a car that has a door in the back. The door swings up, so you can put things in the open area behind the seat.

Manual transmission: not automatic; the driver has to change the gears as the car's speed changes

Sound System: a system that typically includes an AM-FM radio, tape player, CD player, and multiple speakers

Sunroof: a window on the car's roof

Overview

You may:

- rent a car (see chapter on "Traveling In & Out of the U.S.").
- lease a car. A lease is a long-term rental—usually 1-3 years. At the end of the leasing period, you give the car back to the owner; with some leasing contracts, you may buy the car at the end of the period.
- buy a car.

Getting the Best Price

 The list price, or "sticker" price, is different for each car. These prices depend on:

- the Manufacturer's Suggested Retail Price (MSRP); this is the price the company that makes the car suggests you pay.
- extras. You may pay more for a sunroof or a Global Positioning System (GPS). Extras should be listed on the car window, along with the price for each.
- warranty. With a warranty, the dealer will fix major problems for free or at a discount.

Used car prices

These prices also depend on:

- the person or business you buy it from. Cars sold by dealers usually cost more.
- warranties. Cars sold by dealers may come with a warranty; cars sold by individuals may not.

- the model year.
- mileage, or the number of miles the car has been driven. By law, the mileage must be on the odometer of every car—either used or new.
- condition. If you are buying a used car, have a mechanic inspect it (see below).

⊗ Always have a used car inspected *before—not after—* you buy it. Go to a certified mechanic or to a service station with an American Automobile Association (AAA) sign. The mechanic will tell you if the car needs any repairs. The dealer or seller may pay for these repairs.

Other costs

In addition to the price of the car, you pay other costs, including:

- dealer preparation for getting the car ready to drive—such as cleaning and testing.
- insurance (see "Auto/Insurance You Need").
- taxes. Taxes cost a percentage of the car price.
- title and registration fees (see the "Registration" section in this chapter).
- a car inspection fee (see the "Inspection" section in this chapter).

How long it takes

If the dealer has the car you want, and you already have insurance, you may be able to take it home right away. If the dealer has to order the car, you may wait 6 or more weeks.

Getting information

Before you negotiate the price, find out:

- the factory invoice price for new cars.
- the recommended price for used cars.

You may get these prices from:

- books and magazines at the library; ask the librarian at the "Information" desk.
- a consumer magazine—such as *Consumer Reports*.
- your credit union; many credit unions have books on car prices for their members.
- the Internet.

How to buy a car

1. Compare the prices at several auto dealers.

When you enter the showroom, a dealer will ask if you need help. To look around by yourself, say, "I'm just looking, thank you."

2. Ask questions.

It is not impolite to ask a lot of questions and then say, "I want to look around some more" or "I want to think it over."

3. Test drive the car.

The dealer will let you take a short drive in the car.

4. Bargain for a good price if the dealer does not have a single-price policy.

Tell the dealer you know the factory invoice or the recommended price. Also tell the dealer what price you expect to pay.

5. Get a bill of sale *in writing* before you buy a car.

The bill of sale tells the price, the make and model of the car, and all the extras.

6. Discuss financing.

If you discuss financing with the dealer, also check out the terms with banks and other lenders.

7. Pay for the car or make a down payment.

Most dealers prefer a cashier's or certified check. You also may pay with:

- a credit card. If you pay with a credit card, the dealer may charge about 3% extra—the amount dealers usually pay the credit card company.
- cash. Many dealers do not like cash.

Registration

⊗ By law, you must get insurance for your car (see "Auto/Insurance You Need").

If you buy the car from a dealer, the dealer will register the car and send away for the car title (paper that shows you own the car). If you buy from an individual, go to the nearest Motor Vehicle Administration (MVA) or Department of Motor Vehicles (DMV) office to register the car.

 Call your state's MVA or DMV and ask what to bring. Most offices require:

- a photo ID.
- a bill of sale. For a new car, also bring the manufacturer's statement of origin; you will get this document from the dealer. For a used car, bring the title from the former owner.
- the name and number of your car insurance policy.
- cash, check, or credit card to pay for the registration fee.

 You will pay:

- taxes.
- a title fee.
- a tag or registration fee.
- a lien recording fee and contract, if your car is being financed.

Inspection

In most states you must have your car inspected for:

- safety—including lights, brakes, and signals.
- emissions, or the amount of pollution coming from your car.

Call and ask what days are the best to go. Try not to go during the last week of the month, when the stations are busy. Call the MVA or DMV and find out:

- where to go.
- how often to go.
- how much it will cost.
- what to bring. Usually, you need
  - your car registration.
  - your safety inspection notice, if you have one.
  - your emissions inspection notice, if you have one.
  - money. Ask if you can pay with a credit card.

Leasing a Car

Advantages

Easy return. Sometimes, leasing costs less than buying a new car. For example, suppose you need a large loan to buy a car. If you decide to trade the car in after a few years, the price you get for it will be much less than the price you paid; in fact, after you sell the car, you still may not have enough money left to pay off the loan.

Lower deposit. The down payment for a car loan may be 10%–20% of the price. With a leased car, the deposit is lower; sometimes, you pay no deposit at all.

Disadvantages

The total cost of leasing a car is often more than the cost of buying a new or used one. When you add up the cost of the deposit and the monthly payments before you lease, keep in mind:

- equity. When you return the car, you get no money for it. If you get an "open lease" (see "Your leasing agreement" section in this chapter), you may buy the car; but leasing a car and then buying it often costs more than buying it right away.

- penalties. When you return the car, you may pay penalties, or fees, for:
  - returning the car before the lease is over. Ask whether your employer will pay the penalty if you go back to your home country early.
  - extra "wear and tear" on the car—for example, if the seats are dirty or the outside paint has scratches on it.
  - extra miles. You will pay a fee if you have used more than the number of miles in the agreement.

⊗ If you cannot afford to buy a new car, find out the price of a used one; used cars are often easy to sell. Often, leasing saves money only if you keep the car for a short time.

How to negotiate a leasing contract

1. Get general information about leasing a car.

Learn more about the advantages and disadvantages of leasing.

2. Shop around.

You can lease a car from:

- special leasing agencies.
- short-term rental car agencies.
- new car dealers.
- used car dealers.

Tip: The large dealerships often will negotiate better prices because they have a lot of inventory.

Use the Internet to see what prices the dealers are offering. Visit the dealers with good prices. Bring a print-out of the on-line information; be sure to point out any discounts in the print-out.

3. Negotiate the price.

Do not tell the dealer you want to lease right away. Ask: How much does the car cost to buy? Negotiate. Then ask about leasing and negotiate again.

4. Compare the costs of leasing and buying.

Remember to compare the total cost.

5. Read the contract carefully before you sign.

Your leasing agreement

How long is the lease? If possible, find out how long you will need the car. The longer you lease the car, the less you will pay for each year.

How much will you pay? What is the deposit, or down payment? How much will you pay each month? What "extras" will you pay for?

What will you pay to break the lease?

Can you buy the car at the end?
With a closed lease, you cannot buy the car at the end; with an open lease, you can. If you may want to buy the car, find out the price. You may save money if you agree to buy the car ahead of time.

What are the warranties? You should get the same manufacturers' warranties for leasing as for buying. Your dealer may ask whether you want to pay for extra warranties; make sure you need these warranties before you buy them.

How much can you drive? With some agreements, you cannot drive more than a certain number of miles—for example, 15,000 miles a year. If you plan to drive the car much less, you should get a lower price. If you plan to drive more miles, find out whether you will pay more.

Can you take the car to another city? If you plan to move to another city, make sure you can take the car with you.

What will you pay for "wear and tear"? The lease should say:

- what is normal "wear and tear" and what is excessive (too much). You will pay extra for any excessive "wear and tear."
- how much you will pay for specific types of "wear and tear."

How will you pay for the tax? The tax can be as high as 10% of the price of the car. Who pays for the tax? If you pay, will the price be in your monthly payments?

What insurance comes with the car? How much money will you get if the car is in a serious accident? Will you get gap insurance—that is, enough money to pay the leasing company for the car?

Words to Know

American Automobile Association (AAA): a club for car drivers. It provides services—such as emergency repairs.

Bill of sale: a document that tells the price, make, and model of the car

Car Navigation System: see Global Positioning System

Cargo van: a large car, mostly used for transporting boxes, carts, and luggage—rather than people

Contract: a written legal agreement between two people or businesses

Dealer preparation: what the dealer does to make the car ready

Deposit: (see "Down payment" below)

Down payment: the money you pay when you buy or lease the car. You borrow the rest (see chapter on "Credit Cards and Loans").

Emissions: gases that come from the back of a car

Financing: getting a car loan from a bank or dealer

Gap insurance: a type of insurance. It pays for the difference between the amount you get from your insurance company and the money you lose because of an accident, illness, or other incident

Global Positioning System (GPS): an electronic system in your car that gives you directions while you drive. You type in the address where you are and the address where you are going; the system's voice tells you each time you need to make a turn. Most GPS's are good for the whole country.

Inspection: a safety check on the car. All cars must pass inspection.

Lease: to rent a car for a long time. Often, you can buy the car in the end.

Lien contract: a document that shows the car is yours and who financed it

Lien recording fee: money that you pay the Motor Vehicle Administration to record that your car was financed

Make of a car: the company that makes the car—such as Ford or General Motors

Manufacturer's Suggested Retail Price (MSRP): the price the car maker suggests you pay. You may negotiate this price.

Mark-up: the amount of money the dealer adds to the price of the car after the car comes from the factory

Mileage: the number of miles the car has been driven

Model: the style of car—for example, Ford Taurus station wagon or Toyota Celica GT

Model year: the 12-month period when a new model is sold—usually starting in September

"No-claim letter": a letter from your car insurance company that shows you are a safe driver

Odometer: the meter that shows how many miles have been driven

Registration: listing your car with the state

Single-price policy: a policy that sets the price for a car. You cannot bargain to lower the price.

Sports utitility vehicle: a large family car, with extra room in the bank. This car does not have a trunk.

Sunroof: a window in the car's roof

SUV: (see sports utitility vehicle).

Test drive: a chance to drive the car before you buy it

Title: a document that says who owns the car

Trade in (a car): sell an older car in order to buy a new one

Minivan. a large car, usually for transporting small groups of people.

Warranty: a guarantee that your car will work. If it doesn't, you can get it repaired for a discount or for free.

___Finding Work___

Ana Maria Castillo

222 Rockcreek Road, Arlington, VA 22052
703/999-2345   amcastillo@xyz.com

OBJECTIVE

To develop and implement training programs.

EDUCATION

M.A. Linguistics. University of Buenos Aires, Argentina, 1985.
B.A. Spanish Literature. University of Buenos Aires, Argentina, 1983.

WORK EXPERIENCE

9/95–present. U.S. Agency for International Development, American Embassy, Buenos Aires, Argentina. Training Coordinator.

- Developed a training program for staff development, using resources from the Mission and developing countries.
- Design and execute workshops on subjects such as management and interpersonal communication.

8/90–6/95. The American School, Buenos Aires, Argentina.
Spanish Program Coordinator.

- Developed pre-kindergarten through 4th grade curricula for children in Argentina and developing countries.
- Trained incoming Spanish teachers.

LANGUAGES

Native Spanish; fluent English; working knowledge of French.

REFERENCES AVAILABLE UPON REQUEST

Sample Cover Letter

May 8, 2005

Dr. Steven Smith, Director
Training Services of America
123 Apple Street, NW
Washington, DC 20000

Dear Dr. Smith:

I am writing in response to the advertisement in *The Washington Post* on Sunday, April 17, for the position of education specialist. Enclosed is my résumé and a newspaper article describing the Spanish program I developed for the American School in Argentina.

I believe I can contribute to the development of your language program for two reasons. First, my master's degree in linguistics—with a specialty in Spanish dialects—is particularly suitable for the curriculum of your South American locations. Second, I have a proven track record; during the five years I was coordinator and staff trainer at the American School, student enrollment doubled.*

I look forward to speaking with you and will call next week.

Sincerely,

(signature)

Ana Maria Castillo
222 Rockcreek Road
Arlington, VA 22052

Enclosure

Note: The writer tells how and why she will be successful at the job she wants.

Making It Legal

Overview

⊗ You may lose your right to live and work here if you do not follow all the immigration rules and general laws (see the chapter on "Your Legal Status").

Immigrant Status (permanent immigrant status). You are legally authorized to work without restrictions.

Non-immigrant status (non-permanent immigrant status). If your visa allows you to work, you may live and work here only until the expiration date on your I-94 card. Be sure to notify the United States Citizenship and Immigration Service (USCIS) or contact an attorney if your status or residence changes or if you need an extension.

Who may work

Professionals with jobs often may get work authorization for several years. If your employer is willing to be your sponsor, you may be able to become a permanent resident with a "green card" or a "pink card." Talk to an attorney or call the United States Citizenship and Immigration Services (USCIS) if:

- you plan to stay longer than the date on your visa.

- you plan to change jobs—even within the same organization (see chapter on "Your Legal Status").

F-1 Students cannot work the first year. After the first year, you probably can work as long as you follow certain rules; check with the international students' office at your school. In general, you can work:

- on campus—up to 20 hours a week during the school year and full-time during vacations and holidays.
- off campus—up to 20 hours a week during the school year and full-time during vacations and holidays. The international students' office may help you find an employer who is willing to do the paperwork.
- during vacation and after you graduate—for a total of 12 months; the work should be related to your studies.

Spouses. The rules for spouses vary—for example:

- spouses of diplomats. Your country may have an agreement with the U.S. allowing you to work.
- spouses of international organization employees. Your organization may sponsor you for a job.
- other spouses. The rules vary. For example, spouses with E or L visas now are allowed to work; ask an immigration attorney or international student advisor about the procedure for getting work authorization.

Getting USCIS approval to work can take 2–3 months or longer.

Documents you need

Legal documents. The type of documents you need in order to work depends on the visa. Ask your international students' advisor or an immigration attorney.

Proof of qualifications. To prove that you are qualified, bring:

- translated diplomas/transcripts.
- training certificates from vocational-technical training programs.
- occupational licenses. Some professions need state licenses. To get the license, you need to take an exam. Contact the state licensing board.
- letters of recommendation from past employers explaining what you did and how well you did it.
- samples of your work—for example
  - books or pamphlets about you or that you have written.
  - your portfolio, if you are an artist, illustrator, or decorator.
- copies of any awards and honors you have received.

Looking for a Job

How to look

1. Complete the necessary legal forms.

2. Write your résumé and get samples of your work.

Show your portfolio and résumé to someone who is familiar with American hiring culture.

3. Get job counseling if necessary.

4. Look into job opportunities in your area.

See section on "Job counseling services" in this chapter.

5. Practice interviewing.

Ask someone familiar with American culture to play the role of the interviewer. The practice interview will help you understand the expectations of an American interviewer.

6. Call a possible employer.

You might say, "Hello, my name is Ana Maria Castillo. I am calling in response to the ad for a Spanish translator. Is the job still available? How can I apply?"

7. Send a cover letter and your résumé.

8. Go in for interviews.

Where to look

Want ads. Read the "Help Wanted" ads in:

- the classified section of the newspaper every Sunday.
- the "Professional Opportunities" listing in the business section of the newspaper.

Employers. Find out which companies may have the kinds of jobs you want. Look in the Yellow Pages directory, search on-line, or go to the library. Many cities have books listing the most popular kinds of jobs and the companies that use professionals in those jobs. Ask each company if it:

- has the kind of job you want.
- is hiring or plans to hire soon.

If the answer is "yes," ask for an interview.

Internet. More and more companies are using the Internet for hiring new workers. Use the "Chapter Information" (Appendix B) to find job sites or just put in the word "jobs" and the name of your profession to find a good site.

Some companies may ask you to fill out an on-line form. Fill out the form honestly; if you have the skills the company is looking for, include them on the form. Americans expect you to include every skill you know you have; especially do not leave out any management experiences.

Note: The form is just a first step. The employer will look over all the forms

and choose whom to interview. Often, employers interview two or three people, then offer the job to only one of them. Even if you are chosen for an interview, you still may not get the job.

Networking. Talk to as many people as possible about your job interests and keep a list of possible contacts. Talk to friends, relatives, business associates, and neighbors.

Associations. If you join an association or professional organization, you will meet others in the same profession. Look in *The Encyclopedia of Associations* at the library for a list of associations. Call the main office of the association you want to join and ask for the number of the local branch near you.

Most associations have:

- meetings about once a month.
- conventions with people from all over the country.
- training workshops where you can learn more about your field.

Many companies expect you to send your résumé:

- by fax. If you do not have a fax machine, use a private service—such as Mail Boxes, Etc.
- electronically. You also may need a different résumé for companies that scan electronically for certain key words.

If possible, get an e-mail address and search for jobs on the Internet. Some career counselors estimate that more than one-half of the job openings are on the Internet. If you do not know how to use the Internet, you may:

- ask a career counselor for help.
- look up an Internet service that explains what to do.

Note: You may access the Internet at most libraries and many printing shops, such as Kinko's.

International groups. You may get help in finding a job from an organization or center such as "The China Human Resources Group" or the "The Japan-America Society" (see "Organizations of Special Interest to Internationals/Chapter Information" in the Appendix). Look in the business section of the White Pages; find all the organizations that start with the name of your country.

Job counseling services

Schools and colleges. Vocational schools, community colleges, and universities usually have a job counseling program, placement office, or career center. Also, talk to a counselor in the international students' office. Generally, colleges provide free job services to their students, including:

- self-assessment testing for help in planning your career.
- a career reference library with books that explain how to look for a job and what kinds of jobs you can get.
- job listings of government agencies and private companies with available job positions.
- help in writing your résumé. Some career centers send résumés out to possible employers.
- on-campus recruitment programs. Employers visit the campus and talk to students.

The Continuing Education or Adult Education Department of many colleges also offers classes for people who want to find a job or start a career. These classes include:

- résumé writing.
- finding the best career for you.
- improving job skills.

State and county employment service offices. Some services are free; others may cost up to $40 for one counseling session or up to $20 for a group session.

Private employment agencies. These agencies interview you and help you find a job. There is usually no fee to you—just to the company that hires you.

Private counseling companies. These companies test your skills and help you decide which career is best. Their programs may cost $1,000 or more.

Your résumé

Your résumé (see first page of this chapter) should include:

- your objective, or the kind of job you want.
- your name, address, email address, and phone number.
- jobs you have had in the past. Include every relevant job you have had, how long you worked there, where the job was, and what you did (your duties). Try not to have time gaps, or holes, in your résumé; make sure every year is included. If

You can find books on specific careers, methods of finding a job, writing résumés, and interviewing at the public library. Most bookstores also have books for the local area.

you skip a year or two, the interviewer probably will ask you to explain.

- your education. Include undergraduate and graduate degrees and special training classes that show you can do the job.
- special skills, such as languages you speak or experience you have had with computer programs. However, do not say you are "an expert" if you are still beginning to learn the skill; if the interviewer starts to ask you questions about it, you might be embarrassed.
- names, dates, and publishers of any articles or books you have written, even in another language.
- references. Ask first if the person will agree to be a reference. You may write references (names and telephone numbers) on the résumé, or simply write "References available upon request."
- names of professional organizations you belong to.

Tip: Be sure to include and explain any jobs you have had as a manager of a project or facility; you will be more likely to get a responsible job if you have had the experience.

 Your résumé should be no longer than two pages.

The Interview

Getting ready

Learn as much as you can about the job before the interview.

- Look up the company on the Internet.
- Prepare questions to ask the interviewer. These questions
  - help you learn more about the job.
  - show the interviewer you are interested.
- Review your own skills and how they will help you do the job.
- Practice the interview. Find a professional or an American friend to help you prepare.

 Be on time! You may be a few minutes early, but never be late!

When you go to the interview, bring your résumé. Even if you have already sent your résumé to the interviewer, bring it along; the interviewer may not have it handy. Also bring letters of recommendation, samples of your work, and copies of any awards and honors (see "Documents you need" in this chapter.

Getting a job is hard—especially for someone from another country. A professional career counselor will help you understand what to do and what to expect. For example, some counselors will interview you for practice so you feel comfortable with American ways. Most professionals also look over your résumé and make suggestions. This help is important because the American procedures and customs may be very different from those in your country.

Do not give the references to the employer unless she or he asks for them.

How to interview

1. **Prepare for the interview.**

See "Getting Ready" in this section.

2. **Be on time for the interview—better 5-10 minutes early than late.**

3. **Introduce yourself when you walk in. Shake the interviewer's hand.**

4. **Let the interviewer decide when to start talking about the job.**

Some interviewers like to start by talking about popular subjects—such as the weather, current events, sports, or international affairs.

5. **Answer the interviewer's questions directly.**

Explain why you want the job and why you will be good at it.

4. **Ask questions.**

For example, for a job as a translator you might ask, "How long is a typical translation project? Who are your typical clients?"

5. **Thank the interviewer for taking the time to see you.**

Ask when you may call to find out if you got the job.

6. **Send a thank-you letter to the interviewer.**

Tell why you can do a good job.

? ***May I ask questions about money?*** It is not impolite to ask what the pay will be; but do not negotiate at this time. Wait until the employer offers you the job.

Staying Active

If you cannot find a job, you may stay active by:

- taking adult education classes (see chapters on "Making Friends" and "Colleges and Universities").
- working as a volunteer. Doing volunteer work is an important first step. If possible, find a job that is related to your field; for example, if you were a doctor or nurse at home, volunteer in a hospital or other medical facility.

After you have volunteered in one place for 2-3 months, ask for a reference letter explaining what you did and how well you did your job. This letter may convince an employer that you are a good worker—even if the job you did is not related to your profession.

To find information on volunteer jobs, check your local newspapers (see chapter on "Making Friends").

Words to Know

Association: a group of people who have the same interests or do the same kind of work

Career center: a place at school that has information and people to show you how to look for a job

Cover letter: a letter that you send with your résumé to apply for a job. The letter explains the details of your résumé.

Employment agency: a company that helps you find a job

Interview: a formal meeting between you and the person or company representative you want to work for

Letters of recommendation: letters from past employers stating how well you did on the job

Local branch: a small office of an organization. The branch is in a different place from the main office.

Networking: meeting and talking to people who do the same kind of work

Occupational license: a certificate from the government that says you are qualified to do a special job

Portfolio: examples of your drawings or photographs of your work, professional articles you have written or that others have written about you

Recruitment programs: programs in which employers visit a school and interview people for jobs

Reference: a person who can recommend you for a job—usually someone who has been your manager or employer

Résumé: a CV; a document that describes your education, jobs, and qualifications (see first page of this chapter)

Self-assessment test: a test that helps you find out what jobs you can do well

Special interest group: a group of people with common interests—such as the environment or international relations

Transcript: a printed official copy of your educational record—the courses you took, and your grades

United States Citizenship and Immigration Services (USCIS): a division of the Department of Homeland Security. The USCIS has responsibility for immigrant and non-immigrant visas, procedures for coming into the U.S., working permits for international residents, and financial benefits for immigrants.

Vocational school: a school that gives training in practical skills—for example, carpentry or electrical work

Want ads: job advertisements in the classified section of the newspaper

Work authorization: official permission for you to work for pay

Workshop: an educational meeting—usually lasting a day or less

Your Children

Your Young Child

Day care International

3425 Franklin Avenue
Falls Church, VA 22134
(703) 437-8900

Child

Name Jung Kwon **Nickname** John

Sex M **Birthday** 7/24/05 **Home Phone** 703/010-4124

Father's Name Ho Young **Work Phone** 202/000-8100

Mother's Name In-Ae **Work Phone** 703/000-2301

Emergency Information

Name of Child's Physician: Dr. David Miller

Phone: 703/371-5161

Name of contact persons if parents cannot be reached (2 names)

(1) **Name:** Peter Kwon **Phone** 703-001-5117

(2) **Name:** Tae Sun Lee **Phone** 703-001-8988

Persons authorized to pick up child:

Mother, Father, Peter Kwon, Tae Sun Lee

Persons not authorized to visit or pick up child:

Allergies: Chocolate, Bee Stings

Babysitters

Where to look

Other parents. Ask your child's day care or nursery school if you can post a note on the bulletin board. Often, other parents will share their baby-sitter with you.

Hospital and university nursing schools. Call the school's main office or the Dean's office.

Nearby universities. Ask for the career center or student job office.

Newspaper ads. Your local newspaper probably has ads for baby-sitters.

Babysitter agencies. These may cost more, but agencies can get good sitters right away. Look in the Yellow Pages under "Babysitters."

 First call the babysitters and get the names of three or more references. Call all the references and ask:

- How long did this babysitter work for you?
- Were you satisfied?
- What were the babysitter's strengths?
- What were the weaknesses?

Listen carefully. Do not be afraid to ask more questions. Ask the babysitter

to meet you and your child in your home.

Nannies/Au Pairs

Overview

Nannies. A nanny takes care of your children all day and does light house-work for the children such as washing their clothes or cleaning up their rooms. Usually, a nanny is an experi-enced professional with special train-ing. Some nannies live with the child's family ("live-ins"); others have their own home ("live-outs").

Au pairs. An au pair is usually a student from another country who comes to the U.S. for one year. Most au pairs live with the child's family.

Au pairs work about 45 hours per week. They take care of the children and do light housework. The hours may be flexible, depending on what you need.

How to find nannies/ au pairs

Agencies. Professional agencies will find you a nanny or au pair for a fee. Most check work experience, personal references, child-care experience,

When you leave, give the babysitter, nanny, or au pair:

- the name of the child's doctor.
- the name of your health insurance company and your policy number.
- the telephone number where you can be reached.
- a neighbor's name and phone number
- the address of your house

child-care training, and first-aid training. Some agencies also check criminal and medical records; check to be sure. Also call the American Institute for Foreign Study (AIFS).

Other agencies have lists of nannies—and tips on interviewing and hiring. Be sure you have enough names of nannies to choose from. The cost is much less.

Nanny schools. You may get lists of nannies looking for jobs by asking nanny schools for a list of their graduates.

The Internet. Most nanny agencies are on the Internet. Look for "Nanny Agencies."

Interviews and references. The candidates for your nanny job will come to your house for the interview. Ask for at least three references if you have not gone through an agency (see section on "Babysitters" in this chapter).

 Write out an agreement with the candidate, listing details such as the salary, number of hours, and the kind of jobs you expect the nanny or au pair to do.

 Make sure the person you hire has legal permission to work in the U.S. Remember: Hiring illegal aliens in the U.S. is a crime.

Website services are about $250-$300. If you use an agency, you will pay placement fees. For example, you may pay a registration fee of about $50-$250 to see the names on the agency's list. If the agency finds a nanny, you probably will pay the agency $1400-$2500.

Nanny. You pay the nanny a salary each week. You also pay some taxes for the nanny and possibly part of her health insurance. An agency will help you calculate these costs.

Au pair. When you hire an au pair, you pay:

- insurance fees.
- airfare to the U.S. and back.
- a weekly salary (usually less than the salary of a nanny).
- tuition for classes and spending money.

Preschools

Day care centers. Most provide all-day, all-year care. Children may go to most day care centers at any age. Look in the Yellow Pages directory under "Day Care," "Nurseries," or "Child Care."

Nursery schools. Many have half-day programs; most are closed during the summer. Often, nursery schools accept children who are:

- two years or older.

You may send your child to a co-operative (co-op). Co-ops are centers and schools where parents share the work. In most co-ops, parents help the teacher in the classroom 1-2 times a month. Co-ops often cost less than other centers or schools.

- ready for school. Children must be ready to leave home for a short while and play in the same room with others.
- toilet-trained.

Look in the Yellow Pages directory under "Schools/Preschools & Kindergarten," "Nurseries," or "Child Care."

What to look for

Go to the school or center without an appointment to see what it is like on an average day.

You may get information about day care centers and nursery schools from:

- educational counselors.
- guidebooks in local bookstores.
- the National Association for the Education of Young Children (NAEYC), which publishes pamphlets explaining how to choose good care for your child. It also lists schools and centers that meet its high standards.
- people you know.

The staff's training.

- The director should have at least two years of college classes in Early Childhood Education (ECE) and 1–5 years of experience in a child-care center.
- The teachers should have some college training in early childhood education and a year's experience.

The staff's attitude. Do they like children?

The program. Look for a balanced program—for example, a balance between:

- indoor and outdoor play.
- playing alone, in a group, and with a teacher.
- playing and working, or learning.

Multilingual. Some schools have staff that speak two or more languages. To find the name and number of these schools, look in the Yellow Pages directory under "Schools."

Montessori schools often have many educational toys and games, with more free play than group activities. Each child is supposed to learn at his or her own pace. The Montessori philosophy is popular in the U.S. and in Europe; but any school can say it is "Montessori." To be sure a school really uses the Montessori methods, check the classroom yourself or call the Montessori Institute.

The other children. Find out their:

- ages. Some centers have a wide range. Be sure there is enough care for each age group.
- backgrounds. Are there other children from different countries?

Relationship with parents. Check to see if:

- you may visit anytime.
- there are parent-teacher conferences.
- you receive daily or weekly reports with details that tell what your child is eating and how he or she is behaving.
- the staff welcomes suggestions from parents.

Space and equipment. Look around the whole center, inside and outside. Be sure:

- the center is clean and cheerful.
- the equipment and toys are safe. Toys for young children should be washed daily.
- the outdoor play area is a large, fenced space.

Place. If the school or center is far away, make sure:

- the center will pick up your child for an extra fee.
- some of the parents live near you and will car pool.

Meals and snacks. Be sure the food is healthful. If your child cannot eat certain foods, find out what the center will give him or her instead.

Your child's reaction. See how your child likes the school when you visit.

Nursery schools

Calendar. Usually, the school year begins in September and ends in early June.

Each nursery school has different hours; but most run from 9 am–12 noon. Often, you may choose to send your child two days, three days, or five days a week. Some schools have full-day programs (7 am–6 pm) for working parents.

Class size. Usually, each class has about 14–15 students.

Who is accepted. Generally, nursery schools accept only children who are ready for school. Some nursery schools also:

- interview the child.
- give an Intelligence Quotient (IQ) test.
- require that the child speak or understand English.

Time: Many nursery schools and day care centers have a waiting list. Usually, they take the child who is first on the list. With some schools and centers, you may need to apply a year or more ahead of time.

Licensing. Good programs are usually licensed. To find out if a school is licensed, call the school and ask if it is licensed.

If you are already in the U.S., start looking for a nursery school about a year in advance—in September or October of the year before. Most day care centers accept children any time.

How to apply

1. **Call the school to make an appointment for a visit.**

Ask if you can bring your child.

2. **Visit the school.**

Talk to the director or principal. Take a look around.

3. **Fill out an application form.**

Send it to the school, along with the application fee.

4. **Put down the names of some references if necessary.**

Get the names of people who know you or your child. Call your references and ask if you may use their names.

5. **Have your doctor sign the school's health forms.**

6. **Take your child to the school for an IQ test if necessary.**

Most schools do not require this test.

Day care

Calendar. Day care centers operate either all year round or during the school year (from September to June).

Many day care centers are open five days a week. Some centers, or "day-out" programs, let you leave your child for just one or two mornings a week.

A few day care centers have "latch-key" programs; that is, you may leave your child for an hour or two almost any time you like. "Latchkey" programs cost more per hour than regular, full-day programs.

The full-time hours are usually 7 am–6:30 pm. Half-day programs are usually 9 am–1 pm.

Adult/child ratio. The National Association for the Education of Young Children recommends that all groups of children have at least two adults for each group, with the following maximum sizes for groups:

- 0–2 years old. 6-8 children.
- 2–3 years old. 10-14 children.
- 4–5 years old. 16–20 children.

Licensing. In some cities, the license is voluntary; some good schools may not apply for the license. In other cities, *all* good centers are licensed. Call the school and ask if it is licensed.

Special Needs

Most cities have services that test children for delays, or slow growth, in:

- speech/language, gross motor skills.
- audio/visual skills.
- psychological profiles.

Ask your pediatrician for a program in the area where you live.

Family Activities

Story-time

The library is one of the best places to meet other parents and have fun with your child. Almost all public libraries have story-time activities for children of all ages. For example, some libraries have a special story hour for babies less than one year old; for many parents, meeting each other is the most important part of the activity. Public libraries are run by the city or the county; all activities are usually free.

For a list of public libraries, look up "Libraries" in the City or County government section of the White Pages directory. You may go to any public library for these activities—even those in other counties or cities. Call and ask about programs for the whole city or county; often, one library in the system specializes in young children.

Parent/child classes

Classes run by the city or county are often low-cost (under $50) or free. Private classes in doctors' offices or in play centers are generally more—usually about $16-$20 a session.

Infants. All major cities have classes for parents of babies up to 12 months of age. With most classes, you may bring your baby. These classes generally give parents the chance to:

- get professional advice on the everyday growth of their children. For example, common topics are: finding a good doctor, starting new foods, and managing a crying baby. Look for a class run by a social worker or other professional with special training in infant care.
- meet and talk to other parents. Many times, the parents in a class continue to meet on their own long after the class is over.

You may find parenting classes in:

- the Adult Education Department of your school system. Look under "Schools/Adult Education" in the City or County government section of the White Pages directory.

- the Recreation Department of your City or County. These classes are generally in community centers around town. Look under "Recreation (Department of) in the City or County government section of the White Pages directory.
- doctors' offices and hospitals. Ask your pediatrician if he or she knows of any classes in the area; also call a hospital near you and ask. Look in the Yellow Pages under "Hospitals."
- play centers such as Gymboree Play Programs. Look in the mall where you shop or find the number in the Business section of the White Pages directory.
- the YMCA and YWCA. Look in the Business Section of the White Pages directory for your local number.

Toddlers (2-3 years old) and pre-school (4-5 years old). Children and their parents may go to classes with all kinds of activities—including art, music, and exercise. In addition to the Recreation Department and play centers, ask the YMCA and YWCA. Along with exercise and gym classes, the "Y" often has swimming classes for beginners. The cost is usually $35–$75.

Playgrounds

Most neighborhoods have playgrounds where parents sit around, watch their children, and make friends. Find the one nearest you; it is a wonderful way to meet your neighbors and find out more about programs for young children in your area.

Words to Know

Agency: an organization that will find a nanny or au pair for a fee

Application fee: money you pay to apply to a school

Audio/visual skills: (a child's) ability to see, hear, and speak well

Au pair: a person from another country who lives with your family and takes care of your child

Babysitter: a person who takes care of your child part-time or once in a while. The child may be of any age.

Bulletin board: a board in a public place where you can put a message

Car pool: a group of people who go in the same car. Workers may "car pool" to the office or parents may "car pool" their children to school.

Cooperative (co-op): a day care center or school where parents share the work in the classroom and often pay less in tuition than other nursery schools

Day care center: a center where small children stay while their parents work

"Day out": a day care center where you leave your child for just a few mornings a week

Gross motor skills: a child's ability to make large movements—such as running, throwing a ball, or jumping

Illegal alien: a foreigner who does not have government permission to be in the U.S.

Infants: a very young baby—usually until 10–12 months old

Intelligence Quotient (IQ) test: a test that measures how smart someone is

"Latchkey" program: a program that lets you leave your child for an hour or two—before or after school

License: a document that shows the center is approved by the government

Montessori (school): a school where children spend a lot of time playing and exploring on their own

Nanny: a person who takes care of your child all day in your home

Nursery school: a school where very young children go, usually for a half day

Parent-teacher conference: a meeting between the parent and the teacher

Preschool: a school for children who are younger than five years old

Psychological profile: a test that shows how someone acts and feels

Reference: a person you call to find out someone's ability to do a job

Social worker: a person with professional training in family matters

Toddlers: usually children who are 18 months–3 years old

Toilet-trained: able to use the toilet; not needing diapers anymore

Waiting list: a list of people who want to join a program or school

Your Older Child

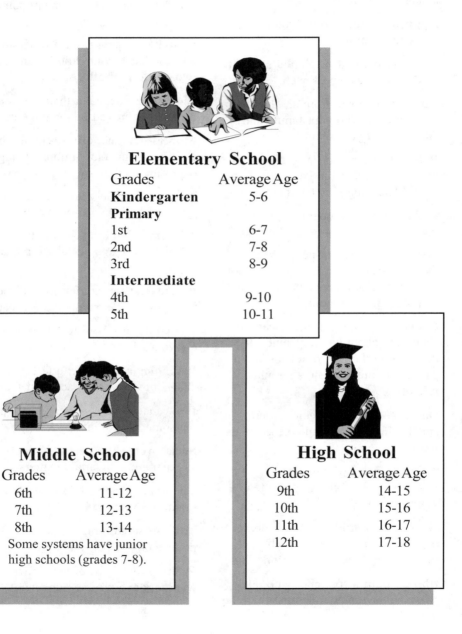

Elementary School

Grades	Average Age
Kindergarten	5-6
Primary	
1st	6-7
2nd	7-8
3rd	8-9
Intermediate	
4th	9-10
5th	10-11

Middle School

Grades	Average Age
6th	11-12
7th	12-13
8th	13-14

Some systems have junior high schools (grades 7-8).

High School

Grades	Average Age
9th	14-15
10th	15-16
11th	16-17
12th	17-18

The School System

Overview

Usually, children go to school from the ages of 5-6 through 17-18. At the end of the school year, most children move up from one grade to the next.

In most schools, the children get report cards 2–4 times during the year. The report cards tell if the child is passing—that is, doing well enough to move up to the next grade. You, the parent, must sign this card.

Calendar

Most schools begin in late August or early September and end in the middle of June. During the school year, the schools are closed for 1½–2 weeks in the winter—from the middle or end of December until January 2nd. Schools are also closed for one week in the spring, around Easter time, and on most national holidays.

Hours

Each school has different hours. The day starts between 7:30–9 am and ends between 1:30–3:30 pm. Students—except those in half-day kindergarten—often eat lunch at school; in a few schools, children may go home to eat and come back again.

Tip: Many schools have after-school care for children with working parents.

Public Schools

The county or city manages the public schools. These schools are free and accept all children. To talk to someone at the school, call the "Information" number; look in the county or city section of the White Pages directory under "Schools." To get a list of private (non-government) schools, look in the Yellow Pages directory under "Schools."

Finding a school

In general, children go to the public school in the neighborhood where they live. First find out which public school is best for your child. Then find a home in the neighborhood for that school.

To find a good school, talk to:

- a relocation center or service.
- a real estate agent.
- an educational counselor (see section on "Tutors/Counselors" in this chapter).

Your child may be able to go to some special programs (see section on "Academic programs" in this chapter).

Other places to look are:

- local bookstores
- the Hello! America publication *"Choosing Elementary and Secondary Schools: Questions Parents Need to Ask."* This booklet has a checklist for comparing schools and a section with resources for more research.

- the Internet. For example, the local Chamber of Commerce often lists the Scholastic Achievement Test (SAT) or other standardized test scores for each school in the area.

Academic programs

Levels of instruction. College-bound students must complete certain courses—such as a foreign language, algebra and geometry, and physics or biology.

Often, you can tell the level of instruction by looking at:

- College Admissions Tests such as
  - SAT or American College Testing (ACT) scores. Find out the school's scores from the guidance office.
- the percentage of students going to college and the colleges they attend.
- the kinds of courses offered. Most high schools have honors and Advanced Placement (AP) classes.

International Baccalaureate (IB). The IB program prepares students for the International Baccalaureate exam. Ask the school's guidance office if there is an IB program and how your child can get in.

Special-interest schools. Many cities and counties have schools for children with special interests or talents in subjects such as foreign languages, computers, math, science, or the arts.

English as a Second Language (ESL) programs. In general, public schools have good ESL programs.

Children from non-English-speaking countries usually take an English test before they start school so they can be enrolled in an ESL program at their level. Call to find out how to register.

Special needs. To find out about programs for the handicapped or learning disabled, talk to the principal or director of your child's school ahead of time.

If your child has trouble reading, writing, or paying attention, see if he or she can be tested for a disability. Ask:

- the principal or director.
- a private counselor.
- a learning center.

To contact other parents of special-needs children, contact the Council for Exceptional Children or the International Dyslexia Association.

Gifted and Talented. Many school systems have enrichment programs or programs for gifted and talented elementary-school students. Generally, the school systems use academic tests and teacher recommendations to choose the children for these programs. To contact other parents with gifted and talented children, contact the Gifted Child Society.

Registering your child

Non-English records must be officially translated. Some schools will translate these records for free. Bring:

- medical records, or proof that your child has had all the required vaccinations (shots) and a physical exam. Often, the school can tell you where to go for free vaccinations and exams.

- school records from the your home country.
- birth certificate or passport.
- proof of residency (either a utility bill or a document showing you rent or own a home in the area).

How to register

1. **Call up the school's international student office or the "Information" number for your school system.**

Make an appointment to register your child. Find out what documents you need.

2. **Have your child tested.**

When you go to the international student office, your child may take a test in English and, sometimes, math. This test will help the teachers decide your child's program (see "Academic placement" on this page).

3. **Call up the school your child will attend.**

Ask about the orientation session so you can meet the principal and find out more about the school.

4. **Find out about open houses.**

Many schools have an "open house," or a day to meet with all parents.

Transportation

If you do not live near the school, a school bus may take your child. Ask for a bus schedule; find out if the school has "activity buses" for after-school programs or sports. Generally, public school buses are free.

Academic placement

Be sure your child is in the right class. For example, if your child had a different math program in your home country, he or she may be placed in remedial math classes (classes for children who have trouble learning), when instead of a remedial class, your child might just need to catch up with the aid of a tutor (see section on "Tutors/Counselors" in this chapter).

The Parent-Teacher Association (PTA)

The Parent-Teacher Association helps you become more involved in your child's school. All parents are encouraged to come to the meetings and join the association. In general, a strong PTA means a better school. For example, the PTA may:

- raise money for school equipment or for field trips.

- talk about school matters with principals and teachers.
- hold meetings where parents get to know each other.

Join the PTA; volunteer your time if you want to meet people.

? *What if my child is not doing well in school?* Make an appointment to talk to the teacher. If you keep trying and cannot get an appointment, speak to the principal. If you still have problems after talking to the teacher, you may want to talk to an educational counselor.

Private Schools

$ Private schools may cost between $2000 (mostly religious schools) and $25,000 a year—with an extra $15,000 for boarding. Most have scholarships.

Kinds of schools

Bilingual schools teach in English and another language. Call your embassy or consulate to find a school with your language.

International schools have children from many different countries— including the U.S.

Religious schools teach religion along with other subjects.

Special schools have programs for children with special needs—such as children who are physically handicapped or learning disabled. Most of these schools also accept children without special needs.

Magnet schools for very good students.

Charter schools or independent public schools.

How to look for a school

1. **Find out if the school is accredited.**

Also find out if the school is a member of a professional organization. To be a member, a school must pass a special review.

2. **Visit the school.**

Make an appointment with the admissions office; ask if you should bring your child. At the school, talk over the program with the head of the school or the admissions director.

3. **Call the school's references.**

The best references are people you know—co-workers, neighbors, or friends. You also may ask the director, during the interview, for the names and telephone numbers of parents whose children attend the school.

? *What if I need help finding the best school?* Educational counselors may be able to help. Many can give you advice about both private or public schools.

Applying for admission

If possible, contact schools a year in advance. You probably will need to send your application and school records by the end of February for enrollment the following school year, in September.

When you apply to a private school, you will need:

- a birth certificate/passport (sometimes required).
- translated school records.
- a health form signed by a doctor. The form comes with the application.
- letters of recommendation from former teachers or people who know your child.
- an application fee.

Tip: Some schools accept only 10%–20% of the students who apply. Many parents apply to several schools at the same time.

Test scores. Some common tests are:

- the Secondary School Admissions Test (SSAT) for grades 5–11. Students take this test in local private schools and in test centers around the world.
- achievement tests for grades 10, 11, and 12. These test skills in subjects such as languages, math, history, and science.
- the Test of English as a Foreign Language (TOEFL). This test is given in many countries. Call the TOEFL office for times and places.

Writing samples in the child's own language. Each school has different requirements.

Getting accepted

Most schools mail you a letter—usually by March or April. If your child is accepted, you probably will need to send part of the tuition at this time.

Tutors/ Counselors

If your child has special needs, call the Council for Exceptional Children.

What they do

Private tutors and centers. Many tutors or centers teach several subjects. Some teach only reading and writing; others teach only math. Tutors may specialize in teaching English as a Second Language (ESL) or in preparing students for tests such as the SAT or SSAT.

Educational consultants. These consultants may:

- help you find the right school for your child.
- help you solve problems your child may be having in school.
- test your child to evaluate
  - his or her academic skills.
  - his or her IQ.
  - the possibility of a learning disability.

What to look for

Most good tutors are certified to teach in the state where they are teaching. Look for a special degree in one of these subjects:

- elementary education or a high school subject, such as math or English.
- English as a Second Language.
- reading, speech and language, or math
- special education (for children with learning or physical disabilities).

Some really good tutors are not certi-fied—particularly tutors for high school students. Be sure that the tutor knows the subject and seems to like and motivate students the same age as yours. Then give it a try!

 Tutors usually charge $35–$75 an hour. In some cities the fees are much higher.

Fun Activities

School clubs

Schools offer clubs for outdoor activities and community services such as Boy Scouts and Girl Scouts; other popular clubs are science, drama, school newspaper, and interna-tional clubs such as the Model U.N.

City/county recreation

 If possible, sign up at least 2 or 3 months beforehand; the most popular classes fill up quickly.

Most county and city recreation departments offer programs for children of all ages—including sports, music, drama, and arts. Call the Recreation Department for the latest programs; to find the number, look under "Recreation" in the county or city government section of your phone book.

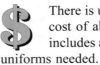 There is usually a one-time cost of about $20–$50, which includes any equipment and uniforms needed.

Junior Sports Leagues

Many counties have sports leagues for children of all ages. Often, businesses in the county pay for the uniforms and other equipment. Parents usually coach the players and help organize the games.

Volunteer programs

Many teenagers work as volunteers after school or during the summer—for example, as helpers in the hospital or readers for the blind. Call a nearby hospital or ask the school about pro-grams that might interest your child.

Words to Know

Academic placement: the right learning level for the point at which the child is learning

Accredited: approved by the govern-ment; meeting certain standards

Achievement tests: tests used by colleges and some private secondary schools for admitting students

Advanced placement (AP) classes: classes that let a student earn college credit while still in high school. You must pass a special test at the end of the course.

Boarding school: an elementary or secondary school where the students live on the campus, away from their homes.

College-bound: going to college

Charter School: charter schools are independent public schools that are not part of the ordinary public-school system. Most charter schools are for pupils from low-income areas or for pupils with special needs and interests. Many charter schools are run by parents or private educational organizations.

Elementary school: a school with a kindergarten and grades 1–5 or 6.

Gifted and talented programs: challenging, or higher-level, programs

Grade: a letter (A, B, C, D, or E) that tells how good the student's work is; also, a school level—such as the first grade, second grade (see first page of this chapter)

Handicapped: having a physical or mental condition, for example, being blind, deaf, or unable to walk.

International Baccalaureate (IB) diploma: a diploma that can be earned in addition to the regular high school diploma. Usually, the IB program is more challenging than most other high school programs. Many foreign colleges and universities accept an IB diploma.

Learning disabled (LD) students: students with special needs—for example, students who have trouble reading, writing, or paying attention

Magnet school: a school for students with special skills and interests

Parent-Teacher Association (PTA): a group for parents and teachers

Private school: a non-public school. Most students pay to attend.

Public school: a school that is paid for by taxpayers and run by the city or county. Public schools are free.

Report card: a record of a student's classes and grades

Secondary school: a middle or high school. Any school with grades 6 or 7 through 12.

Tuition: the cost of an educational program. The tuition does not include other expenses—such as uniforms or books and materials.

Tutor: a teacher who helps one or more students learn a specific subject outside regular classroom time. Students learn from a tutor, in addition to their regular classroom teacher.

Hello! America Publication List

¡Hola Estados Unidos! (Hello! USA in Spanish)

Check our website or call to receive notification of availability.

StaySafe!!

A 16-page booklet for American residents traveling or relocating outside the U.S. Practical tips on protecting yourself, your family, and your possessions in a variety of situations. Appropriate for both relatively safe and high-risk countries. The special section on "Teaching Your Children about Safety" explains how to instill good safety practices to children of any age, without increasing their anxiety. (available in packets of 10)

Choosing Elementary and Secondary Schools

A 32-page booklet for any parent relocating anywhere in the world. This comprehensive booklet contains 20 *Plus One* questions parents need to ask about all educational programs. Advice about what to do and what *not to do* from educators, parents, and students. Addi-tional sections on special education, private day schools, and programs for families moving internationally (available in packets of 10).

Jobs and Careers for International Spouses

For American spouses moving internationally. Provides valuable information on getting a job or finding a satisfying alternative while you are away. The section on cultural differences in the job-search process is a must for anyone planning to look for a job in another country (available in packets of 10).

Pets on the Move

An 8-page booklet for individuals and families relocating with pets—including dogs, cats, birds, and horses. Comprehensive and practical information about transporting your pet safely and helping it adjust to its new home. A special section on international relocation explains rules and regulations you need to know ahead of time (available in packets of 25).

American Customs

A free newsletter about American culture and language

Holidays
Major sports events
Festivals and celebrations around the U.S.
Common idioms and expressions
Tips on everyday living

Visit our web site at: www.hellousa.com

*Hello! America, Inc.*7962 Old Georgetown Road, #B; Bethesda, MD 20814-2475
Tel: 240/497-1088   Fax: 301/215-4171   E-mail: judy@hello-america.com

Higher Education

English as a _Second Language_

What to Learn

 Basic English

 Conversation

 Reading and writing

 Words for work

 Test of English as a Foreign Language (TOEFL)

ac-cent (ak´sent) Accent reduction

How to Learn

 Classes

 Cassettes

 TV

 Phone

 Books

 CD-ROM

 Internet

How to Choose a Program

Program. Think about these questions:

- What do I want to learn? Some institutions offer courses in preparation for the Test of English as a Foreign Language (TOEFL)—along with American culture. All institutions with intensive programs offer courses in everyday conversation, speaking, reading and writing.
- Is my goal to get a job or to study in a college or university?
- Will the school get me ready for the English-language tests I will take?

Quality. How good is the program? First, make sure the school is accredited—that is, approved by a professional organization. Then find out:

- What do the other students think? Ask people who have studied in the U.S. Ask the school for the names of students from your country so that you may call them.
- Who are the teachers? Do they have degrees or certification for teaching English as a Foreign Language (EFL) or English as a Second Language (ESL)? How long have they been teaching?
- Will you be learning at your own level? Does the school give placement tests to see where you should start?
- Do you have a contract that sets the learning goals, so you know
  - what you will learn.
  - how long it will take.
- Will you get college credit for the program (see chapter on "Colleges and Universities")?

- How big are the classes? Does each teacher have 15 students—or 50?
- Does the school offer separate classes for speakers of certain languages—such as Spanish, Korean, and Vietnamese?

Intensity. Find out how many:

- weeks or months the program lasts.
- hours of classes you must take.
- hours of homework you will have each week.

Location. If you already have a home in the U.S., find a school you can get to easily—either by bus, subway, or car. If you are coming for an intensive program, ask:

- Is the school in a big city or a small town? Which do you like best?
- Will you like the weather?

Cost. In general, public schools do not cost as much as private schools. Ask:

- How much will I pay for each hour of class?
- When must I pay?

Intensive Courses (F-1 Visas)

With intensive English programs, you study 20 hours or more per week. Often, these programs can help you get an F-1 visa. You also can take an intensive program if you come to the U.S. with another type of visa—for example, as a family member of a student or employee.

What to look for

Also think about the following:

Extra-curricular activities. Will you be able to find non-academic activities you are interested in? Ask:

- Can I play the sports I like—such as tennis, basketball, or soccer?
- Are there classes or clubs for the arts—such as photography or painting, theater, or music?
- Is there a religious organization I can join?

Time. Some schools have monthly programs; others offer courses for 4-5 month semesters.

Services. Can the school give me personal help? You may want to get advice about careers and jobs in the U.S. Ask if the school can help you:

- understand immigration forms and rules.
- find a place to live.
- understand the tax rules (see chapter on "Paying Your Taxes").
- understand the health insurance program the institution offers.

Dormitories. Many schools have dormitories for their students. If not, find out where most international students live and how much these apartments cost. Also find out if the school will help you find a roommate if you want one.

Applying

You can find out more about English-language schools from:

- travel agents.
- the Internet. Many language schools are on the Web.
- the schools themselves. Call the U.S. Consulate or Embassy to find out if someone from the school will be visiting your country (see "Applying/Colleges and Universities").

To find out more about how to apply, see "Colleges and Universities."

Part-time Courses

Part-time courses have less than 20 hours a week of study. Most large metropolitan areas have many programs. Look in the Yellow Pages directory under "Language Schools."

The immigration laws are strict. Be sure you know and obey them. Tell your foreign student advisor when you are changing your address, course of study, or when you are leaving the U.S.

Do not stay longer in the U.S. than your visa allows or you may not be able to come back for 10 years or more.

If you enter the U.S. with an I-20 document from a specific language school, you must attend that school for a specified amount of time.

For more information about immigration rules see "How to avoid common problems/Your Legal Status."

Places to learn

Community Colleges. You may take ESL classes at a community college for:

- credit. Credit courses count toward a college degree. These courses are in a college's regular catalog. You usually need to be enrolled at the community college in order to take them.
- non-credit. These courses do not count toward a degree; but often you get a certificate, which may help you get a job. These courses are listed in the "Continuing Education" or "Adult Education" catalog. You do not need to be accepted into the university to take them.

Courses at community colleges cost less for residents of the county or city than for non-residents. Usually, you are a resident if you have lived in the county or city for more than 6 months or a year. In some counties and cities, you are a resident only if you have paid taxes in that time period. Students here on an F–1 or F–2 visa are usually not considered residents—even if they have been in the U.S. a long time.

Public schools. Call your local high school or look for information on these courses at the library. You will not get college credit for these courses.

Private language schools. Look in the Yellow Pages directory under "Language Schools."

Note: A few large schools have networks all over the world. You may be able to start learning English in your home country and then continue the same program after you get to the U.S.

Home study. You may find many of the following materials in libraries, bookstores (especially travel and foreign-language bookstores), and on the Internet:

- books.
- audio cassettes. If you read English but want to improve your listening skills, try "books on tape." You can listen to these books at home or in the car.
- videos. One interesting way to improve your English is to watch movies or operas in your own language and read the English subtitles.
- CD-ROMs.

Tip: Many schools offer online courses.

You also may learn from:

- a course by phone from one of the private language schools. You will get books and other materials by mail. Then you have a lesson with the teacher on the phone.
- TV courses—usually on cable. Call the community colleges, 4-year colleges, and universities in your area.
- Internet courses. You may take:
  - just one or two courses.
  - all the courses for a B.A., B.S., and many graduate degrees. You also may find more informal classes, such as a chat room where you exchange messages with a native English speaker. The chat program gives you lesson plans or suggested topics.

- individual (private) lessons. Some private schools have instructors who come to the students' homes for an extra fee. Usually, you will pay the cost of a private, or individual, lesson, plus the instructor's traveling time.

Advanced English programs

The following advanced courses are commonly available.

Vocabulary—idioms, common expressions, and the meaning of word parts such as "pre" and "post."

Reading and writing—reading more quickly, organizing and outlining, punctuating and spelling.

Public speaking—speaking more clearly in formal or business situations—such as in business meetings or group presentations.

Skills for the workplace (also called English for Specific Purposes, or ESP)—words used for a specific subject or job—such as law, business, computers, economics, or medicine. You may take these classes privately or in a group. Other schools teach work skills along with English—for example, accounting, typing, and word processing on the computer.

Accent reduction—speaking in a way that Americans can understand more easily. Look for a program with:

- qualified teachers.
- a test to find out your accent level.
- small classes (no more than 5–10 students in a class).
- books, cassettes, or other materials to take home.

- 3 to 5 or more class hours a week.

Advanced TOEFL—giving speeches, writing research papers and business letters.

English-Language Tests

Test of English as a Second Language (TOEFL)

You must take the TOEFL to get into most college programs or to get a job that requires good English skills. The same schools that teach EFL or ESL usually have TOEFL courses. Test preparation companies also may help.

Test centers. You may take the TOEFL at test centers around the world and in major U.S. cities. To get a free list of these centers, call the TOEFL office and ask for the TOEFL *Bulletin of Information* (see "English As A Second Language/Chapter Information" in Appendix B).

You will take the TOEFL on the computer, so you will get your scores right after you finish. You may get a schedule from the center where you want to take the test.

Test of English for International Communication (TOEIC)

Many businesses use the TOEIC to see how well you use English in everyday or business situations. Call International Communication Incorporated for more information on the schedule and cost.

Words to Know

Accent reduction: changing the way you speak so that others can understand what you say more easily

Accredited: approved by a professional organization, such as the Teachers of English to Speakers of Other Languages (TESOL). Accredited schools meet the standards set by the organization.

Certificate: a document that you get for finishing a class or course of study

Chat room: an Internet site that lets you exchange messages with a native English speaker.

Community college: a public, 2-year college that offers an Associate (A.A.) degree (see chapter on "Colleges and Universities")

Conversational English: a class where you practice speaking—rather than reading and writing

Credit: a unit of academic study in a degree program

Dormitories: rooms in which students live. Usually, the dormitories are on campus.

English for Specific Purposes (ESP): a program that teaches words used for a specific subject or job—such as law, business, computers, or medicine

English as a Foreign Language (EFL) and English as a Second Language (ESL): Both programs teach the same skills. EFL classes are for foreign students who will return to their home country; ESL classes are for immigrants. Both types of students may be in each class.

Intensive class: a class with more than 20 hours of study per week

Non-credit: courses that do not count toward a college or university degree

Placement test: a test that helps the college determine the right level of instruction for you. If you do well, you will be placed in an advanced class.

Private institution: an institution that gets its money from tuition and private individuals and organizations—rather than the government

Public institution: an institution that gets a lot of money directly from the government. For example, community colleges get most of their money from the county government.

Resident (of a city or county): a person who has lived in the city or county for 6 months or a year—depending on the city or county. Some cities and counties also require that you have paid taxes during that time.

Scholarship: money you get to help pay for school

Subtitle: words at the bottom of a movie screen. The subtitles translate the language spoken in the film

TOEFL (Test of English as a Foreign Language): a test of your listening, grammar, reading, vocabulary, and writing skills in English. The TOEFL is mainly for students applying to colleges or universities.

TOEIC (Test of English for International Communication): a test of your English skills in business or everyday situations. The TOEFL is more popular than the TOEIC.

Colleges and Universities

AAR University

In the space below, evaluate a significant experience or achievement that has special meaning for you.

Last summer, I volunteered as a paramedic in the Peruvian partnership program. I chose this program because I thought it would help me decide if I wanted to be a doctor.

Those 6 weeks in Peru changed my life. At first, deep down, I felt that I was "above" the Peruvians I lived and worked with. Then, partway through the summer, I began to treasure their deep caring for me and for each other. I made friends with the neighborhood teenagers, who became closer to me than many of my friends back home. I began to admire my new family because they never argued with each other, even though they were very poor. And I envied the nurses in my clinic because they were so loving toward their patients, even though they knew so little about modern medicine.

When I came home again, my life seemed empty. So I began to choose my friends more carefully, picking out the ones who had the warmth I now longed for. I also started to choose activities that focused on my professional goals and on my desire to help others.

Now I am sure I want to be a doctor—the kind of doctor who makes a difference in her patients' lives. I know I will be a good doctor because I will learn everything I can about modern techniques. But I will also remember the lesson I learned in Peru: Modern techniques aren't enough. To be really good, you have to care.

Overview

Calendar

Colleges and universities offer courses for two semesters each academic year. The fall semester usually begins in late August or early September and ends in December. The spring semester usually begins in January and ends in late May. Some courses are also offered during shorter summer semesters.

Each semester ends in a 1–2-week examination, or exam, period. Vacations include 2–4 weeks in the winter, and one week in the spring (see chapter on "Holidays"). Some colleges have quarters (four sessions per year) or trimesters (three sessions per year).

Credit

Most colleges and universities use the credit system; that is, you get credits for every class you finish successfully. For example, you may get three or four credits for a class that meets for one hour, 3–4 times a week. To graduate from a 4–year, undergraduate institution, you need a minimum of 120 credits, plus laboratory time for many science courses.

At the graduate level, credit requirements depend on the degree and the field you are studying.

Transfers

American students often transfer credits from one college to another. For example, you may want to transfer credits:

- from an accredited college or university in your home country. Contact the admissions office of the U.S. college.
- from one U.S. college to another. Many students study 1–2 years in a college, then transfer to another college. Other students take 1–2 courses in another university—for example during the summer; then they transfer their credits. Contact the international students' office of the college you are now attending.

The immigration laws are strict. Be sure you know and obey them. Tell your student advisor when you are changing your address, or course of study, or when you are leaving the U.S.

Do not stay longer in the U.S. than your visa allows or you may not be able to come back for 10 years or more.

If you enter the U.S. with an I-20 document from a specific college or university, you must attend that school for a specified amount of time.

For more information about immigration rules see "How to avoid common problems/Your Legal Status."

Programs

Undergraduate programs.

Associate of Arts—often called an Associate degree (A.A.). This is a 2-year program used for credit toward a Bachelor degree or as training for certain jobs—such as the job of a secretary, technician, or physical-therapist assistant. The community college is the most common type of college offering an associate degree.

Bachelor degree. 4–year program offered at most colleges and universities. In the U.S., the Bachelor-degree program is usually less specialized than in other countries. In fact, most bachelor-degree students must take a liberal-arts program for the first two years so they will be "well-rounded" in both the arts and sciences.

The most common programs are the:

- Bachelor of Arts (B.A.).
- Bachelor of Science (B.S.).
- Bachelor of Fine Arts (B.F.A.).

You need a B.A., B.S., or B.F.A. degree to get into a graduate program.

Graduate programs.

Master degree, or 2–year to 3–year program for earning a specialized degree—for example:

- Master of Arts (M.A.).
- Master of Science (M.S.).

Professional, or specialization in a professional field—for example:

- Juris Doctorate (J.D.) for practice of law.
- Master of Business Administration (M.B.A.).

Doctorate, the highest degree offered by a university—for example:

- Ph.D. (Doctor of Philosophy).
- Ed.D. (Doctor of Education).
- Eng.D. (Doctor of Engineering).

Post-doctorate. A non-degree program for people who already have a doctorate but want to research a specialized area related to their degree.

Non-credit programs.

Most of these classes are open to anyone who wants to come. F-1 visa students may not take these classes as part of their program:

Audited courses. Academic classes you attend without getting a grade or credit toward a college degree. You do not take any tests or write papers.

Professional classes. Many 2-year and 4-year colleges have "adult education" programs for specific professions. Most of these classes are at night or on the weekend. Some programs give certificates to those who complete the class. Call a college or high school near you and ask for an "Adult Education" catalog.

Enrichment programs. Courses for personal enjoyment or development

Most students do not study in the same university for undergraduate and graduate work. Even if you go to a little-known college, you may be accepted into a "top" graduate school if you do well in your undergraduate studies.

(see "Fun Classes and Clubs/Making Friends").

Applying

Submit your application materials on time—before the deadline. With some colleges, you must apply for a visa at least one year in advance; others require only six months.

With most institutions, you may:

- apply electronically (on-line) if the mail will take too long.
- fax the application papers if the mail will take too long. Be sure you send the original application and other forms by mail afterwards.

Note: Some colleges have rolling admissions; that is, the college decides on each application about 6 weeks after it arrives. You will get a letter accepting or rejecting your application soon afterwards.

To apply for a 4–year or graduate institution, you need:

- an application. Often, this includes an essay (see first page of this chapter). Call or write to the admissions office; ask the office to send you an application. Be sure to say you are a foreign student.
- official transcripts. Allow plenty of time to order your transcripts from your home country. Send only original copies (no photocopies!) with notarized English translations of the following transcripts:
  - college or university.
  - high school (for undergraduate admission).
- letters of recommendation from professors, advisors, or employers.
- medical and immunization records, with English translations.
- a statement of financial ability. To prove that you are able to pay for your U.S. education, you may need to fill out a form. You may also need documents such as bank records and salary statements.
- a satisfactory health plan. Be sure the amount and type of your plan satisfy the requirements of the college. If you do not have a good plan already, you may buy one through the college.
- admissions test scores—most commonly, the Test of English as a Foreign Language (TOEFL) for anyone coming from a country where English is not the main language.

Note: For many 2–year colleges you need only a satisfactory TOEFL score and a high-school diploma or its equivalent. You may not need any other admission test scores or letters of recommendation.

Read "International Organizations/Chapter Information" in Appendix B for places to get information about:

- applying to college.
- cultural activities.
- applying for a job.

Getting information

Centers, libraries, and organizations. You may get general information about U.S. colleges for free or at a low cost (under $5). If you are in your home country, call the U.S. Embassy, the U.S. Consulate, or the Ministry of Education. Find out if your country has an advising center. Ask if there is a(n):

- Fulbright Commission or Foundation.
- binational center.
- exchange organization, such as the Institute of International Education or AMIDEAST.
- American university library.

College guidebooks. All major bookstores in the U.S. have guidebooks with general information about choosing and applying to U.S. colleges. These books also have lists of most colleges, with details such as:

- majors, or academic programs.
- sports and other extracurricular activities.
- types of housing.
- costs.
- admissions tests you need to take.
- location.

For personal services to help you find the best college, visit the Hello! America website on the Internet.

Websites. You may get a list of all the courses offered and admissions forms on the college website. A few colleges also have videos and CD-ROMs detailing their offerings. Some websites also help you fill out the application forms.

Academic and foreign-student advisors. You may talk to:

- an advisor or counselor at the high school or college you are now attending.
- private advisors or organizations.
- the advisor for the college you are interested in.

A counselor may help you:

- choose the right college.
- complete the forms.
- study for the admissions test.
- find financial aid (see section on "College Costs" in this chapter).

College fairs. College representatives often talk to students in local high schools or at college fairs around the world. If you are still living in your home country, call the U.S. Embassy or the Ministry of Education to find out if any representatives are coming to your country.

Campus visits.

Tours. With a tour, you walk around the campus and see the classrooms, dorms, sports facilities, and labs. Call ahead and ask about the schedule.

Orientation sessions. A group of students interested in the college meet with a student or advisor to discuss the college.

Most undergraduate students apply to 2–10 colleges. Check with the admissions office or international students' office for each college you apply to. Ask how you can get admitted; also be sure to find out about the cost.

Interviews. You meet alone with an admissions counselor or student to talk over the program or any other concerns you may have. With some colleges, the interview does not help you get admitted; with other colleges, you need to make a good impression.

Call ahead of time and ask if you need to set a time for the interview; ask if the interview helps you get accepted to the school.

The admissions tests

The tests. The most common tests for admission to an undergraduate program are:

- Test of English as a Foreign Language (TOEFL).
- Test of Written English.
- American College Testing Program Assessment (ACT).
- Scholastic Assessment Test (SAT).
- SAT II (tests on subjects such as math, English, history, biology, chemistry, or a foreign language).

Common graduate-program tests are:

- Graduate Management Admissions Test (GMAT) for business and management programs.
- Graduate Record Exam (GRE).
- Test of Spoken English (TSE), a 20-minute tape-recorded test of your English-speaking skills. Students applying for teaching and research assistantships often must take this test.
- Law School Admissions Test (LSAT).
- Medical College Admissions Test (MCAT) for medical school.

Preparing. You may prepare for any of these exams by:

- getting test-preparation books and cassette tapes from a library or bookstore.
- taking a test-preparation course
  - at a college.
  - at a private institute.
  - from a private tutor.

What to look for

Quality.

- Does the college have a strong faculty in the subject you want to study?
- Is the college accredited? Look in the college guidebook or ask.
- Does the college have many general resources and facilities—such as libraries, laboratories, research centers, athletic facilities, computer centers, and career counseling?
- What does the institution offer foreign students? For example, does it have a foreign student office with counseling, special activities, and a lounge where you can all meet informally?

Cost.

- How much are tuition and other expenses (see section on "College Costs" in this chapter)?
- What scholarships or loans can this college offer you?

Note: Most colleges offer scholarships only at the graduate level for international students.

Standards.

- What are the admissions qualifications (both personal and academic)?
- Does the college admit a limited
  number of international students?

Requirements.

- What are the language requirements?
- Which courses do you need to take?
- How many credit hours do you
  need to complete?
- Will you be able to transfer any
  credits for college courses you took
  in your home country?
- Do you need to have a certain grade
  point average (GPA) to stay in the
  college?
- How much time do you have to
  finish the program?

Student body.

- Are the students from all over the
  U.S. or from one area of the country?
- How many international students
  study there?

Size.

- Is the college large or small?
- How many students are in a class?
  What is the faculty/student ratio—
  that is, how many students are there
  for each teacher?

Public vs. private (see box below).

**Location, extra-curricular activities,
and services** (see chapter on "English
as a Second Language").

How to Apply

**1. Choose two or three
colleges or universities.**

You may apply to more than one
college or university at a time. But
you may accept only one.

**2. Follow the application
procedures.**

Fill out the forms, take the admissions tests, and have interviews if
necessary.

American colleges and universities may be public or private. Public institutions
get most of their money from the local or state government—whereas private
institutions rely on sources such as tuition and gifts. Most 2-year community
colleges are public; four-year institutions may be public or private. Usually,
the tuition at a private school costs more.

Note: You get a tuition discount at a public institution if you are a resident of
the city, county, or state. For example, a resident of Massachusetts pays less
tuition at the University of Massachusetts than a non-resident; residents of
Montgomery County, Maryland, pay less tuition than non-residents at Montgomery College.

Usually, you are a resident if you have lived in the city or county longer than
6–12 months before you enrolled. In some places, you must have paid taxes
in the past year to be considered a resident. International students to the U.S.
are usually considered non-residents.

3. **Wait for an acceptance letter and an I-20 form.**

Return the acceptance form to only one college or university.

4. **Request a visa at a U.S. Embassy or Consulate.**

The Embassy or Consulate will give you a visa. Be sure to read all the immigration rules.

5. **Tell the college or university when you will arrive**

The college will send you registration materials and orientation information. Arrive in the U.S. at least a week ahead of time so you can get settled.

College Costs

Before you come to the U.S., you must prove that you can pay for your college tuition and living expenses. You may fill out a "Financial Certificate" that tells your "source of funds."

The college estimates the costs for 9 months of study. Costs vary; generally, private colleges cost more than public colleges.

Tuition. You may pay:

- for each credit hour. For example, if a college charges $200 per credit, a 3-credit course will cost $600.
- a flat rate, or set amount, for full-time study—that is, more than 12 credit hours.

Sample of 2004–2005 Expenses for 12 Months*

Tuition and Fees (Based on $326 per credit for 24 credits.)	$ 8,280
Books and Supplies	$ 800
Room and Board**	$15,700
Mandatory Health Insurance	$ 545
Personal Costs	$ 3,050
Total:	**$28,375**

* This estimate is for the 2004–2005 academic year at North Shore Community College near Boston.

**Room and Board costs can be subtracted if a sponsor provides a signed and notarized letter stating he or she will provide you with room and board while attending college.

Note: If your spouse or unmarried minor child (under 18 years of age) will accompany you to the U.S. (F-2 status), add $3,330 per person to the estimate of expenses.

Financial aid

Scholarships, grants, and fellowships. You do not pay these back.

Assistantships. The college pays you to assist a professor with research, teaching, or administrative work.

Student employment. The college gives you a job. Check with the Student Employment Office.

Loans. Ask the college or a private bank. International students are rarely eligible for a loan from a U.S. bank.

 Non-citizens cannot get a scholarship or loan from the federal or state government. But you may get help from:

- the college itself—especially for athletes. Some religious institutions also offer loans or scholarships.
- another organization in the U.S.— for example, an organization with research jobs in a particular scientific field.
- an organization inside your own country.

Ask your guidance counselor, a private scholarship search company, an advising center, or your embassy.

Senior citizen discounts (usually for people 60 years or older).

Words to Know

Accredited: approved by the government or an independent agency; meeting certain academic standards

Admissions: applying to a school or college; doing all the necessary procedures to be admitted—such as filling

out the application, having an interview, and taking the SAT

Advising centers: information centers outside the U.S.

Advisor: a special member of the faculty (college staff) who helps students plan their academic or career programs

Assistantship: financial aid for a graduate student

Associate degree (A.A.): a degree offered at 2-year colleges

Audit: to take a course without receiving a grade or credit

Bachelor degree (B.A. or B.S.): a degree for finishing a 4-year program

College: a place for undergraduate study

Community college: a public, 2-year college that gives an Associate degree.

Credit hour: a unit of study earned by a student

Deadline: a specified date or time when you must complete or submit something; also called a "due date"

Extra-curricular activities: non-academic activities—such as sports teams or student clubs

Faculty: the teachers

Fellowship: financial aid, usually given to a graduate student on the basis of merit, need, and/or experience

Full-time: a student taking more than a set amount of credit hours per semester—at least 12 hours or credits at the undergraduate level and 9 hours or credits at the graduate level

Grade point average (GPA): The average of grade points earned for all completed courses. Usually, A=4 points; B=3 points; C=2 points. For example, a student who has two As and one B has a GPA of 3.7 (4+4+3 divided by 3).

Grant: financial aid given to an undergraduate or graduate student—usually awarded to those who need the money the most

Higher education: post-secondary (after high school) education

Master degree (M.A., M.B.A., M.S.): the first graduate degree awarded after completion of a Bachelor of Arts or Science.

Major: a special subject area—such as psychology, economics, international business, or physics. Undergraduate students usually take most of the courses in their major during their junior and senior years.

Matriculate: to apply and enroll in a degree program

Medical College Admissions Test (MCAT): the most common admissions test for medical schools

Private (institution): getting its money from individuals and organizations, or the government

Professional school: an institution for the study of business, medicine, dentistry, law, physical therapy, or other professional areas

Public (institution): getting most of its money directly from the government. For example, community colleges get most of their money from county governments.

Resident (of a city or county): a person who has lived for more than 6 months or a year and/or paid taxes in a city or county. Most foreign students cannot become residents.

Rolling admissions: a type of admissions procedure; the college decides on each application about 6 weeks after each application's arrival.

Scholarship: educational financial assistance awarded to an undergraduate or graduate student. You do not pay back the money.

Scholastic Assessment Test (SAT): a common college-admissions test

Semester: a 14–16 week period of study. Many colleges have fall and spring semesters and a short summer semester.

Test of English as a Foreign Language (TOEFL): a college admissions test that tests the English-language skills of foreign students.

Test of Spoken English (TSE): a 20-minute tape-recorded test of your skills in speaking English. You might take this test if you are applying for a research or teaching assistantship.

Test of Written English (TWE): a 30-minute college admissions test that tests your skills in writing English

Transcript: an official copy of your school record showing the courses you took and the grades you got

Transfer: to get credit for college courses you have taken at another university

Tuition: the cost of a course

Two-year college: a college where you can get an Associate degree or certificate

Undergraduate: a person who is studying for an Associate or Bachelor degree. You need an undergraduate degree for admission to a graduate program.

University: a place for undergraduate and graduate study. Research is an important focus of the institution.

___Staying Safe___

Your pocketbook or wallet

- **Always** keep your wallet or pocketbook with you. Strap your pocketbook across your shoulder if you can.
- **Always** keep your pocketbook closed, with the locks facing you.
- **Always** keep your wallet inside your jacket pocket.

Your credit cards

- **Always** call the company right away if your card is lost or stolen.
- **Always** keep the number of your credit card at home.
- **Always** tear up the black carbon paper into little pieces.

Your money

- **Never** carry large amounts of cash. Carry a credit card or checks instead.
- **Never** count out large amounts of money where others can see you.

The subway

Most subways are safe—even late at night. But:

- **Always** check the area outside the subway before you go there at night.
- **Always** stand with other people in the station.
- **Always** stand away from the edge of the platform.
- **Never** pay attention to people who are arguing loudly; their partner may try to steal your wallet.

In your home

- **Always** make sure the area is safe at night before you buy or rent a home (see "Residential Areas/Finding a New Home").
- **Always** lock your doors and windows. Most people have double locks (locks that close two times).
- **Never** leave valuables near an open window.

Your children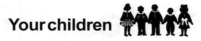

Most people who kidnap children are not strangers—they are divorced or separated parents. But tell your children:

- **Always** dial 911 in an emergency.
- **Never** talk to or get into a car with strangers.
- **Never** let strangers into your home if they are alone.
- **Never** tell a stranger on the phone that they are alone. (Tell them to say you "cannot come to the phone.")

Your car

- **Always** keep the doors locked—when you are driving or leaving the car.
- **Always** put your luggage, tapes, and other valuables in the trunk *before* you reach a parking lot. (If you put your valuables in the trunk and walk away, someone may see you and get into the trunk.)
- **Always** carry a copy of your car registration papers in your wallet. Show these papers to the police if someone steals your car.
- **Always** have your key ready as you walk toward the car. Look inside quickly; then open the door and get in.
- **Never** leave the keys in the car.
- **Never** let strangers in the car.

At the automatic teller machine

- **Always** be sure no one can grab you when you are using the machine.
- **Always** look around before you open the door or use the machine.

In a hotel

- **Always** keep your valuables in the hotel safe.
- **Never** leave valuables in the room when you are gone.

In an Emergency

Call 911

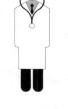

Fire	Medical Emergency	Crime

Fire

1. **Call:** 911

2. **Say:**
   - "I would like to report a fire."
   - "Please come to… (your address)."

3. **Tell:**
   - which room the fire is in.
   - how big the fire is.
   - how the fire started.

Medical Emergency

1. **Call:** 911

2. **Say:**
   - "I need an ambulance right away."
   - "Please come to… (your address)."

3. **Answer questions** about the accident or sickness.

Crime

1. **Call:** 911

Call if:

- you think someone is committing a crime— *do not wait* until a crime has happened.

2. **Say:**
   - "I would like to report a (break-in, mugging, or other crime)."
   - "Please come to… (your address)."

3. **Answer questions** about the crime.

Help will come in 5-10 minutes.

Resources

Introduction: Author's Favorites

The Northeast

Liberty Bell : Independence National Historical Park. 313 Walnut St., Philadelphia, PA 19106
www.nps.gov/inde
Ph: 215-597-8787

Metropolitan Opera House: Lincoln Center, New York, NY 10023
www.metopera.org
Ph: 212-362-6000
Fax: 212-870-7695

Niagara Falls: New York State Parks Information Center.
www.infoniagara.com
Ph: 716-278-1796
Fax: 716-278-1744

Statue of Liberty:
www.nps.gov/stli
Ph: 212-363-3200

Amish country: Pennsylvania Dutch Visitors Bureau.
www.amishfarmandhouse.com
Ph: 800-723-8824
www.padutch.com

Harvard Yard: Harvard Information Center, 1350 Massachusetts Ave., Cambridge, MA 02138.
www.news.harvard.edu/guide/
Ph: 800-447-6277 or 617-495-1573
(MA Dept. of Travel & Tourism)
Fax: 617-495-0905

Whitewater rafting: New England Outdoor Council, P.O. Box 669, Millinocket, ME 04462.
www.neoc.com
Ph: 800-766-7238 or 207-723-5438
Fax: 207-723-4397

The South

Kentucky Horse Park: 4089 Iron Works Parkway, Lexington, KY 40511.
www.kyhorsepark.com
Ph: 800-678-8813 or 859-233-4303
Fax: 859-233-9924

The White House: 1600 Pennsylvania Ave., NW, Washington, DC 20500. White House Visitors Center, 15th & E Sts. NW
www.whitehouse.gov/history/tours
Ph: 202-456-7041 or 202-456-2121
Fax: 202-456-2461

The Kennedy Space Center Complex: Mail Code DNPS, Kennedy Center, FL 32899.
www.ksc.nasa.gov
Ph: 321-452-2121
Fax: 321-452-3043

National Air & Space Museum: Smithsonian Institution, Washington, DC 20560
www.nasm.si.edu
Ph: 202-357-2700
Fax: 202-357-3726

Graceland: P.O. Box 16508, Memphis, TN 38116-0508
www.elvis.com/graceland
Ph: 901-332-3322 or 800-238-2000

French Quarter : 1000 Bourbon St., PM Box 263, New Orleans, LA 70116
www.neworleansreservations.com
Ph: 504-523-1246 or 800-523-9091
Fax: 504-527-6327

AstroWorld /WaterWorld: Six Flags AstroWorld/WaterWorld, 9001 Kirby Drive, Houston, TX 77054
www.sixflags.com/parks/astroworld
Ph: 713-799-8404
Fax: 713-799-1491

Disneyworld: 7100 Municipal Dr., Orlando, FL 32818
www.disneyworld.com
Ph: 407-824-4321

World Of Coca-Cola: 55 Martin Luther King, Jr. Dr., Atlanta, GA 30303-3505
www.woccatlanta.com
Ph: 404-676-5151

Pinehurst Resort: P.O. Box 4000, Village of Pinehurst, NC 28374
www.pinehurst.com
Ph: 910-295-6811 or 800-487-4653
Fax: 910-235-8488

The Midwest

Mount Rushmore National Memorial: P.O. Box 268, Keystone, S.D. 57551
http://www.travelsd.com/parks/rushmore
Ph: 605-574-2523
Fax: 605-574-2307

Mackinac Bridge: 333 I-75, St. Ignace, MI 49781
www.mackinacbridge.org
Ph: 906-643-7600
Fax: 906-643-7668

Mackinac Island: Chamber of Commerce, P.O. Box 451, Mackinac Island, MI 49757
www.mackinac.com/TouristInfo
Ph: 906-847-6418
Fax: 906-847-3571

The Gateway Arch: 707 North First St., St. Louis, MO 63102
www.stlouisarch.com
Ph: 877-982-1410 or 314-982-1410
Fax: 314-982-1527

Henry Ford Museum & Greenfield Village: 20900 Oakwood Blvd., Dearborn, MI 48124-4088
www.hfmgv.org
Ph: 800-835-5237 or 313-982-6100

Art Institute of Chicago: 111 South Michigan Ave., Chicago, IL 60603-6110   www.artic.edu
Ph: 312-443-3600
Fax: 312-443-0849

Mall of America: Mall of America, 60 East Broadway, Bloomington, MI 55425
www.mallofamerica.com
Ph: 952-883-8800
Fax: 952-952-8803

The West

Old Faithful: Yellowstone National Park, Information Office, P.O. Box 168, Yellowstone, WY 82190
www.yellowstone-natl-park.com
Ph: 307-344-2004 or 307-314-7381
Fax: 307-344-2386

Golden Gate Bridge (San Francisco, CA)
www.goldengatebridge.org
Ph: 415-380-9876 or 877-GGB-TOLL (toll free in the San Francisco Bay area)
Fax: 415-380-2879

Grand Canyon National Park:
P.O. Box 129, Grand Canyon, AZ 86023
www.kaibab.org, or www.the grandcanyon.com/home.cfm

Mt. Denali: Division of Tourism, Dept. AP, P.O. Box 110801, Juneau, AK 99811-0801
Ph: 907-465-2010
Fax: 907-465-2287

Native American Art: Santa Fé Chamber of Commerce, P.O. Box 1928, Santa Fe, NM 87504
www.santafechamber.org
Ph: 800-777-2489 or 505-983-7317
Fax: 505-984-2205

Vail Skiing Resort: P.O. Box 7, Vail, CO 81658 www.vail.com
Ph: 800-525-2257 or 970-476-9090
Fax: 970-479-4377

Song-and-dance shows: Las Vegas Chamber of Commerce: 3720 Howard Hughes Parkway, Las Vegas, NV 89109-0937
www.lvchamber.com
Ph: 702-735-1616
Fax: 702-735-2011

1. Before You Come

Neighborhood Information

American Chamber of Commerce. Links to large U.S. cities and counties www.chamberofcommerce.com. (see also "Chapter Information/ Finding a New Home)

What to Bring In

U.S. Customs Department: Rules for importing and exporting items such as pets, meats, vegetables and fruit, alcohol, automobiles, and medications.
www.customs.treas.gov/about/about.htm

Immigration Regulations (see "Chapter Information/Your Legal Status")

2. When You Arrive

Social Security Administration: Telephone numbers and addresses of Social Security Offices near you.
www.ssa.gov
Ph: 800-772-1213

3. Getting Connected

Telephone Connections

www.intelius.com or *www.switchboard.com* These are two of the many sites that will find the contact information for all U.S. individuals and businesses. Unlisted telephone numbers may be found for a fee of $29.95-49.95.

Internet Connections

ConnectNet: This free service, funded by AOL, gives you a list of places in your area where you can access the Internet. Call if you need to connect your own computer; call or use the website to get a list of Internet cafés and other computer terminals. A map on the website shows the locations.
www.connectnet.org
Ph: 866-583-1234

Calling Cards (see "Chapter Information/Communications at Home")

4. Your Legal Status

Legal Assistance

American Immigration Lawyers Association: Will refer you to an attorney in your area. 918 F St., NW, Washington, DC 20004.
www.aila.org
info@aila.org
Ph: 202-216-2400
Fax: 202-783-7853

Government Offices

Federal Information Center: Information on applying for local federal jobs, federal income taxes, immigration services, Social Security benefits—and other federal agencies, programs and services.
www.info.gov
Ph: 800-688-9889

U.S. Citizenship and Immigration Services (USCIS): Forms for applying to immigrate to the U.S. and reporting information such as changes in address or student or job status after your arrive.
www.uscis.gov

U.S. State Department: Telephone numbers, addresses, and websites of U.S. embassies and consulates around the world.
http://usembassy.state.gov For contact information of foreign embassies in the U.S. look up
www.embassyworld.com/embassy_usa/htm

U.S. State Department: Explains visa rules and regulations—including qualifications, applications, and restrictions about who may or may not enter and who may or may not work. You can download a visa application from this site.
http://travel.state.gov

Social Security Administration:
www.ssa.gov
Ph: 800-772-1213

5. Traveling In & Out of the U.S.

Airport Security

U.S. State Department. Country-specific information sheets; travel warnings; and public announcements concerning security situations, health concerns, driving and road safety, and links to foreign embassies worldwide.
www.travel.state.gov
Call 202-647-5225 for latest travel announcements. In an emergency:
888-407-4747.

Where to Stay

Hostelling International-American Youth Hostels: Information on hostels here and abroad. For travelers of all ages. 8401 Colesville Road, Suite 600, Silver Spring, MD 20910.
Ph & fax: 301-495-1240
www.hiayh.org

Telephone and Computer/ Internet Connections (see "Chapter Information/Getting Connected")

U.S. Routes (see "Chapter Information/Getting Around")

6. Getting Around

www.mapquest.com: Provides maps and directions to and from any U.S. destination. If possible, check with someone who knows the route.

American Automobile Association (AAA)
www.aaa.com For your local telephone number, look up "AAA Emergency Road Service" in your phonebook.
AMTRAK:
www.amtrak.com
Ph: 800-USA-RAIL (800-872-7245)

Greyhound Bus Lines:
www.greyhound.com
Ph: 800-229-9424 or 402-330-8552.
En Español: 800-531-5332

7. American Holidays

www.hellousa.com. Monthly holiday section explains how Americans celebrate national and religious holidays.

9. News, Sports, & Entertainment

Sports

www.sports.yahoo.com: General information for all major U.S. sports—including game schedules, team rankings, and game scores.

National Basketball Association: www.nba.com

Major League Baseball Association: www.majorleaguebaseball.com

Major Football Association: www.nfl.com

National Hockey Association: www.nhl.com

U.S. Soccer Association: www.ussoccer.com

Ethnic Newspapers.

Lists over 200 ethnic newspapers from all over the world, in their original languages.

www.onlinenewspapers.com

11. Making Friends

(see "International Organizations ")

12. Food Shopping

U.S. Department of Agriculture (Meat and Poultry Hotline): Provides food product safety information including a chart of home refrigerator storage times.
www.fsis.usda.gov/oa/pubs/dating.htm
Ph: 800-535-4555

The National Food Safety Database of the University of Florida: Comprehensive information on food safety—including a chart called "Safe Food Storage Times and Temperatures." Click on "Consumer-Related Information," then "Storing and Handling Food."
http://foodsafety.ifas.ufl.edu/consumer.htm

14. Your Mail

United States Post Office: Information on topics such as rates, regulations, and zip codes. Online ordering of stamps, postcards and phone cards. Help in finding a Western Union agent near you.
www.usps.com

Western Union:
www.westernunion.com
Ph: 800-325-6000

15. Money Matters

Travelex/Thomas Cook: Offers a variety of services, including currency exchanges, international money transfers, and international calling cards. The site gives up-to-date currency-exchange rates and lists U.S. locations and telephone numbers. If you are still in your home country, ask locally for a Thomas Cook location. www.travelex.com

Ph: 800-CURRENCY (800-287-7362)

Western Union: On-line money transfers with a credit card.
www.westernunion.com
Ph: 800-325-6000

16. Paying Your Taxes

Internal Revenue Service (IRS): Tax publications, including Publication 519, a Tax Guide for Aliens. Forms and explanations for paying your federal taxes. You may also pay online.
www.irs.gov
Ph: 800-829-3676

17. Finding a New Home

Chamber of Commerce Official Global Locator
www.chamberofcommerce.com

MSN Home.
http://houseandhome.msn.com. Advice on buying and renting homes—including how much you can afford. Statistics include educational levels, income, and safety for neighborhoods for most cities.

National Association of Realtors:
www.realtor.com
Ph: 800-874-6500 or 312-329-6001
Fax: 312-329-5960

19. Telephone Services

Services

AT&T:
Home phone service: 800-222-0300
Calling cards. Ph: 800-225-5288
Cell phones. Ph: 800-888-7600
www.att.com

MCI:
General Service: Ph: 800-444-3333;
www.mci.com
Cell phones: Ph: 800-254-8991;
www.wireless.com

Sprint:
Calling cards: Ph: 800-480-4727;
www.sprint.com
Cell phones: Ph: 800-877-4646;
www.sprintpcs.com

Nextel:
Ph: 800-208-4645;
www.444Phone.com

Consumer Advice

Telecommunications and Action
Center. *www.trac.org/index.html*:
Consumer tips on choosing long-
distance calling plans and calling
cards. Database of area codes and
their locations.

Directory of U.S. business and residential telephone numbers

www.intelius.com or
www.switchboard.com Databases
of business and home telephone
numbers in all U.S. areas

*Federal Communications Commis-
sion*: The U.S. government agency
that handles complaints about some
illegal radio, TV, or telephone practices. The FCC also provides fact
sheets and other information for
consumers.
www.fcc.gov
fccinfo@fcc.gov
Ph: 888-225-5322
Fax: 202-418-0232

Consumer World
Reports comparing a variety of
products—incuding telephone services, TVs, and jewelry.
www.consumerworld.org

20. Insurance

Financial-status ratings of insurance companies

A.M. Best Co.: A.M. Best Rd.,
Oldwick, NJ 08858. You must sign on
to become a member to use the
service.
www.ambest.com
Ph: 908-439-2200
Fax: 908-439-3296

Weiss Research: 4176 Bruns Rd.
Palm Beach Gardens, FL 33410
www.weissratings.com
You must pay a small fee to use the
service.
Ph: 800-289-9222 or 561-627-3300
Fax: 561-625-6685

Tips on cutting insurance costs

*Insurance Information Institute of
America*: Information about all types
of insurance including auto,
homeowners, life and business (also
available in Spanish). Explains com-
mon insurance terms. 110 Williams
St., New York, NY 10038
www.iii.org
Ph: 212-346-5500 or 800-942-4242
(National Insurance Consumer
Helpline)
Fax: 212-791-1807

21. Medical Care

Consumer Health

1-800-DOCTORS: Help in finding a doctor or dentist who speaks your language. All doctors and dentists have certified credentials that are approved by the organization. *Note:* Only doctors who pay for this service are on this list.
www.800doctors.com
Ph: 800-362-8677

National Health Information Center: Help in finding the organization that can answer special health questions on subjects such as: AIDS, cancer, alcoholism, diabetes, allergies. P.O. Box 1133, Washington, DC 20013-1133
www.health.gov/nhic/
Ph: 800-336-4797
Fax: 301-984-4256

22. Credit Cards and Loans

Credit Cards

Bankcard Holders of America. www.CardWeb.com. Click onto "Find a Card" on the left side. Ph: 301- 631-9100. Call for a paper copy of the information on the website. The cost is $5.

Credit Reporting

Monitrust: Provides a personal credit report from all major reporting organizations. 500 Bi-county Blvd., Suite 146. Farmingdale, NY 11735
www.monitrust.com
info@monitrust.com
Ph: 631-719-4568 or 866-648-7878
Fax: 800-953-8236

23. Buying or Leasing a Car

Determining the Price

American Automobile Association (AAA):   Look up the phone number for the AAA office in your area. www.aaa.com (national)

Kelley Blue Book: Advice about new and used cars. Also, information about recalls and safety ratings. www.kbb.com

Consumer Reports New and Used Car Price Service: Information about new cars, including the list price, the dealer cost of the car, and the price of options. Consumer Reports, 101 Truman Avenue, Yonkers, NY 10703-1052
www.consumerreports.com
Ph: 800-934-3414 (to order a report) or 914-378-7300
Fax: 408-370-5315

Publications on buying or leasing a car

Federal Trade Commission: Publishes a guide on leasing a car. Publication Department, CRC-240, Washington, DC 20580
www.ftc.gov
Ph: 877-382-4357 o r 202-326-2222

National Automobile Dealers Association: Publishes: a "blue book" with used car prices.   8400 Westpark Dr., McLean, VA 22102. www.nada.com
Ph: 800-544-6232
Fax: 410-594-1327

24. Finding Work

America's Job Bank: Provides over 750,000 nationwide job listings.
www.ajb.dni.us

Applying for Employment Authorization Document (EAD)
http://uscis.gov. Click on "Immigration Forms," "I-765," then "Application for Employment Authorization."

25. Your Young Child

Nannies and Au Pairs

American Institute for Foreign Study (AIFS): Recruits young women from around the world for one year. River Plaza, 9 W. Broad St., Stamford, CT 06902.
www.aifs.com
aupair.info@aifs.com
Ph: 800-727-2437

Home/Work Solutions, Inc.: Prepares tax returns for famlies employing household workers. 2 Pidgeon Hill Dr., Sterling, VA 20165.
www.4homehelp.com
Ph: 800-626-4829
Fax: 703-404-8155

American Background Information Service: Screens nannies and au pairs. 629 Cedar Creek Grade, Winchester, VA 22601.
www.americanbackground.com.
Ph: 800-669-2247 or 540-665-8056
Fax: 540-667-8461

Child Care and Nursery Schools

North American Montessori Teachers Association (NAMI): For teachers, schools, and parents. Provides a list of Montessori schools throughout the U.S. and Canada. 13693 Butternut Rd., Burton, OH 44021
www.montessori-namta.org
staff@montessori-namta.org
Ph: 440-834-4011
Fax: 440-834-4016

Child Care Aware: Assists parents in locating quality child care and child care resources throughout the country. Offers information related to child care including licensing of child care providers. This program is part of the National Association of Child Care Resource and Referral Agencies. 1319 F St., NW, Suite 500, Washington, DC 20004
www.childcareaware.org
Ph: 800-424-2246

National Association for the Education of Young Children (NAEYC): Publishes standards for day care centers, nursery schools, and elementary schools (grades Kindergarten–3) throughout the country. 1509 16th St., NW, Washington, DC 20036.
www.naeyc.org
Ph: 800-424-2460 or 202-232-8777
Fax: 202-328-1846

The Child Development Web. Tells where to go for free testing and other services in your area—in case your child may have difficulties in speech, vision, hearing, or psychological adjustment. Many programs also include parenting classes.
www.childdevelopmentweb.com

26. Your Older Child

Public and Private Schools

Hello! America, Inc.:   Publishes *Choosing Elementary and Secondary Schools: 20 Plus Questions Parents Need to Ask.* Helps parents decide which schools meets their child's needs. Individual schools not rated.
www.hellousa.com.

Independent Baccalaureate North America (IBNA):   475 Riverside Dr., Room 1600, New York, NY10115.
www.ibo.org
Ph: 212-696-4464
Fax: 212- 889-9242

Independent Educational Consultants Association (IECA): Consultants for children and teenagers of all ages for all types of schools—elementary and secondary, public and private.   3251 Old Lee Highway, Suite 510, Fairfax, VA 22030
www.iecaonline.com.
requests@iecaonline.com
Ph: 800-808-IECA or 703-591-4850
Fax: 703-591-4860

Private schools

Association of Boarding Schools (TABS): Lists of boarding schools, application forms and information. 4455 Connecticut Ave., NW, Suite A-200, Washington DC 20008
www.schools.com
tabs@schools.com
Ph: 202-966-8705 or 800-541-5908
Fax: 202-966-8708.

National Catholic Educational Association (NCEA): 1077 30th St., NW, Suite 100, Washington, DC 20007
www.ncea.org
nceaadmin@ncea.org
Ph: 202-337-6232
Fax: 202-333-6706

Montessori schools:
www.montessoriconnections.com

National Association of Independent Schools (NAIS): 1620 L St. NW Washington, DC 20036-5695.
www.nais-schools.org
Ph: 202-973-9700
Fax: 202-973-9790

Private School Admissions Testing

Independent Secondary Entrance Examination (ISEE), c/o Educational Records Bureau (ERB), 220 E. 42nd St., Suite 1100, New York, NY 10017
www.erbtest.org
Ph: 800-989-3721 or 212-672-9800

Secondary School Admission Test (SSAT): Test registration form, sample test questions, and details about test sites, dates, and fees.   862 Rt. 518, Skillman, N.J. 08558
www.ssat.org
Ph: 800-442-7728 or 609-683-4440
Fax: 609-683-4507

Special needs

Council for Exceptional Children: For parents of handicapped and gifted children. Information includes *Help for Children* (a booklet with comprehensive list of hotlines and resources). 1110 N. Glebe Rd., Suite 300, Arlington, VA 22201-5704

www.cec.sped.org
service@cec.sped.org
Ph: 800-CEC-SPED or 703-620-3660
Fax: 703-264-9494

The Gifted Child Society: 190 Rock
Rd., Glen Rock, NJ 07452-1736
www.gifted.org
Ph: 201-444-6530

The International Dyslexia Association: Information for parents,
educators, and physicians—including
a list of branches near you. 8600
LaSalle Rd. Chester Building, Suite
382, Baltimore, MD 21286-2044.
www.interdys.org
Ph: 800-ABCD123 or 410-296-0232
Fax: 410-321-5069

Publications

Petersen's Guides, Inc.: Wide
range of high-school programs, with
topics from preparing for college to
wilderness exploration. Includes lists
of private secondary schools.
P.O. Box 67005, Lawrenceville, NJ
08648
www.petersons.com
Ph: 888-892-6288 or 609-896-1800
Fax: 609-896-1811

Porter Sargent Publishers: Publishes books on topics such as private
schools, special education, and international education, including the
Handbook of Private Schools.
11 Beacon St., Boston MA 02108.
www.portersargent.com
info@portersargent.com
Ph: 800-342-7470 or 617-523-1670
Fax: 617-523-1021

27. English as a Second Language

(See "Chapter Information/College &
University Admissions Tests" and
"English Language Tests")

English Language Tests

TOEFL (Test of English as a Foreign Language) and *TSE (Test of
Spoken English)*: Educational
Testing Service, P.O. Box 6151,
Princeton, NJ 08541-6151.
www.toefl.org
Ph: 609-771-7100
Fax: 609-771-7500

TOEIC (Test of English for International Communication): TOEIC
Service International, The Chauncey
Group International, Ltd., 664
Rosedale Rd., Princeton, NJ 08540
www.toeic.com
Ph: 609-720-6647
Fax: 609-720-6550

*TESOL (Teachers of English to
Speakers of Other Language)*:
700 S. Washington St. Suite 200,
Alexandria, VA 22314-2751.
www.tesol.org
Ph: 703-836-0774
Fax: 703-836-7864

28. Colleges and Universities

Independent Education Consultants Association: Lists of consultants—including those who help with
college admissions. 3251 Old Lee
Hwy., Suite 510, Fairfax, VA 22030
www.iecaonline.com

requests@iecaonline.com
Ph: 800-808-IECA or 703-591-4850
Fax: 703-591-4860

Institute of International Education (IIE): Reference library with information about scholarships and studying in the U.S. Regional offices around the country; each region has its different services. 809 United Nations Plaza, New York, NY 10017
www.iie.org
Ph: 212-883-8200
Fax: 212-984-5452

(See "College & University Admissions Tests," "English Language Tests" and "International Organizations" in this Appendix)

College & University Admissions Tests

ACT Assessment: Test designed to assess high school students general educational development. ACT, P.O. Box 414, Iowa City, IA 52243
www.act.org
Ph: 319-37-1270
Fax: 319-339-3032

GRE (Graduate Records Examination): P.O. Box 6000, Princeton, NJ 08541-6000.
www.gre.com.
Ph: 609-771-7670
Fax: 609-771-7906

LSAT(Law School Admissions Test): P.O. Box 2000-M, 661 Penn St., Newtown, PA 18940-0993.
www.lsat.org.
Ph: 800-342-7470 or 215-968-1001
Fax: 215-968-1119

MCAT (Medical College Admissions Test): P.O. Box 4056, Iowa City, IA 52243.
www.aamc.org
Ph: 319-337-1357
Fax: 319-337-1122

Miller Analogies Test: The Psychological Corporation, 19500 Bulverde Rd., San Antonio, TX 78259
www.tpcweb.com
scoring_services@harcourt.com
Ph: 210-339-8710 or 800-622-3231
Fax: 888-211-8276

SAT: Educational Testing Service: Rosedale Rd., Princeton, NJ 08541.
www.collegeboard.org
etsinfo@ets.org
Ph: 609-921-9000
Registration from abroad by fax: 609-734-5410

Books to Read (Students)

English Language and Orientation Programs in the United States, Carl DeAngelis. Institute of International Education. 809 United Nations Plaza. New York, NY 10017-3580. Over 1,000 programs and course offering of U.S. accredited higher educational institutions, U.S. private secondary schools, and U.S. language schools.

Funding for U.S. Study, Institute of International Education, 809 United Nations Plaza, New York, NY 10017-3580. Describes 600 grants, scholarships, fellowships, internships.

The International Student Handbook, by Allan Wernick. The American Immigration Law Foundation, Attn: Publications, 400 Eye St. NW, Suite 1200 Washington, DC 20005

U.S. Taxation of International Students and Scholars—A Manual for Advisers and Administrators. by Bertrand M. Harding, Jr. and Norman Peterson. NAFSA: Association of International Educators. 1875 Connecticut Ave. NW, Suite 1000. Washington, DC 20009-5728

International Organizations

African American Institute: 833 United Nations Plaza, New York, NY 10017
www.aaionline.org
aainy@aaionline.org
Ph: 800-745-3899 or 212-949-5666
Fax: 212-682-6174

AMIDEAST Information Services: Information for students and trainees from the Middle East. 1730 M St., NW, Suite 1100, Washington, DC 20036
www.amideast.org
inquiries@amideast.org
Ph: 800-368-5720 or 202-776-9600
Fax: 202-776-7000

The Asia Foundation: 465 California St., San Francisco, CA 94104
www.asiafoundation.org
webmaster@asiafound.org
Ph: 415-982-4640
Fax: 415-392-8863

China Human Resources Group: Recruits individuals for management and technical positions in China-related businesses. 29 Airpark Rd., Princeton, NJ 08542
chrg@usa.com
Ph: 609-683-4521

China Institute in America: English and Chinese language exchange programs. For Chinese students, scholars, business professionals and families. 125 E. 65th St., New York, NY 10021
www.chinainstitute.org
Ph: 212-744-8181

National Association of Japan-America Societies. Programs and services including an online job bank with links to different geographic areas. 733 15th St., NW, Suite 700, Washington, DC 20005
www.us-japan.org
Ph: 202-783-4550
Fax: 202-783-4531

YMCA International Program Services: Summer and training programs. Helps international students on international flights at major airports nationwide. Homestay tour programs for visiting students. Publications: 71 W. 23rd St., New York, NY 10010
www.ymcainternational.org
ips@ymcanyc.org
Ph: 888-477-9622 or 212-727-8800
Fax: 212-727-8814

Special Features

Index

Note: Page numbers in bold type have illustrations. See Appendix C for a complete list of illustrtions.

Sample 1.

check register **123**, 128
[An illustration of a check register is on page 123.]

Sample 2.

cars
    leasing 204–206
["The main category is "cars."; "leasing" is the subcategory.]

Sample 3.

catalogs. *See* shopping
[The information for "catalogs" is in the "shopping" category.]

Sample 4.

electricity. *See* homes: utilities
[The information for electricity is in the "homes" category under the subcategory "utilities."]

Sample 5.

checking account 129. *See also* checks
[First look under the "checking account" category. Then look under "checks" for more information.]

Sample 6.

gas. *See* homes: utilities; service stations
[The information for "gas" is under two separate categories—"homes," and "service stations."]